The Queer Gree

Marios Psaras

The Queer Greek Weird Wave

Ethics, Politics and the Crisis of Meaning

Marios Psaras

ISBN 978-3-319-82075-0   ISBN 978-3-319-40310-6   (eBook)
DOI 10.1007/978-3-319-40310-6

Printed on acid-free paper

This Palgrave Macmillan imprint is published by Springer Nature
The registered company is Springer International Publishing AG
The registered company address is: Gewerbestrasse 11, 6330 Cham, Switzerland

To my family, the blood and the chosen

ACKNOWLEDGMENTS

An earlier version of the material on *Hardcore* that appears in Chap. 1 was published as Marios Psaras, 'Soft Fantasies, Hardcore Realities: Greekness and the Death Drive in Dennis Iliades's *Hardcore*', in M. Photiou, T. Kazakopoulou and P. Phillis (eds), *Contemporary Greek Film Cultures*, Special Issue of *Filmicon*, 2, 2014, 133–155, and is reprinted here by kind permission of *Filmicon*. An earlier version of the material on *Strella/A Woman's Way* that appears in Chap. 3 was published as Marios Psaras, 'No Country for Old Faggots: Breaking with the Parental Home and Exploring Queer Utopias in Panos Koutras's *Strella* (2009)', in Tonia Kazakopoulou and Mikela Fotiou (eds), *Contemporary Greek Film Cultures from 1990 to the Present* (Oxford: Peter Lang, 2016), and is reprinted here by kind permission of Peter Lang.

I would like to express a deep gratitude to my mentors Robert Gillett and Libby Saxton for the many inspirational conversations about film, ethics and queerness, their astute remarks on my text and for always pushing for clarification. I am also grateful to Rosalind Galt and Lydia Papadimitriou for their helpful comments and insights on my doctoral thesis, from which this book was developed.

Finally, I am greatly indebted to a number of people that have surrounded me with unflagging support and encouragement—intellectual and personal—and without whom this book would not be possible: Stavros Makris, Christos Andreou, Alen Toplišek, Avgi Lilli, Maria Kountouri, Tonia Siamptani, Nandia Tomasidou, and of course my parents, Andreas and Pandelitsa Psaras. This book is dedicated to them.

CONTENTS

LIST OF FIGURES

CHAPTER 1

Introduction: The Meaning of the Crisis or the Crisis of Meaning

On 6 December 2008 15-year-old student Alexis Grigoropoulos was killed in cold blood by an armed policeman in the Exarcheia area of central Athens. Within hours angry protesters and demonstrators took to the streets of the Greek capital and put themselves at risk in violent confrontations with the police. The demonstrations soon escalated into a massive series of nation-wide riots that lasted for more than three weeks, paired with solidarity demonstrations and riots in many cities around the world, from London to São Paolo. Expressing 'a general rage against state arbitrariness and police impunity', as Kostis Kornetis observes (2010, p. 174), this unprecedented movement in the history of contemporary Greece history, later dubbed the 'December Events' of 2008, comprised protests ranging from peaceful sit-ins at Syntagma Square outside the Greek parliament, to the occupation of university buildings, daily clashes with the police and the indiscriminate destruction of public and private property.

The December Events drew heavily on the revolutionary rhetoric of past dissident movements, particularly of student movements both at home and abroad, such as the anti-dictatorial Polytechnic movement in Greece in 1973 and May '68 in France, in the form of slogans, banners and graffiti that voiced such distinctive demands as 'Bread, Education, Freedom' and 'We don't ask for much, we want it all!' However, as Kornetis argues, this polycephalous movement, which in no time managed to gather together such different and, to an extent, even opposing social groups as anarchists, teenagers, immigrants, hooligans, radical intellectuals and unspecified others, soon made clear its intentions to separate itself from the revolutionary

© The Author(s) 2016
M. Psaras, *The Queer Greek Weird Wave*,
DOI 10.1007/978-3-319-40310-6_1

legacy of the past, conveying 'an anti-heroic tone and a rather critical attitude' (2010, p. 177). A giant graffito cried 'Fuck May 68, Fight Now!', while an aggressive leaflet expressed the rioters' 'acute resistance against the cannibalization of a historic tradition', stating 'the mandarins of harmony, the barons of quiet, law and order call on us to be dialectical. [...] We saw them in May, we saw them in LA and in Brixton, we have been watching them for decades licking the bones of the Polytechnic' (2010, p. 177).

Clearly, the December uprising was an anti-foundational, anti-authoritarian yet heterogeneous movement, which deployed modern technology, particularly social media such as online blogs, Facebook and Twitter, in order to mobilize thousands of discontents across the country, thus turning what could have been an isolated urban incident into a national event or, better, to use Kornetis's words, 'from a local to a global, or more fittingly, a "glocal" movement' (2010, p. 185). Nevertheless, the movement's profound heterogeneity as well as the absence of clear determinant content made it difficult for analysts and critics to provide meaningful interpretations of its emergence. Stathis Gourgouris for instance notes:

> The deeper historical and political significance of the December insurrection may still elude us, though there is no doubt that this event will remain a key reference in radical history and in the history of youth movements worldwide. The hermeneutical work in this case is made harder by the fact that the insurgent actors demanded precisely that we dismantle our ways of interpreting and representing the world. (2010, p. 371)

Indeed, as Kornetis tells us, 'many analysts called December "a crisis of meaning," others an identity crisis, a nihilist outburst, or a collective psychodrama, and juxtaposed it to the euphoric utopianism of 1968' (2010, p. 182). Following Slavoj Žižek's insight regarding the 2005 French uprising in the Parisian suburbs, Kornetis similarly suggests that, 'if 1968 was "a revolt with a utopian vision," 2008, just like 2005 in the *banlieues* of Paris, was "just an outburst with no pretence to vision"', a mere 'insistence on *recognition*, based on a vague, unarticulated *ressentiment*' (2010, p. 182). At the same time, however, as Kornetis contends, this visionless outburst reverberated with Kenneth Clark's analysis of such events as 'subconscious or conscious invitation to self-destruction [...] reflecting the ultimate in self-negation, self-rejection, and hopelessness' (1970, p. 108).

Nevertheless, I would argue that psychoanalytically infused interpretations of self-negation and self-rejection mask theoretically reactionary responses that seek to annihilate or merely fail to conceive of the political ramifications of the events, and thus evade the assumption of political responsibility by precisely reducing the protester to the status of a hopeless irrational rioter.

Disappointingly though unsurprisingly, this was also the official state response to these events, as Greek politicians and especially the conservative government of the time did indeed avoid having to take responsibility for the events. However, the 2008 riots were only the beginning of this establishment's end, as its scams and deceptions could no longer remain hidden. The 2008 global economic meltdown led to the sudden exposure of all the deficiencies of the Greek economy, which the country's governments had for years swept under the carpet. Exposed to the inherent anomalies and imbalances of the newly formed European monetary union, which, fearing its own collapse, immediately withdrew all its previous concessions to the Greek economy, the scandalously corrupt Greek economic-political structure had no choice but to condemn the country to a massive and extremely painful material and ideological breakdown. Towards the end of 2010, Greek politicians, in an effort to avoid the country's default and its exit from the eurozone, asked the so-called Troika, that is the International Monetary Fund, the European Commission and the European Central Bank, for a bailout. In exchange, the Troika demanded the implementation of unprecedented austerity measures that have resulted in an explosive rise in unemployment and a corresponding deterioration in every aspect of people's daily lives, including such vital areas as the country's health and educational systems. In the years that have followed, the economic crisis has only further deepened leading to unpredictable social and political turbulence not only in Greece but across Europe, challenging and questioning the neoliberal foundations of its monetary union, as well as the once-lauded vision itself of the united Europe.

Despite the overabundance of public discourses, widely propagated by printed and electronic Greek and foreign media, and the proliferation of public demonstrations and riots in Greece's capital and major cities, the prevailing affective, as well as cognitive, response to the catastrophe has been characterized by an extreme sense of confusion, frustration and disenchantment with politics for a society that has traditionally been very politicized. In the face of the abrupt calamity, an unparalleled inarticulacy has emerged, reinvoking the nihilistic spirit of the December Events, which has now grown and overrun even the last remaining pockets of optimism. Nevertheless, where language falls short in verbalizing the lived experience, both individual and collective, of this modern Greek tragedy, cinema emerges as the unexpected medium through which the aesthetic provides a paradoxical cognitive and affective access to this unprecedented encounter with the 'crisis of meaning'. Appropriately, the cinematic movement that is said to articulate this encounter bears the epithet 'weird'.

'Is it just coincidence that the world's most messed-up country is making the world's most messed-up cinema?' wonders *The Guardian* journalist Steve Rose in his article '*Attenberg, Dogtooth* and the Weird Wave of Greek Cinema', asking whether 'the brilliantly strange films of Yorgos Lanthimos and Athina Rachel Tsangari [are] a product of Greece's economic turmoil' (2011). In this article, Rose makes the case for identifying a 'Greek Weird Wave', pointing to 'the growing number of independent, and inexplicably strange, new Greek films', including Yorgos Lanthimos's *Dogtooth* (2009), Panos Koutras's *Strella* (2009) and Athina Rachel Tsangari's *Attenberg* (2010), which he places at the top of what he calls the 'strangeness scale', as well as other 'slightly less weird' but equally unorthodox films, such as Yannis Economides's *Knifer* (2010), Syllas Tzoumerkas's *Homeland* (2010) and Argyris Papadimitropoulos and Jan Vogel's *Wasted Youth* (2011). The correlation between the country's severe financial crisis and a particular corpus of its cinematic production emerges as, indeed, an interesting hypothesis generating a number of epistemological and ethical questions with regard to the meanings and interpretations of the crisis, but most significantly with regard to its social, cultural and affective manifestations. In effect, much as the collapse of the Greek economic-political structure has brought about an unprecedented deterioration in the material quality of Greek people's daily lives, so it has brought about an irrevocable destabilization and demythologization of established national narratives that have long been central to the production of national identity and history, exposing them as fantasmatic ideological regimes, in many ways accountable for the present catastrophe.

Clearly, such a critique could not but permeate the country's cinematic production, not only because of cinema's inherently emancipatory potential, but also because Greek cinema has invariably invested in or critically engaged with the nation's favorite narratives. Nevertheless, it is questionable whether the so-called 'Greek Weird Wave' is indeed a direct 'product of Greece's economic turmoil' (Rose, 2011). For, despite its intrinsic (thematic and formal) alignment with its historical moment, the current cinematic trend draws on a long genealogy of local production that has insistently and self-consciously pitted its oppositional aesthetics against the nation's official historicity and self-representation, while also being in dialogue with the global art-house cinema and modernist traditions. However, before attempting to explore the cinematic genealogies that frame the emergence of the Greek Weird Wave, it is important to elucidate the ideological context in which it positions its radical rhetoric.

Arguably, the nation's most characteristic narrative has been the one framed around the problematic triptych 'Fatherland, Religion, Family'. Despite the undeniable controversy that haunts its historical deployment and appropriation by the dictatorial regimes of the country, this particular triad has in significant ways ideologically framed—if not constituted—the nation's modernity, underpinning its self-representational lexicon and producing the institutions of family and religion as keystones of modern Greek society, and indeed as the defining core of Greekness. In what follows, I shall investigate the ideological production of the modern Greek national identity and historicity, with a particular focus on the way traditional patriarchal forms of kinship have been inextricably associated with nationalist discourses as well as with the establishment and consolidation of the capitalist construction of the modern Greek state.

'FATHERLAND, RELIGION, FAMILY': THE BIRTH OF A NATION

In his article 'Inventing Greece' Peter Bien argues that nationalism 'acts as bulwark against death, fate, and contingency, providing a way to cheat those everyday forces' (2005, p. 218). On this he follows Gregory Jusdanis's interpretation of the metaphysics of nationalism. According to Jusdanis: 'Nationalist discourse, with its tales of progress, self-fulfillment, and manifest destiny, allows modern individuals to deny their mortality in the face of change. [...] [N]ationalism allows [people] to forget contingency' (1991, p. 165). As Bien suggests, the phenomenon of Western nationalism has replaced religion in the contemporary era, legitimizing even such self-contradictory acts of violence as martyrdom, and thus providing 'a metaphysical rationale for life and death: a meaning for what would otherwise be our futile, meaningless existence' (2005, p. 223).

The origins of modern Greek nationalism can be traced back to the late eighteenth century and the movement of the Neohellenic Enlightenment, which, according to Gourgouris, created a new tradition, a new identity involving 'a social homogeneity, a linguistic tradition, and a geographical continuity: in other words, a native past' (1996, p. 73). As Bien notes, at the center of this movement was Adamantios Koraïs, a visionary scholar, 'who amalgamated European Philhellenism's adulation of pagan Greece with enthusiasm for the French revolution and an utter revulsion against what he considered the superstitions of the Orthodox Church' (2005, p. 224). Koraïs's visionary version of modern Greece relied on both an idealized past that would constitute the foundation for the modern Greek nation-state as well as an idealized future, wherein the Western ideas of secular liberalism and humanist enlightenment were to be materialized. In a direct appropriation of the Western philhellenes' invention of ancient Greece, Koraïs's idealized and mythicized past obliterated such 'black pages' from ancient Greece's history as slavery, pederasty, internal discord and the brevity of Periclean democracy, which are widely known to us today, yet to a great extent are still silenced in the official Greek national narrative. However, such an idealized version of the past was strategically successful at the time, as Bien notes (2005, p. 226), in conveying to the 'barbarized Greeks of the Ottoman Empire' a temporal continuity and a spatial coherence that would unite them under the flag of the War of Independence in the 1820s.

Perhaps Koraïs's most interesting project was, however, his attempt at a 'linguistic refinement' of the 'Hellenic' language 'from the barbarity of Turkish words that kept them chained to their degeneracy', as Bien notes, a clearly political project that was in accordance with 'the conviction of his time that language is the essence of nationality' (2005, p. 226). Koraïs's *katharévousa*—literally meaning 'purified'—was a remarkable example of language construction in the modern era, which sought to bridge the gap between extreme Atticism, a modification of Ancient Greek proposed by the scholars of the time, and the demotic, the vernacular form of Modern Greek. Widely used for literary and official purposes in the newly formed Greek state, *katharévousa* was the reason for the state of *diglossia* that the Greek language suffered up until 1976, when the demotic was declared as the official language of the Greek state.

As Bien argues, this first form of invented Greek nationality, which was invested in a distortion of both ancient and modern Greek reality, 'provided at the deepest level a metaphysical rationale for life and death' (2005, p. 226), not only for the fighters of the Greek War of Independence but also for the future Greek citizens, thus laying the ideological foundations of the modern Greek nation-state. However, alongside the invention of a glorious ancient past and the project of linguistic 'purification' and unity, the Orthodox Church was also deployed in the production and consolidation of the modern Greek national identity. Historian Thanos Veremis explains that with the creation of the autocephalous national Church soon after Independence, 'the state incorporated the Church and its martyrs into the pantheon of Greek heroes and made them integral parts of the national myth. Thus the Church became an accomplice of the state in its mission to spread the cohesive nationalist creed' (1989, p. 136). Anna Koumandaraki also emphasizes the formative and performative role of the Church in the consolidation of Greek nationalism and the process of national homogenization of the population within the borders of the Greek state. As she explains, according to the first Greek constitution, which was written while the War of National Independence was still under way, Greek citizenship was accorded to 'all people who were members of the Orthodox Church' (2002, p. 41). However, as she clarifies, 'the way nationalist ideology was promoted in Greece entailed the exercise of state power and the severe punishment of all those who tried to question the domination of the Greek state' (2002, p. 42). Hence, the Church's role was more of 'a supplementary force to state power' (2002, p. 42), facilitating through its rituals and public celebrations the construction and consolidation of Greek national identity. This institutional subordination of the Church to the nation-state signaled a significant transvaluation, as Bien argues, 'whereby secular values came to control spiritual ones instead of the other way round' (2005, p. 228). This peculiar association between the Church and the state marked a redefinition of the original version of the Greek national identity espoused by Koraïs and the European phil-hellenes, which now expanded to incorporate the Byzantine heritage. However, as Koumandaraki again observes, in the sphere of ideology this meant the coexistence of 'two obviously opposing civilizations: these were the Ancient Greek civilization and the Byzantine Christian Realm' (2002, p. 45).[1] Then again, the nation is redefined—or reinvented to use Bien's words—once more in the late nineteenth century by the romanticists' re-evaluation of the folk song tradition of the Ottoman period, thus ultimately preparing the ground for the construction of a 'synthetic view' of Greek history 'stressing the continuity from ancient times and the significance of Byzantium and the Turkish period for modern Greece' (Bien, 2005, p. 229).

This process of reinventing the nation continued during the numerous political and military events of the twentieth century (the Balkan wars, the Asia Minor operation, the two World Wars, the Civil War, the Colonels' Junta and so on) and was consistently associated with what Jusdanis identifies as the need for a 'cure for failed irredentist aspirations and wrecked hopes for a modern, democratic, and liberal state' (1991, p. 79). Indeed, the history of the modern Greek state demonstrates, as Bien suggests, how 'political vicissitude serves to open up anew, each time, the chasm of contingency, futility, and meaninglessness that must be filled by an ever-renewed, ever-redefined nationalism, the modern world's primary religion' (2005, p. 230). This never-ending process of inventing Greek nationalism was, ultimately, a process of aestheticization, as Bien argues, having as its indispensable tool 'the notion of Greekness [...] which is aesthetic "because its promised unification of differences occurs in [an] imaginary space", permitting Greeks "to be both Hellenic and Romeic, to christen their children Pericles as well as Maria"' (p. 231), thus ultimately constructing Greece itself as a metaphor.

The status of Greekness as an aesthetic category is probably best encapsulated in the discursive genealogy of the notorious slogan 'Fatherland, Religion, Family', which does indeed help to expose the internal contradictions of the process of aestheticization that Greece itself, as a name, an idea, a narrative, went through in the modern era. Offering a number of examples of the use of the slogan in the service of conservative politics, Effi Gazi (2013) demonstrates how the associations of these concepts, as well as their interconnecting function, came about. Originating from a variety of popular sayings, catchwords and catchphrases dating back to the nineteenth century, the slogan, as Gazi outlines, followed a series of appropriations and invocations throughout the twentieth century, appearing in various conservative and reactionary discourses, from the critique of secular, Western-type modernity as well as of feminist and Marxist ideas by religious and other conservative organizations to the fascist, nationalist and anti-communist agenda of Greece's dictatorial regimes (2013, p. 706). Not strictly a Greek invention, as it crosses the ideological spectrum of numerous Western authoritarian as well as liberal and republican movements, the slogan stands for 'the core doctrines of conservatism: traditionalism, patriarchal family, religious values and morality' as Gazi explains (2013, p. 706).

As Gazi's study elucidates, the national project of constructing and narrating the Greek state and identity was channeled through a moralistic discourse that linked Orthodox Christianity and an idealized version of the traditional patriarchal family with images of national fatherhood and masculinity that reverberate with the fascist and national socialist biopolitics of the interwar period. Intersecting 'not only with gender but with class, as it came to be portrayed as the guardian of property against the threat of socialism' (2013, p. 705), the 'ideal traditional family' was often deployed as a 'firewall against the spread of Marxist and socialist ideas' as well as against the 'immoral' feminist discourse that occasionally threatened the traditional religious and family values. And as such it is still invoked and lauded by both the Church and conservative politicians as the cell that can 'provide harmony to the entire society and constitute a model for the nation' (2013, p. 702).

A genealogical study of such idealized patriarchal versions of the modern Greek family and the way they have been seamlessly incorporated into the discursive production of the country's capitalist state is provided by anthropologists Paul Sant Cassia and Constantina Bada in their study *The Making of the Modern Greek Family: Marriage and Exchange in Nineteenth-century Athens* (2006). Cassia and Bada (2006, p. 8) locate the emergence of the modern Greek family in the first decades of the nineteenth century, and especially after the War of Independence against the Ottomans and the establishment of the first Greek sovereign nation in the 1830s. Cassia reminds us that 'family and kinship are as much questions of morality and values […] as property relations' (2006, p. 16). As he explains, most of the familial economic systems (whether virilocal or uxorilocal) that emerged within modern Greek society were imbued with 'the desire to retain resources intact within the family, or at least to prevent their undue pulverization' (2006, p. 17). The model of household, kinship and marriage that prevailed, especially in the big cities, was that of the *nikokirei*. The *nikokirei* were an emerging, economically powerful class in the newly formed Greek state, who threatened the political monopoly of the *arkhontes*, that is the traditional nobles from the Ottoman period. This class emphasized the nuclear family and the massive endowment of daughters at marriage as a means of securing and pursuing prestige. The *nikokirei* model was particularly supported by the Orthodox Church, which 'was deployed to control the amount of goods offered at marriage' (2006, p. 31) and to oversee the conclusion of marital contracts. As Cassia notices (2006, p. 31), these agreements 'reveal a close, almost phobic, concern with the types and quality of bridal costumes, cash endowments and dowers, all issues which bear on boundary-maintaining mechanisms'.

The emergence and prevalence of the *nikokirei*, as an essentially urban class, also highlights the importance of urbanization and the political and economic significance of the city for an understanding of the evolution of the Greek family, its ethics and concerns from the nineteenth century, as well as its role in Greek politics (2006, p. 9). As Cassia explains:

> within Greece, the growth of the State's bureaucracy, which had to be established ex nihilo after the Ottoman departure, attracted rural notables to the cities, the new centers of power, and increasingly the dispersed mercantile elite. The lack of a common national culture, because of different regional ones whose only common element was the Greek language, and a despisal of the departed Ottoman overloads, meant that a new culture was to emerge in a rapidly expanding urban setting which indelibly influenced the ethics of the family and the significance of kinship in relations between family groups. (2006, p. 8)

Indeed, these 'newly formed urban populations had to rely extensively on kinship links and mutual support' (2006, pp. 10–11) as a way to secure the means of social survival and economic growth, the latter of which, more often than not, translated into access to participation in the state administration.[2] In this way, kinship links inevitably affected the political organization of the country, resulting in a highly corrupt political system, which, favoring clientelism and nepotism, gradually produced an inexplicably gigantic public sector, which was both disproportionate to the private one and overpaid. Koumandaraki laments:

> Whilst Greek society obtained very early in its history modern and European-like parliamentary institutions, these were controlled by political cliques who used these institutions for their own private interests. The prevailing mode of domination placed clientelistic relations at the centre of Greek politics and destroyed the impartiality of the modern political institutions. (2002, p. 41)

Hence, despite laying claim to individualism and personal autonomy the economic-political organization of the modern Greek state has never managed to relinquish its nepotistic foundations, which originated in the traditional forms of kinship and social organization that date back to the pre-modern era. These traditional forms have historically privileged familial bonds over the individual to the extent of fetishization, with the latter often finding him/herself unconditionally subjected to the will of the former. As political scientist Adamantia Pollis (1988) observes in her investigation of the power relations and the distribution of rights within the traditional Greek family, individualism and equal rights collapse in the face of a paternalistic construction that secures both the bodily and social survival of its subjects as well as of itself. Koumandaraki explains Pollis's findings as follows:

> the idea of equal rights does not exist in the traditional family, individual rights being strictly subjected to the hierarchical social position of each of the members. [...] The only recognized rights belong to social groups; they are the rights of the extended family and of the village over the individual, who has certain obligations towards the community. The lack of individual autonomy in the Greek family and/or agrarian community is primarily expressed in the organic unity that keeps it together. Individual autonomy is seen as the threat to the security of this whole. (2002, p. 42)

As is evident from Cassia's study discussed above, this hierarchical subordination of the individual to the traditional familial power systems effected by patriarchy was preserved even after the demographic and economic-political transformation of Greek society in the modern era. For the *nikokirei* model, which supported the capitalist foundations of the modern Greek state, although geographically and ideologically departing from the communitarian models of the extended family and the village, still heavily relied on an intrinsically patriarchal familial organization that imbued and regulated the lives of individuals, particularly of women.

The structural transformation that the organization of kinship underwent in the modern era in Greece has contributed, according to Koumandaraki, to the reinforcement of the Greek national identity and the consolidation of the modern capitalist Greek nation-state. Discussing the material conditions of this transformation, Koumandaraki explains that the demand for accommodation that was created because of the large urbanization movements and the concentration of the majority of the population especially in Athens signaled 'the abandonment of the tradition of the extended family living in one dwelling [...] [something which] reflected a shift towards individualism where self-reliance was closely connected to private property' (2002, p. 49). The acquisition of property as accommodation gradually became 'the symbol of the modern Greek's personal autonomy' (2002, p. 49), while the state's efficient response to the increasing need for accommodation increased the popularity of the right-wing governments.

Although these demographic developments contributed to the reinforcement of capitalism and nationalism at the expense of the old communal links between people, the traditional familial links remain unaffected; as Koumandaraki observes, 'family members tend to live within apartments in the same building or in the neighborhood' (2002, p. 50).

Hence, even if reduced to its nuclear version, the idealized Greek patriarchal family still pervades much of the nationalist discourse, as it is inextricably linked to the nation-state's capitalist organization, considered both as a structural pillar of the country's economy and the quintessential vessel of the nation's morals and values. Indeed, the vacuum left by the dissolution of the old communal ties, owing to urbanization and the social estrangement between individuals, is filled in the modern era with a growing sense of national belonging, which strengthened the Greek national identity. Koumandaraki astutely notices that with 'Greek nationalism [being] a modernizing force which transformed the members of extended families and traditional communities into political citizens with equal social status', the Greek paradigm ultimately verifies Ernest Gellner's theory that nationalism is the 'ideology which fills the gap that urbanization and industrialization create' (2002, p. 50).

In conclusion, the dissolution of the dominant kinship system of the traditional extended family of the Greek village into the nuclear family model as a response to the modern use of space in the big cities, in spite of bringing about a significant socio-political shift, which led to the incorporation of kinship into the material as well as ideological mechanisms of the nation-state, was not, however, accompanied by an equivalent or, at least, simultaneous dissolution of traditional patriarchal gender and sexual hierarchies. On the contrary, these were also to be deployed in the consolidation of the (contradictory) ideologies that have imbued the construction of the modern capitalist Greek nation-state. Indeed, what the above studies reveal is that familial bonds and associated power relations emerge as not only a crucial analytical category for an understanding of gender construction and the organization of domesticity in modern Greece, but also for investigating the material conditions of property transmission patterns, economic growth and social ascendancy within the newly formed state, and, ultimately, how these have affected the social and economic-political foundations of the nation itself. Ultimately, 'Greece' and 'Greekness' have been produced through a paradoxical amalgamation of such different traditions as classical antiquity, Orthodox Christianity and the folk culture of the Byzantine and Ottoman periods, but also through the odd merging of such contradictory relational structures as family, religion and the nation. But this could only be achieved insofar as the first two categories, namely family and religion, were reconceptualized and rendered subordinate to the third, that is the nation. For much as the family had to conform to the material and ideological conditions of the capitalist nation-state, so the Greek Orthodox Church had to turn the spiritual direction of its believers from the ecumenical Christian ethics of the universal loving society towards the nationalist project of racial and, thus, 'moral purification', combating the forces that have at various times threatened the nation physically or ideologically: from the Ottomans, through feminists and communists, to immigrants and queers.

The (Anti-)National Greek Cinema

In contrast to the conformist discourses of the Orthodox Church and the traditional patriarchal family, Greek cinematic production has, throughout its history, evinced a rather more ambivalent attitude towards the nation-state's official ideology. Although it is often regarded as a national phenomenon, owing, as Lydia Papadimitriou contends (2011), to its limited exportability, one can hardly argue that what has been labelled under the term 'national Greek cinema' has been faithfully national or even faithfully Greek. Such a claim certainly resonates with the familiar debate regarding the concept itself of 'national cinema', whose omissions and shortcomings Andrew Higson (2000) has brought to the surface. As Higson claims, the study of national cinemas encourages two problematic tendencies: first, to approach them in relative isolation, thus overlooking the interactions and exchanges between different national cinemas, and second, to focus 'only on those films that narrate the nation as just this finite, limited space, inhabited by a tightly coherent and unified community, closed off to other identities besides national identity' (2000, p. 66). The term 'national cinema' ultimately risks tautology, Higson argues, as it fetishizes the national, obscuring 'the degree of cultural diversity, exchange and interpenetration that marks so much cinematic activity' (2000, p. 64). Highlighting instead the permeability of borders and the 'hybrid' and 'impure' nature of 'modern cultural formations', Higson puts forward the concept of the transnational, which takes into consideration the 'complexities of the international film industry and the transnational movements of finance capital, filmmakers and films' that, indeed, make it difficult to define cinema 'by the limits of the nation-state' (2000, p. 73).

In effect, Greek cinema has always embraced the transnational, as this was inevitably embedded in its modes of production, distribution and exhibition, as well as style and representation, and indeed provides numerous instances that seem 'quite self-consciously to dissolve rather than to sustain the concept of the nation', to use Higson's words (2000, p. 67). Papadimitriou identifies the transnational dimensions of Greek cinema in its very beginnings and, specifically, in the work of the first Greek film practitioners, the Manakia brothers, whose work back in the 1900s was 'in no way specifically Greek', as she pointedly emphasizes, but offered, instead, 'ethnographic recordings of everyday life in the wider Balkan region' (2011, p. 494). However, as she then observes, the history of Greek cinema includes only a limited number of Greek films that display transnational configurations at the level of production and/or distribution, let alone in terms of themes and representations, arguing that 'of those films that deal with the "other", very few have avoided the trap of (negative) stereotyping' (2011, p. 508).

Contrary to this view, Karalis contends that 'Greek cinema was and still is a point of convergence, a space of colliding idioms, as expressed by Hollywood and European traditions', not only because of the enduring involvement of foreign capital and talent in the country's cinematic activity, but primarily because of the way collective efforts to construct a local visual idiom were seriously inflected by the dominant traditions worldwide, thus ultimately engendering 'a heterogeneity of cinematic endeavor' in Greece (2012, p. xvi). Karalis's voluminous historiographical account of cinematic production in Greece, from its inception up until very recently, indeed attests to the multivalent and diverse nature of what has been categorized under the label 'Greek cinema'. On the one hand, as he notes, throughout a century of filmic production in the country, the vast majority of films are uncomplicated genre films, which, following the Hollywood paradigm, are angled towards commercial success and thus less interested in formal and representational experimentation and radicality (2012, p. ix). Such uncomplicated productions, which inadvertently or deliberately turn a blind eye to the stark social realities surrounding the screen, were clearly predicated on a series of institutional attempts on the part of the state to control, through strict censorship laws, the ideas and forms propagated by the medium. On the other hand, many Greek filmmakers have not been reticent about their own political ideas and visions in their works, deploying cinema as a unique platform to express 'opposition—explicit or implicit—to the dominant ideology of the state as it was imposed through education, army, police, news media, and the Christian Orthodox Church' (2012, p. x).

Karalis goes on to argue that 'during most of its history, cinema, both as an industry and as a culture, developed in opposition to the institutions of the Greek state and its policies' (2012, p. x), creating an aesthetic space to raise questions about history, class, gender, identity and cultural memory. Some formally and/or representationally unconventional strands of filmic production especially offered precisely these kinds of oppositional ways 'of looking at established perceptions of reality, of framing the real and of representing conditions of Greek society at particular moments in history' (2012, p. x). Hence, in spite of the Greek state's 'intrusive censorship' and later its 'paternalistic hegemony',[3] which consistently aimed at controlling production and disseminating 'an ideology of oppression, self-marginalization, and folkloric exceptionalism', cinema—unlike any other cultural product in the country—uncovered the 'heterogeneity, pluralism, and diversity' immanent in the Greek social structure, 'in opposition to the official versions of "Greekness"' derived from 'a naive and parochial nineteenth-century historicism' (2012, pp. 286–287).

Greek cinema's distinctive display of 'oppositional aesthetics', as Karalis (2012, p. x) calls it, can perhaps be attributed to the redemptive and emancipatory qualities of the medium itself, whereby a privileging of the visual allows practitioners to break through the constraints of language, in this case of the Greek language as a perennial marker and constituent of Greekness and national exceptionalism. As Karalis explains, the rich literary tradition that characterizes the history of Greek culture, and includes many of the seminal texts of Western civilization, naturally buttressed the nation-state's ideology by affording a vehicle for articulating the nation's 'self-perception in terms of linguistic continuity with the culture of Homer, fifth-century Athens, and the Hellenistic, Byzantine and Ottoman periods' (2012, p. xviii.). Clearly, Karalis's argument here reverberates with the political underpinnings of Koraïs's project of linguistic 'purification' and 'unification', examined above. Indeed language, by privileging the eternal and monumental through this prominent literary tradition, has provided the basis for the nation's construction of historical coherence and cultural unity. However, unlike language, cinema, with its insistence on the fleeting 'images of the ephemeral and the temporary', has for its part exposed this ostensible historical and cultural cohesion as 'a palimpsest consisting of gaps, missing pages, and individual silences' (2012, p. xviii).

Arguably, this oppositional project has been carried out most success-fully by some particularly defiant Greek filmmakers, as well as by specific strands in the history of Greek cinema whose unconventional form and subversive content I aim to address briefly below in an attempt to trace the genealogical lines of the similarly defiant, contemporary trend.

In 1955, Cyprus-born Michael Cacoyannis released *Stella*, a film that fea-tures in its lead character an emancipated and sexually promiscuous female singer, who works at an Athens nightclub. According to Karalis, *Stella* was 'the culmination of the process of bringing Greek cinema to its maturity' (2012, p. 68). Apart from its technical achievements and aesthetic innova-tions, Cacoyannis's film still stands out for its highly subversive exploration of gender and sexuality, as well as for its establishment of 'distinct narra-tive codes to express the polarities between city and countryside'[4] (2012, p. 72). Having studied, lived and worked in London as a young actor and (primarily, stage) director, Cacoyannis's 'Greek' gaze, Karalis argues, was 'built on the narrative strategies of Hollywood, the realistic precision of British documentaries and the psychological complexity of French poetic realism' (2012, p. 69). A year after *Stella*'s release, another exceptional master of classical Greek cinema, Nikos Koundouros, presented to the Greek audience perhaps 'the most subversive and revolutionary text of Greek cinema', as Karalis describes the director's dark exploration of a sinister underworld and of the Greek state's totalitarianism in *The Ogre of Athens* (*O Drakos*, 1956). Blending noir undertones with touches of parody and carnivalesque surrealism, decking out the criminal underworld with uninhibited homoeroticism and exposing the performative nature of the state through the motif of the parades, Koundouros's film constitutes a unique 'political essay on surveillance and domination', which takes on a particular resonance in a politically unstable era of extreme oppression and escalated persecutions (2012, p. 73).

The 1950s and 1960s was arguably the most prolific and commercially successful period for Greek cinema, in line with the roughly contempo-raneous revitalization of other national cinemas (Italian neorealism, 'new waves' in France, Japan, Czechoslovakia and so on). The films produced in Greece were predominantly melodramas, comedies and *fustanellas* (moun-tain films) in the 1950s, and musicals and war films in the 1960s. Among these generic productions, the musical stands out as a particular case in the history of Greek cinema, as it attempted to 'negotiate the tensions and con-tradictions in Greek society that emerged from the rapid process of mod-ernization and social change in the 1960s' (Papadimitriou, 2012, p. 164).

By 'combining plot structures and iconography, as well as music and danc-ing styles from different traditions and origins', such as Hollywood, pre-war western European musicals and *epitheorisi*—that is, the Greek version of revue—the Greek musical 'affirmed and supported the dominant desires of the nation' for adopting and adapting to the Western (capitalist) values and lifestyle of social mobility and wealth accumulation, while simultane-ously preserving traditional Greek values, such as family and patriarchy (2012, pp. 150–151). Perhaps the most distinguished representative of the Greek musical was Yannis Dalianidis, who also directed some of the most psychologically nuanced and sophisticated Greek melodramas. Though meticulously covert, owing to state or self-censorship (family audiences were after all the main target of his producers), a vigorous game of inverted sexual psychodynamics always loomed in the background of his films, as Karalis observes (2012, p. 132). From the 'lustful homoerotic gaze' that wandered over the half-naked bodies of his male actors and dancers to the numerous 'erotic subtexts' of his narratives and his characters' 'repressed hysterias', Dalianidis's films 'were full of gender confusion, erotic symbol-ism, and tense sexual anxiety' (2012, p. 132). Indeed, dealing with such themes as family oppression, sexualized or self-inflicted violence, social exclusion, and also implicitly with incest and homosexuality, Dalianidis's oeuvre at all events projects an insightful, if camouflaged, grasp of the cri-sis of masculinity and (patriarchal) authority in modernized, westernized post-war Greek society, thus anticipating Greek cinema's contemporary explicit renditions of patriarchal cannibalization.

The 1960s also register the first signs of Greek cinematic modernism in the work of internationally acclaimed director Takis Kanellopoulos, whose films, as Panayiota Mini suggests, 'eclectically borrowed formal devices from both Eastern and Western European art cinemas', reworking them into 'a modern aesthetic that reflected on pain, loss and memory' (2012, p. 242). In particular, Kanellopoulos's first film *Sky* (*Ouranos*, 1962), which was nominated for the Palme d'Or at the 1963 Cannes Film Festival, displays what for a Greek film is an unprecedented amalgama-tion of temporal ellipses, lack of narrative details and loose causality. This unconventional film form, in conjunction with the slow panoramic shots of northern Greece's vast snowy landscapes and the long shots of immo-bile silent people, clearly broke with the linear and vibrant representations of national time and space registered in the elaborate sets and straightfor-ward narratives of mainstream studio productions of the period, which showcased the Greece of travel posters and the Parthenon.

In the 1970s, and despite the ubiquitous censorship imposed by the Junta of the Colonels' regime (1967–1974), cinematic production in the country experienced a profound reorientation with the emergence of the—in many ways—defiant New Greek Cinema (known in Greece by its acronym, NEK). However, before going on to discuss the influential NEK, it is worth noting briefly that the movement had an unexpected competitor in the emerging soft porn industry. Filmed on the Greek islands, with both local and international casts, low production values, bad acting and non-existent script, these commercially successful films targeted mainly male audiences both at home and abroad, also fostering the market for so-called 'sex-tourism' that blossomed throughout the 1970s, as Karalis observes (2012, p. 165). Karalis acknowledges the highly sexist ideology and androcentric character of these films, evident in their monolithic representations of non-heterosexual and female desire, and their pervasive de-eroticization of the male body.[5] Nevertheless, astonishingly enough and despite its predominantly phallocentric aesthetics, the soft porn production of the period encompasses some of the most provocative images of homosexuality, transsexuality and lesbian sex in the history of Greek cinema. In addition, the 'funny, ironic, sarcastic, almost carnivalesque celebration of sexual pleasures that some of these films encoded, in a society that struggled officially to regulate sexuality and control desire' aligns them with a long tradition of representations of transgressive sexual excess that dates back to the irreverent Aristophanic comedies, as Karalis boldly suggests (2012, pp. 166–167). However, at the same time, the vigorous presence of the soft porn industry in a politically turbulent decade ultimately exposes the hypocritical nature of the totalitarian state itself, which was after all rumored to have secretly endorsed the blossoming of the genre in order to entertain the sexually repressed (and politically oppressed) male population, thus posing questions regarding the complex entanglement of sex with politics and its diverse deployments in the machinations of the nationalist state.

At the other end of the scale, serious, intellectual and self-reflexive, NEK makes its appearance as a refreshing aesthetic movement. NEK was closed off from the capitalist circuits of the predominantly studio-based industry of the previous decades, instead relying on private and/or state funds for its production and distribution, and almost exclusively on the Thessaloniki Film Festival for exhibition. This context allowed NEK's filmmakers to experiment with the medium and depart from the themes, forms and style of the commercial cinema of the 1950s and 1960s, which itself gradually declined in the face of the rising popularity of television. Films such as Pavlos Tasios's *Yes, Certainly, But ...* (*Nai Men, Alla ...*, 1972), Pandelis Voulgaris's *Anna's Engagement* (*To Proxenio tis Annas*, 1972), Tonia Marketaki's *The Violent John* (*Ioannis o Viaios*, 1973) and Kostas Ferris's *The Murderess* (*I Fonissa*, 1974) mark a gradual transition to a self-reflexive cinema that was both strongly political and formally innovative, thus echoing the political, modernist and art cinemas of Western and Eastern Europe, yet seeking desperately to articulate a distinct national voice (Papadimitriou, 2011, p. 496). As Rea Walldén et al. observe, NEK was 'radical in its intentions', 'questioning aesthetic and political ideologies and institutions, subverting the conventions of narration and representation' and 'breaking with cinematic illusion' (2011, p. 439). However, they find that it was also characterized by 'latent conservatism': '[i]n terms of content, sexism was quite breathtakingly pervasive', while 'the interest in radical formal experimentation' was limited if not non-existent (2011, p. 439). Bridging this gap was the aim of a particular subgroup of filmmakers, such as Costas Sfikas, Stavros Tornes and Antoinetta Angelidi, who, despite working within the framework of NEK, and actively participating in the movement's publications, festivals and events, self-consciously followed a more radical trajectory in their experimentations with form, which places them in dialogue with the international movement of the avant-garde (Walldén, 2012). From the 'firm geometricity' and the 'painting qualities' of Angelidi's films to the 'intentionally inartistic crudeness' of Tornes's, the Greek avant-garde attempted an extreme exploration of both the physical and visual limits of film, thus demonstrating an unambiguous interest in the specificity of cinema as a language and as an art, as well as a desire to transgress the boundaries of the medium (Walldén, 2012). For Walldén, avant-garde cinema is characterized by an 'increased awareness of the political potential of form', to the extent of considering subversive form 'a political statement or even a revolutionary act' in itself (2012). She also singles out the radical work of Angelidi as an example of the feminist avant-garde, which targets the diachronic representation of women in Western art, by criticizing specific representations of femininity as well as the concept of representation per se (2012).

Even though the radical experiments with form initially pertained to the marginal stream of the avant-garde, by the 1980s the formalist tendency gradually became a core characteristic of the entire movement of NEK, a fact that, however, translated into a failure to reach broader audiences. Nevertheless, one of the movement's architects managed not only to remain relevant and inspiring throughout the 1980s but, most importantly, to cross national borders and become Greece's best-known and most critically acclaimed director, and, as Andrew Horton argues, 'one of the most original voices in world cinema' (1999, p. 5). This epithet, which for Greek cinema is extraordinary, is applied to none other than Theo Angelopoulos.[6] In Angelopoulos's oeuvre one can identify a seamless blending of modernist sensibility with references to the classical Greek tradition, the myths and the values of the past, through which the director examines contemporary social and political issues. Distinguished by their deeply historical character as well as by their explicitly leftist viewpoint, his films revisit Greece's and the Balkans' contemporary history and create the space to contemplate such issues as national identity, borders and mobility, migration and multiculturalism. This is achieved by reframing the traditional representational national space as well as by the director's signature treatment of cinematic time. As Horton observes, Angelopoulos's vision of the 'other Greece' has brought forth 'a Greece of rural spaces, long silences, mythic echoes, missed encounters, winter landscapes, wanderers, refugees, actors without a stage or audience, lonely expressways at night, depopulated villages, cheap cafes, and crumbling hotel rooms' (1999, p. 13). And this 'other Greece' is filmed in extreme long shots and long takes, numerous tableaux and prolonged silences that invite the audience not just to experience the screened realities but instead meditate on them and share the filmmaker's underlying vision, which is nothing less than the establishment of 'a [universal] community where individuals flourish without fear and repression', where differences and diversity in beliefs, attitudes and practices are understood and accepted (1999, pp. 15–16).

Angelopoulos's films, as Papadimitriou argues, 'bring to light a very clear movement from the national to the transnational—and from New to Contemporary Greek Cinema' (2011, p. 496), a transition that is effected in the 1990s when the search for identity and cohesion is finally over and Greek cinema experiences an opening to difference at every level. With the fall of Communism, Greece experienced a wave of immigration that forced a hitherto unprecedented engagement with the culturally and ethnically other, while at the same time encouraging an exploration of the diverse identities that have diachronically permeated Greek society and the unearthing of hidden histories, visions and desires. Cinematic production thus abandoned self-referentiality and the all-encompassing search for Greekness that imbued the post-dictatorship state-funded discourse of NEK, and attended more to 'the discovery of the perennial other that had existed within Greek society since its very establishment: the marginalized group, the religious other, the outcast, and the displaced or dissociative individual' (Karalis, 2012, p. xvi). Hence, although Greek cinema has always been infused with images of the other, its recent history demonstrates a proliferation of 'new cultural heroes' (as Karalis calls the immigrants, transvestites, masculinized females and other 'others' now beginning to occupy the foreground), which 'indicate[s] a deep crisis in the traditional values pertaining to masculinity, the vexed issue of "Greekness", and women's self-articulation' (2012, p. xvi).

Meanwhile, Greece's ostensible prosperity at the beginning of the twenty-first century, which was fueled by extensive—if not excessive—external borrowing as a result of the country's entry into the eurozone, engendered an equivalent reinvigoration of 'national sentiment', which Gourgouris (2004) characterizes as 'spontaneous Hellenomania'. This sentiment was, as expected, amplified by the successful, yet outrageously over-budget, 2004 Athens Olympics and the Greek football victory in the European Cup in the same year. As Gourgouris observes, this overwhelming feeling was not so much an instance of nationalist hysteria, but rather a factitious 'adoration of all things Greek' that was 'utterly explosive and all-embracing, unorganized and unguided by any political force, unreflective of any grand image or "Great Idea"' (2004). The same fraudulent prosperity facilitated a renaissance of commercial Greek cinema, marking the 2000s as the decade of the 'Greek blockbuster'.[7] As Papadimitriou notes (2014, pp. 5–6), in this decade Greek cinema 'saw a significant surge in popularity among Greek audiences', which was largely attributed to the fact that major distribution and/or exhibition companies (Odeon, Village, Audiovisual) became interested in financing Greek films, as long as they were 'designed with commercial imperatives at the forefront' (2014, p. 6).

Among the blockbusters that stand out in the 2000s are such high-profile, high-budget productions, as *Politiki Kouzina/A Touch of Spice* (Tasos Boulmetis, 2003), *Nifes/Brides* (Pandelis Voulgaris, 2004), produced under the supervision of Martin Scorsese, and Yannis Smaragdis's *El Greco* (2007)—the most expensive Greek film production up to that point—which, arguably, attempted to register cinematically precisely this euphoric atmosphere and, to some extent, even enhance it through a kind of cultural sanction. All three films are set in the past, featuring elaborate sets and costumes and crowning long-established national narratives of emigration, expatriation and repatriation, with the acclamatory endorsement of widely propagated past and present discourses of the nation's outstanding cultural uniqueness and of its highly esteemed values of family, religion and homeland. As Dimitris Eleftheriotis remarks, specifically with regard to *A Touch of Spice*, 'the film initiated a pleasurable and reaffirming historical and geographical journey that addressed past and present national anxieties, fantasies and aspirations' (2012, p. 21). In addition, the extensive deployment of cutting-edge technology, special effects and market-wise distribution practices, both in Greece and abroad, that made the three films commercially—if not critically—successful, simultaneously elevated them to 'source[s] of national pleasure and pride', and gave 'a promise of a bright future where Greek creativity and imagination find their secure place in the emerging and ruthless global circuit of cultural commodities' (2012, p. 34).

Nevertheless, alongside these lavish blockbusters, whose elegant decor and superb cinematography only enhanced the sense of the mythical that infused their nostalgic narratives, 'an innovative gaze full of curiosity, ingenuity, and contradiction was crystallizing', as Karalis observes (2012, p. 265). Indeed, the beginning of the new century was also marked by a revitalization of independent cinema in Greece, which ignited an uninhibited exploration of new and subversive modes of expression that borrowed from the postmodern aesthetics of the international indie film scene, while also being in dialogue with the traditions of modernist and global art cinema. An exemplary case of both innovation and subversion that sought to map the trivial and the insignificant rather than the historical and the monumental was, arguably, Dennis Iliades's *Hardcore*, the film that this book focuses on in Chap. 2. Released in 2004, the year that perhaps marks the peak of what are now called 'the years of the bubble' in Greece, Iliades's film constitutes a bitterly ironic commentary on the predominant feeling of its time, also predicting its uncertain ending. Corrosively disturbing the collective imaginary at such a moment of national delirium, Iliades's film dimly illuminates Athens' underworld, unapologetically attacking the nation's fantasies, including that of the sacred patriarchal family. Through its postmodern aesthetics the film attempts a formal and thematic deconstruction of, and experimentation with the nation's favorite narratives as well as with Greekness itself. In this way, *Hardcore* in many ways anticipates the so-called 'Greek Weird Wave', suggesting the prior existence of alternative voices that sought to express the 'weird' encounter with the 'crisis of meaning' through the core inscription of a clearly queer content. After all, the destabilization and demythologization of the wonted familial and national narratives is surely a quintessentially queer endeavor.

THE QUEER 'WEIRD WAVE'

The year 2009 constitutes a 'nodal point' for Greek cinema, as Papadimitriou notes, as 'it marks the beginning of both the crisis and of the new international visibility of Greek cinema', initiated primarily by the critical success of *Dogtooth*, the first film in 34 years to represent Greece at the Oscars (2014, p. 4). *Dogtooth*'s successful festival run was followed up by those of numerous other Greek films, which premiered at prestigious international film festivals prior to their opening in Greece, sweeping up several awards and making critics and audiences wonder, indeed, about this new wave of 'weird' Greek films (Scott, 2010; Rose, 2011). However, as Papadimitriou astutely points out, even though Greece's financial crisis ironically served as a vehicle for drawing international attention to Greek cinema, one should be wary of positing direct causal links between the crisis and this particular cinematic trend (2014, p. 2). After all, as Maria Chalkou argues (2012), this new cinema of 'emancipation', as she names it, needs to be understood in relation to a range of factors: the expansion and prosperity of the Greek commercial audiovisual industry in the 2000s, the enduring institutional failure of the Greek film sector, the development of new 'liberating' cinematic technologies, as well as the emergence of 'unprejudiced' and 'decentralized' forms of cinephilia, facilitated through new platforms of distribution and exhibition (DVDs, the internet). All these factors, in conjunction with the ongoing socio-political crisis and the growing tensions in the public domain between constitutional authority and new modes of articulating public discourse—by which she means specifically the alternative, independent and decentralized networks that communicated the 2008 riots—engendered, Chalkou contends, the emancipation of the new generation of Greek filmmakers from established practices, institutions and ideologies, and the emergence of 'challenging aesthetics and unconventional narratives' (2012, p. 259).

Along similar lines, Dimitris Papanikolaou observes, 'there is an interesting trend of cultural expression [being] produced in Greece at the moment, which, even though not always related to the crisis directly, can assume, in the current climate, a radical political position' (2011). Papanikolaou identifies in this cultural trend a consistent collective attempt to undermine and performatively disturb Greece's 'narrative of its national, political, sociocultural cohesion in synchrony and diachrony', thus dubbing the trend the 'poetics of disturbed archival logics' or the 'disturbed archive' (2011). Papanikolaou's deployment of the concept of the archive relies on Greece's international image as 'the quintessential archive of a perennial past', a logic that has consistently been the target of criticism by Greek postmodern thinkers and artists. However, as he points out:

> this type of undermining now has the potential to become a dominant political and culture critique, a full-blown genealogical attack that takes the current state not as a symptom of things that went wrong in the past, but as the very point from which the past should be reviewed, revisited, re-collated, reassembled and reassessed, both in political and in identitarian terms. (2011)

Papanikolaou lists a number of contemporary Greek films, including *Dogtooth*, *Strella/A Woman's Way* and *Attenberg*, which encompass instances of archival disturbance and excess and thus renegotiate the nation's favorite narratives in unpredictable ways. At the center of these films is a genealogical attack on the structural core of Greek society, namely the Greek family, which, as Papanikolaou acutely observes, is either 'short-circuit[ed] by excess' or 'radically reframed' (2011).

Focusing more on the trend's 'challenging aesthetics' than its subversive thematics, Afroditi Nikolaidou observes 'an excessive performative element at work that is constitutive of the formation of these "festival films" as a wave' (2014, p. 22). Drawing on Erika Fischer-Lichte's notion of the 'aesthetics of the performative', which privileges presentation over representation, and immediacy, liveness, physicality, unpredictability and performative repetition over referentiality and essentialism, Nikolaidou identifies the performative specificity of these films in three interconnecting elements that take into account both text and context: promotional strategies for festival participation; thematic motifs and acting style; and, last but not least, stylistic and narrational devices (2014, p. 23). Nikolaidou thus draws attention to the role of the festivals in the formation of this particular wave, to the alternative promotion of the films as art projects and transmedia events, to the 'bodily-centered', deadpan and presentational (rather than representational) narration that relies on repetition and corporeality defying language, *logos* and emotionalism, and, last but not least, to the recurrent thematics of performance that encompass games, re-enactments, public ceremonies and rituals. Drawing on Papanikolaou's notion of the 'disturbed archive', Nikolaidou concludes that the non-representational and more performative aesthetics of these films, ultimately, 'bears the mark of the shock, of destabilization, of discomfort of/for the present', which in turn calls for 'rearrangement, reframing and replotting' (2014, p. 40).

Anna Poupou explores the repercussions of these non-representational and performative aesthetics on the construction of cinematic space and time, something which evidences, as she argues with particular reference to Tsangari's oeuvre, 'a *return* to modernism, but a kind of modernism strongly affected by the experience of post-modernism' (2014, p. 67). Following David Bordwell's concept of 'parametric narration', Poupou explains that despite not straying from the linearity and causality that characterizes classical narration, the films' temporal structure also comprises 'the morphological traits of repetition, austerity and seriality', as well as specific structural parameters that are not necessarily linked or justified by the plot and sometimes even work independently of it (2014, p. 56). In addition, the excessive use of shallow focus in the films creates what Bordwell names 'planimetric' space, which aims at creating both a sense of isolation and enclosure that is consistent with the films' thematics of alienation, and an overall 'distanciated, dedramatized anti-naturalistic, abstract space' that in modernist cinema is often used to foreground a political, ideological or feminist agenda (2014, p. 59). In this way, she argues, more than merely a matter of similar or common thematics related to the social and economic crisis, the trend 'is also a matter of stylistic and narrative choices by a generation of filmmakers who are in dialogue with the global art-house scene and the modernist genealogies' (2014, p. 67).[8] Indeed, the effect of distanciation and defamiliarization achieved through such non-representational constructions of cinematic space and time, in conjunction with the central thematics of alienation and the anti-naturalistic, detached, deadpan acting style, ultimately create 'the feeling of the uncanny, a mixture of anxiety, fear or inexplicable "strangeness" related to un-familiar or ex-familiar situations that now became strange' (2014, p. 61).

As evident in the above analyses, existing research and criticism on the 'emancipatory' or 'weird' trend of contemporary Greek cinema focuses more on either a delineation of the contextual parameters that frame its production, distribution and critical success or a critical evaluation of the films' innovative aesthetics and the cinematic traditions that inform them. Valuable as these analyses may be for an understanding of the conditions of emergence of the specific cinematic trend, they are nonetheless characterized by epigrammatic—if not hesitant—interpretations of the particular ways these films explore, communicate and comment upon Greece's contemporary socio-political climate. The present book aims precisely at bridging this gap by means of a closer investigation of the way the films' performative and non-representational aesthetics create this 'feeling of the uncanny', exploring the particular meanings of this 'inexplicable "strangeness" related to un-familiar or ex-familiar situations that now became strange' (Poupou, 2014, p. 61), as well as the particular meanings of this 'present' that they destabilize and discomfort, the particular discourses that they seek to 'disturb' (Papanikolaou, 2011), or 'rearrange', 'reframe' and 'replot' (Nikolaidou, 2014). Interestingly, many of the critics and scholars listed above even refrain from using the qualifier 'weird' to refer to the particular trend; Nikolaidou, for instance, prefers the term 'Greek New Wave', since, as she notes, 'the term "weird" has many connotations and provides a characterization that needs further exploration and con-textualization' (2014, p. 21). However, the term 'New Wave' could be equally problematic as it recalls specific cinematic traditions that flourished around the world in the post-war era (Iranian New Wave, French Nouvelle Vague, Japanese New Wave, to name a few), thus failing to appropriately contextualize the current trend and grasp its synchronic aesthetic value.

Contrary to the above reservations, this book would like to embrace the epithet 'weird', although not unconditionally. What I am arguing for is rather a re-appropriation of the specific qualifier that draws on its seman-tic relation to another formerly derogatory, yet now re-appropriated term, namely the 'queer'. In other words, I would suggest a bold maneuver from the 'weird' to the 'queer' as a useful metonymic gesture that illu-minates the underlying rhetoric of the contemporary trend as precisely an acerbic queer critique in response to the ongoing national crisis. The re-appropriation of the term 'weird' as metonymic with 'queer' is not, however, so much invested in the films' representation of non-normative desire and sexual practices—although, such images frequently permeate their frames—as in the radical 'queer sensibility' that, arguably, imbues their non-representational, performative, 'weird' aesthetics and their treatment of the familiar familial and national space and narratives. On this I draw on Rosalind Galt's (2013) conception of the 'default cinema',[9] which refers to a strand of contemporary global art cinema that responds to recent histories of economic crisis by means of a radical 'queer' critique that infuses both its form and content. Galt's conception is theoretically anchored to Lee Edelman's critique of heteronormative and homonorma-tive conceptualizations of time and space, encapsulated in the axiomatic 'queer refusal of meaning',[10] as well as to Teresa de Lauretis's delineation of queer textuality as one 'that not only works against narrativity, the generic pressure of all narrative toward closure and fulfillment of meaning, but also pointedly disrupts the referentiality of language and the referentiality of images' (2011, p. 244). Through a (queer) defiance of narrativity and identity, as well as through a repudiation of normative conceptualizations and representations of time and space as meaningful and productive, 'default cinema', Galt argues, materializes the 'queer refusal to signify', as precisely a formal and thematic repudiation of the intertwined meanings and narratives of neoliberal capitalism, patriarchy and heteronormativity. Galt's 'default cinema' is primarily placed within the context of cinematic cultures of the economically ailing global South, while she uses as an exemplary case of this category a filmic example from Argentinean cinema, namely *Suddenly/Tan de repente* (Diego Lerman, 2002), which she finds defiant not only in textual but also in contextual terms, as the film is not 'fully legible', as she notices, within the 'neoliberal circulatory regime' of mainstream distribution and the major film festival circuit (2013, p. 70).

Clearly, Galt's conception emerges as a particularly useful analytical framework for an understanding of radical cinematic responses to the machinations of contemporary neoliberal capitalism. However, the different context in which European crisis cinema, and particularly the contemporary Greek trend, is produced, promoted and distributed, gives rise to particular theoretical challenges. On the one hand, unlike Argentina, Greece still strives to avoid defaulting on its loans, and to renegotiate the terms of its bailout within the neoliberal narrative of 'austerity', though there has been no sign of any diversion from the trajectory of deterioration in material conditions for Greek citizens', let alone any sign of economic growth. On the other hand, as the above critics of contemporary Greek cinema demonstrate (Chalkou, 2012; Nikolaidou, 2014; Papadimitriou, 2014), the current cinematic trend has crucially relied on the international film festival network for its promotion and distribution, if not even for its formation as a 'wave'. The contextual differences notwithstanding, this book takes its cue from Galt's delineation of the queer sensibility of 'default cinema' to suggest that the contemporary trend of Greek cinema similarly explores the situation around and after the eruption of the economic crisis, and, most importantly, the all-encompassing 'crisis of meaning' that it has unearthed, by virtue of a queer perspective through which the narratives of neoliberal capitalism, nationalism and patriarchy must be reviewed and re-examined, indeed by proffering a 'queer refusal of [their] meaning[s]'.[11]

In the book's chapters, this argument is supported through close textual analysis of a selection of contemporary Greek films, pertinent but
not exclusive to what has been categorized under the label of the 'Weird
Wave', that brings to the surface the multiple ways these films in effect
refuse, denaturalize and reframe Greece's familiar familial and national
space and time, both through their subversive thematics and through
their unconventional, non-representational form. At the same time, the
book investigates how these films turn the spotlight on the medium itself,
reconfiguring mainstream and canonical modes of representation, and
reframing its dominant affective mechanisms. My analysis of the films
draws on a range of methodological approaches from queer theory, film
theory, ethical philosophy and psychoanalysis, which, though stemming
from a different context, nonetheless turn out to be highly pertinent to
the specific case of Greece and Greek cinema, which, as is evident from
the historical account outlined above, has always 'flirted' with the West.

Chapter 2 carries out a psychoanalytic reading of Dennis Iliades's
Hardcore (2004), drawing on Edelman's notion of *sinthomosexuality* to
investigate the way the film deconstructs and negates the fantasies that
frame familial and national subjectivity through a suggestive spatiotemporal construction that dramatizes the fundamental psychoanalytic
pendulum swing between desire and the drive. Chapter 3 examines the
queer challenges that Yorgos Lanthimos's *Dogtooth* (2009) poses to the
traditional patriarchal narrative, as both a metaphor for the nation and
its structural quintessence, as well as to the concept of narrativity per se.
Chapter 4 reads Panos Koutras's *Strella* (2009) as an exemplary cinematic
case of the 'aesthetic queer utopias' modeled by José Esteban-Muñoz,
which invites the viewer to reframe and reimagine traditional ideologies
and representations of family and the Greek national space, both formally
and through its subversive thematics. Chapter 5 conducts a phenomenological analysis of Athina Rachel Tsangari's *Attenberg* (2010), which,
drawing on Sara Ahmed's *Queer Phenomenology* (2006), explores the way
the body's queer meanderings across a hostile and unproductive familial
and national space ultimately expose it as discursive rather than 'natural'.
Chapter 6 brings Derrida's *hauntology* as well as Judith Butler and Athena
Athanasiou's notion of 'dispossession' to bear on Yorgos Lanthimos's *Alps*
(2011), proposing a reading of the film as a queer critique of the way the
social space (familial, national and so on) produces regimes of recognition
that render some lives valuable and/or grievable, and others disposable—
a critique which also poignantly unveils the spectral presences that haunt

our sense of the self and the other. Finally, Chap. 7 examines the ways in which Ektoras Lygizos's *Boy Eating the Bird's Food* (2012) engages with both film and queer ethical models inspired by Emmanuel Levinas's notion of 'responsibility', interrogating mainstream totalizing narratives of victimization and inviting a reinvention of the humanist premises of the biopolitical.

By investigating the films' formal and thematic attack on the traditional meanings, narratives and representations of the family and the nation, and the canonical mechanisms and strategies of the medium, this book ultimately aims to construe the underlying rhetoric of the contemporary Greek cinematic trend as precisely a radically queer and ethical one, which not only aims to deconstruct and reframe the nation's and the medium's dominant and oppressive discourses, but also to invite a radical opening to difference, a radical openness of meaning itself towards the unthought and the indefinite.

NOTES

1. Arguably, the eras that expose in the most vivid manner the irony at the heart of this extraordinary conflation between the contradictory pagan Ancient Greek culture and the Judeo-Christian Orthodox tradition in the construction of Greek nationalism are the ones which showcase an extreme nationalist discourse at the forefront of the state's agenda, namely the eras of the country's dictatorial regimes. Ioannis Metaxas's regime, as well as that of the military Junta (1967–1974), put forward an eminently dangerous nationalist discourse, which, nonetheless, suffered from severe internal contradictions, owing to the eclectic appropriation of selected elements from traditions that differ historically and philosophically, including those just mentioned. Ironically, as Koumandaraki notices, 'in both cases the Greek Church did not react against the regime; on the contrary, amongst its leaders there were many sympathizers. In fact, in both cases the church, with its doctrines and religious practices, was used by the regime in order to support the authoritarian exercise of power' (2002, p. 48).

2. Government employment has always been quite popular among Greek citizens because of the stability and the generous financial benefits that the public sector offered its employees as compared to

the private sector. However, the recent economic crisis has significantly impaired the privileged status of public sector workers.
3. As Karalis explains (2012, p. xii), 'the Greek state functioned either
as the main sponsor of or the main obstacle to [cinema's] development' in the country, with 'heavy taxation' and/or 'lack of protec-
tionism', with 'imposition of strict political control' (especially
during the dictatorship years) or with 'a patronizing approach'
(after the dictatorship and up until the end of the 1980s). However,
from the 1990s and onwards, Karalis notes, international funding
has become more available, through European programs or con-
sortia with European or American companies, which has liberated
Greek cinema 'from its imposed or self-imposed tutelage to the
Greek state' (2012, p. xiii).
4. *Stella*'s assertive depiction of transgressive female sexuality and
renegotiation of traditional gender roles, as these are enmeshed
with issues of national space, are further discussed in Chap. 4,
which argues that Cacoyannis's film constitutes the quintessential
filmic pre-text of Panos Koutras's *Strella*.
5. As Karalis notes, in the soft porn films of the period assertive female
sexuality was relegated to representations of 'sexually active women
as whores, whose bodies were the easy prey of the male gaze'
(2012, p. 163), while gay male sexuality was often modeled on
and, thus reduced to, the heterosexual binary active/passive, with
the 'passive' partner depicted 'as an effeminate screaming queen
with an insatiable thirst for rough sex with hairy, oily, and foul-
mouthed Mediterranean men' (2012, p. 166).
6. Angelopoulos's international acclaim is evidenced by the numerous awards that he has won throughout his career, the most distinguished including the Palme d'Or at the 1998 Cannes Film Festival
for his film *Eternity and a Day* (1998), and the Grand Prize as well
as the FIPRESCI Prize for the film *Ulysses' Gaze* (1995) again at
Cannes in 1995.
7. An epithet coined by Michalis Kokonis (2012), grounded in the
lavish production values, the methods of distribution/promotion
in the market and, of course, the highly profitable returns of many
Greek films released in the 2000s.
8. Poupou draws specific parallels between the new trend and the
works of celebrated modernists such as Chantal Akerman, Jean-
Luc Godard and Robert Bresson, as well as of more contemporary

auteurs such as the Dardenne brothers, Michael Haneke and Ulrich Seidl.

9. Galt borrows from the language of economics, as she notes, to coin 'default cinema' as the one 'in which the radical refusal to pay intersects with the queer refusal to signify' (2013, p. 62).

10. Edelman's groundbreaking 'anti-sociality' and 'anti-futurity' thesis, as unfolded in his controversial *No Future: Queer Theory and the Death Drive* (2004), is further examined in Chap. 2.

11. After all, Galt herself makes a passing reference to *Dogtooth* as an instance of 'queer disturbance of meaning ' (2013, p. 65).

BIBLIOGRAPHY

Bien, Peter (2005) 'Inventing Greece', *Journal of Modern Greek Studies*, 23/2, 217–234.

Cassia, Paul Sant, with contributions by Constantina Bada (2006) *The Making of the Modern Greek Family: Marriage and Exchange in Nineteenth-century Athens* (Cambridge: Cambridge University Press).

Chalkou, Maria (2012) 'A New Cinema of Emancipation: Tendencies of Independence in Greek Cinema of the 2000s', *Interactions, Studies in Communication & Culture*, 3/2, 243–261.

Clark, Kenneth B. (1970) 'The Wonder is There Have Been so Few Riots', in August Meier and Elliott M. Rudwick (eds.) *Black Protests in the Sixties* (Chicago: Quadrangle Books).

de Lauretis, Teresa (2011) 'Queer Texts, Bad Habits, and the Issue of a Future', *GLQ: A Journal of Lesbian and Gay Studies*, 17, 243–263.

Edelman, Lee (2004) *No Future: Queer Theory and the Death Drive* (Durham and London: Duke University Press).

Eleftheriotis, Dimitris (2012) 'A Touch of Spice: Mobility and Popularity', in Lydia Papadimitriou and Yannis Tzioumakis (eds.) *Greek Cinema: Texts, Histories, Identities* (Bristol: Intellect), pp. 18–36.

Galt, Rosalind (2013) 'Default Cinema: Queering Economic Crisis in Argentina and Beyond', *Screen*, 54/1, 62–81.

Gazi, Effi (2013) ' "*Fatherland, Religion, Family*": Exploring the History of a Slogan in Greece, 1880–1930', *Gender and History*, 25/3, 700–710.

Gourgouris, Stathis (1996) *Dream Nation: Enlightment, Colonization, and the Institution of Modern Greece* (Stanford, CA: Stanford University Press).

Gourgouris, Stathis (2004) 'Euro-Soccer and Hellenomania' at http://www.lsa.umich.edu/UMICH/modgreek/Home/Window%20to%20Greek%20Culture/Culture%20and%20Media/CaM_Gourgouris_EuroSoccer.pdf, date accessed 22 April 2016

Gourgouris, Stathis (2010) 'Ανησυχία. μια καταγραφή του αυθόρμητου τον Δεκέμβριο του 2008 and We Are an Image of the Future. The Greek Revolt of December 2008 (review)', *Journal of Modern Greek Studies*, 28/2, 366–371.

Higson, Andrew (2000) 'The Limiting Imagination of National Cinema', in Mette Hjort and Scott Mackenzie (eds.) *Cinema and Nation* (London: Routledge), pp. 63–74.

Horton, Andrew (1999) *The Films of Theo Angelopoulos: A Cinema of Contemplation* (Princeton: Princeton University Press).

Jusdanis, Gregory (1991) *Belated Modernity and Aesthetic Culture: Inventing National Literature* (Minneapolis: University of Minessota Press).

Karalis, Vrasidas (2012) *A History of Greek Cinema* (New York: Continuum).

Kokonis, Michalis (2012) 'Is there Such a Thing as a Greek Blockbuster? The Revival of Contemporary Greek Cinema', in Lydia Papadimitriou and Yannis Tzioumakis (eds.) *Greek Cinema: Texts, Histories, Identities* (Bristol: Intellect), pp. 39–53.

Kornetis, Kostis (2010) 'No More Heroes? Rejection and Reverberation of the Past in the 2008 Events in Greece', *Journal of Modern Greek Studies*, 28/2, 173–197.

Koumandaraki, Anna (2002) 'The Evolution of Greek National Identity', *Studies in Ethnicity and Nationalism*, 2/2, 39–53.

Nikolaidou, Afroditi (2014) 'The Performative Aesthetics of the "Greek New Wave"', in Mikela Photiou, Tonia Kazakopoulou and Philip Phillis (eds.) *Contemporary Greek Film Cultures*, Special Issue of *Filmicon*, 2, 20–44.

Papadimitriou, Lydia (2011) 'The National and the Transnational in Contemporary Greek Cinema', *New Review of Film and Television Studies*, 9/4, 493–512.

Papadimitriou, Lydia (2012) 'Music, Dance and Cultural Identity in the Greek Film Musical', in Lydia Papadimitriou and Yannis Tzioumakis (eds.) *Greek Cinema: Texts, Histories, Identities* (Bristol: Intellect), pp. 147–166.

Papadimitriou, Lydia (2014) 'Locating Contemporary Greek Film Cultures: Past, Present, Future and the Crisis', in Mikela Photiou, Tonia Kazakopoulou and Philip Phillis (eds.) *Contemporary Greek Film Cultures*, Special Issue of *Filmicon*, 2, 1–19.

Papanicolaou, Dimitris (2011) 'Archive Trouble', in Penelope Papailias (ed.) *Beyond the "Greek Crisis": Histories, Rhetorics, Politics*, Special Issue of *Cultural Antrhopology*, http://www.culanth.org/fieldsights/247-archive-trouble, date accessed 22 April 2016.

Pollis, Adamantia (1988) *Κράτος, Δίκαιο και Ανθρώπινα Δικαιώματα στην Ελλάδα [State, Law and Human Rights in Greece]* (Athens: Institution of Mediterranean Studies IMM).

Poupou, Anna (2014) 'Going Backwards, Moving Forwards: The Return of Modernism in the Work of Athina Rachel Tsangari', in Mikela Photiou, Tonia

Kazakopoulou and Philip Phillis (eds.) *Contemporary Greek Film Cultures*, Special Issue of *Filmicon*, 2, 45–70.
Rose, Steve (2011) 'Attenberg, Dogtooth and the Weird Wave of Greek Cinema', *The Guardian*, http://www.guardian.co.uk/film/2011/aug/27/attenberg-dogtooth-greece-cinema, date accessed 22 April 2016.
Scott, A.O. (2010) 'Dogtooth: A Sanctuary and a Prison', *New York Times*, http://www.nytimes.com/2010/06/25/movies/25dog.html?_r=2&, date accessed 22 April 2016.
Veremis, Thanos (1989) 'From the National State to the Stateless Nation, 1821–1910', *European History Quarterly*, 19/2, 135–148.
Walldén, Rea (2012) 'The Avant-Garde, in Cinema, in Greece', in *AΩ International Online Magazine*, http://www.onassis.gr/online-magazine/issue-22/article-8.php, date accessed 22 April 2016.
Walldén, R., E. Hamalidi, and M. Nikolopoulou (2011) 'A Second Avant-Garde Without a First: Greek Avant-Garde Artists in the 1960s and 1970s', in S. Bru, L. van Nuijs, B. Hjartarson, P. Nicholls, T. Ørum and H. van den Berg (eds.) *Regarding the Popular: High and Low Culture in the Avant-Garde and Modernism* (Berlin: De Gruyter), pp. 425–444.

CHAPTER 2

Hardcore: Of the Death Drive

An imposing shot of the Parthenon. The camera slowly dollies out and the image of the perennial marker of the nation's glorious—if mythical—past is revealed to be nothing but a picture hanging on the wall. The film's two protagonists, Martha (Katerina Tsavalou) and Nandia (Danae Skiadi), enter the frame from each of its two sides, thus framing the iconic monument, while looking off-screen at an undisclosed spectacle, whose atrocious nature is nonetheless evident in the splatters of blood that cover Nandia's face and clothes as well as in Martha's enigmatic gaze (Fig. 2.1). Low-key lighting and suspenseful non-diegetic music accentuate the scene's overarching feeling of agitation. This is how Dennis Iliades introduces us to *Hardcore*'s (2004) relentless cartography of Athens' underground spaces, a journey that is mastered and directed not only by (queer) desire but also by the inescapably deadly trajectory of the drive. Martha's suggestive look grows darker as the camera dollies in and frames her in a medium shot—the Parthenon always in the background. The story begins with a voice-over, thus establishing from the very beginning one of the film's central narrative elements, for Katerina Tsavalou's suave, deadpan voice will guide (or better misguide) us throughout this cinematic game of hide and seek. 'Usually fairy tales are crystal clear. It's impossible to both love and not love someone. You need to take a position',[1] the voice-over says. The film abruptly cuts to a series of spotlights that turn on simultaneously for the camera, which in turn quickly tilts down to reveal among the shadows of a theatrical audience Martha, whose suggestive gaze is fixed on the stage (or is it on the extra-diegetic audience?). A shot of the stage

Fig. 2.1   Blood-spattered Parthenon

then shows us in slow motion a burning Ancient Greek warrior crossing the frame in circular movements right in front of Nandia, who is standing motionless, wearing a short grey chiton against a black backdrop that features a Corinthian column. As the warrior vanishes into the black abyss the film cuts back to Martha's close-up and her voice-over: 'However, I know it's possible. I felt this way with Nandia. I felt it every day. It was much stronger than me. Perhaps, our own fairy tale had expired.'

In less than three minutes, the viewer is introduced, through a fast-paced montage of fascinating cinematic eloquence, into the main thematic axes and formal structure of *Hardcore*. For Iliades's film is as much about Martha and Nandia's narratives of desire as it is about the nation's narratives that both haunt the queer subject and are haunted by it, and which are invoked here in the form of banal nationalism. In effect, this chapter reads *Hardcore* as an aesthetic polemic against Greece's familiar and highly valorized familial and national narratives through the conceptual lenses offered by contemporary queer theorizations of time and space, as well as by post-Lacanian psychoanalysis. Investigating the way in which the film's form and narrative stage the fundamental psychoanalytic dialectic between desire and the drive, and the way this dialectic is reflected on, and/or appropriated in contemporary theorizations of queer spatiotemporality, I wish to offer not simply a queer reading of Iliades's film, but most importantly a reading of the film as *queer*, especially in the way it ultimately targets and deconstructs normative and hegemonic conceptualizations of familial and national space and time.

Based on the eponymous novel by Aleka Laskou,[2] *Hardcore*, the first feature film by director Dennis Iliades, tells the story of teenage runaways Martha and Nandia, who meet at a brothel, where they both work as prostitutes. At first, Martha is envious of Nandia's success with boys and clients, but her envy gradually shades both into love and into hate. The girls soon develop a close relationship, which exceeds the boundaries of friendship, supporting each other against the adversities of street life. Drawn into a vicious circle of drugs, prostitution and violence, inflicted both upon and by them, romantic Martha and opportunistic Nandia manage to escape conviction by presenting themselves as victims rather than perpetrators, yet fail to achieve prosperity. When Nandia's vanity condemns them to the flashy yet corrupted world of show business, jealous and neglected Martha suffocates her to death and escapes to an unknown destination, away from the city.

Hardcore entails a corrosive critique of both blood and chosen family, of both heteronormative and homonormative accounts of relationality, of sociality per se. The protagonists are simultaneously victims and perpetrators, who wander about constricted and decaying or luxurious yet corrupted urban spaces only to satisfy their sexual drives, their drug addiction or their vanity. Clearly, the film draws on New Queer Cinema's aesthetics in its mixing of styles and genres, in its portrayal of sexuality as fluid and unpredictable, in its sharp exposure of the performative character of gender, as well as in its self-conscious unapologetic (mis)appropriation of visual culture, the allusions to which in some cases become explicit, as we will see below. Time and space are rendered wasted, unproductive, destructive—indeed, queer—but, at the same time, beautifully visualized and frenetically edited through the film's postmodern style, which have made critics describe Iliades's film as 'a great-looking movie that owes a major visual debt to modern music videos and American indie films' (Digital Vault, 2008), as well as compare Iliades himself to such directors as David Lynch and Quentin Tarantino (Zervopoulos, 2004).

Further to their enthusiastic reception and welcoming of Iliades's 'flashy directorial style' (Raffel, 2004), critics also attempt to investigate and complicate the way film form is unavoidably implicated and interrelated with the narrative and the film's dark queer thematics. Digital Vault blogger (2008) admires how 'grimy scenes of hooker life juxtapose nicely against more sensitive, almost naturalistic moments', while Raffel (2004) describes the film as 'nothing less than a captivating viewing experience [...] gritty and often disturbing in its attempt at realism', which 'even in its darkest hour [...] chooses to bring us out of its misery with a flashy sitcom-like parody'. Nevertheless, he concludes (2004), 'you'll be hard-pressed to crack much more than a slight smile, knowing the darkness that ultimately lies ahead'.

Even more fascinating is the way Iak Jane (2005) verbalizes the film's oscillation between light and darkness, dream and reality, as attuned to characterization and with it to the film's overall preoccupation with the perils and fantasies of queer life. Jane observes:

> The cinematography is at times stark and harsh and at other times quite soft and pretty, [thus resulting in] a movie filled with contrasting imagery, which makes sense considering that the storyline is based around the contrast between the two main characters. Nadia's got ambition, drive and energy—she wants to be remembered and be a somebody, she loves the attention and she loves to have people want her. Martha on the other hand is the quiet type who yearns for something resembling a normal family, if there is such a thing. (2005)

Jane's wording invokes some of the central concepts that guide this chapter's reading of *Hardcore* as a narrative and formal embodiment of the perennial dialectic between desire and the drive; namely, drive, yearning, family, 'normality'. However, unlike Jane, I would suggest that the oscillation between desire and the drive is not represented in *Hardcore* through some clearly delineated characterization that incarnates respectively each of the two—say Martha as an embodiment of fantasy and desire and Nandia as an embodiment of the drive. The pivotal psychoanalytic pendulum is rather staged here through an ambivalent construction of cinematic space, a complicated treatment of queer spatiotemporality that, on the one hand, imagines it as constructive and productive, while, on the other, exposes it as destructive, wasteful and caught up in a relentless negativity associated with the death drive.

According to Lacanian psychoanalysis, the acquisition of Language marks the child's entrance into the Law of the Father and the Symbolic Order, the quintessential agent of prohibition that regulates the subject's pleasures and structures the fundamental kin positions through the incest taboo. Desire is directed towards the substitution of the impossible sexual relationship with the mother, and thus the fantasmatic overcoming of the fundamental lack in the Other. However, desire has to be continuously deferred so as to ensure the concealment of this lack as well as of the Symbolic Order's inconsistency. For the Symbolic Order's consistency relies precisely on this fantasy that supports desire. Hence, as Slavoj Žižek argues, desire is 'already a certain yielding, a kind of compromise for-mation, a metonymic displacement, retreat, a defence against intractable drive' (1995, p. 172). In this way, Žižek explains (1995, p. 134), the psychoanalytic opposition:

> between desire and drive consists precisely in the fact that desire is by defini-tion caught in a certain dialectic, it can always turn into its opposite or slide from one object to another, it never aims at what appears to be its object, but always 'wants something else'.

On the other hand, 'a drive is precisely a demand that is not caught up in the dialectic of desire, that resists dialecticization' (1995, p. 21). Unconditional demand is that which defines the pure drive, which is inert and constantly circulating 'around its object, fixed upon the point around which it pulsates' (1995, p. 134), which is none other than *jouissance*. And *jouissance* in Lacan is that ever-elusive, impossible enjoyment, beyond the pleasure principle and bordering on pain, which is rendered impossible precisely because it threatens the Symbolic Order, by exposing its imma-nent vulnerability to the partial and self-destructive drives.

Before bringing psychoanalysis to bear on queer spatiality it is impor-tant to be clear that the invocation of queer space does not necessarily entail any particular locality with or community of queers, organized around clearly delimited physical or virtual spaces. In a collective volume on queer spatiality entitled *Queers in Space*, Gordon Brent Ingram warns us against understandings of queer space as alternative '"communities" of individuals who possess only vaguely similar desires, practices, and sen-sibilities, and who demonstrate a great disparity in their vulnerability to economic and cultural inequities' (1997, p. 36). Instead, he envisions queerscape as 'a landscape of erotic alien(n)ations, ones that shift with demographics, social development, political economies, interventions of the "state", aesthetics, and—yes—desire' (1997, p. 31). Ingram's notion of 'queerscapes' encompasses a dynamic between 'marginality' and 'erotic alienation' as the immanent forces that both create and transform them. If marginality is the condition that results from the domination of heterosexuality, namely a decentralization of queer desires, acts and communalities, then alienation is the affect produced 'in the people who do not experience sufficient benefits from [this domination]', and thus form alternative social networks that, in turn, 'can produce more marginalization—especially in times of more organized homophobic repression' (1997, p. 29). In this way, Ingram argues, 'one process feeds off the other: an erotic marginality leads to an internalized and environmental alienation, and this constitutes the core, the queerness, the queasy antipodean, of "queer space"' (1997, p. 29). Ingram also explains how excess and instability have been associated with canonical descriptions of queer spatiality, which may vary from 'exceptional starkness replicated in warehouse aesthetics [...] to exceptional richness and complexity rivaling the decorum of royal courts' (1997, p. 30). At the same time, invisibility and 'the closet' have been adopted as individual strategies for 'coping with queer intensification and the compounding of marginality and alienation', although this has only led to the 'feedback loops' between the two spatial forces being 'lengthened and internalized' (1997, p. 30). Accordingly, Ingram's 'queerscape' emerges as always already a space of social and political confrontation, where the 'heterosexist' dichotomies of public and private space are questioned, and public space queerly reclaimed. In his words, 'the thorough queering of the landscape will mean that the existing poorly recognized barriers to equitable use of public space will be removed' (1997, p. 29).

Ingram's optimistic invocation of a kind of linear and teleological narrative of queer futurity in this outline of queer spatiality as something that ultimately frees up productive social and political forces is, however, devastatingly challenged by the so-called anti-social thesis in contemporary queer theory, inaugurated by Lee Edelman in his controversial book *No Future: Queer Theory and the Death Drive* (2004). The anti-social thesis argues that the dialectic of desire is precisely what constitutes and temporalizes politics as a fantasmatic structure of perennial deferrals that merely ensure the perpetuation of the Symbolic Order. The metonymic register of politics as fantasy takes shape in Edelman within a Lacanian context, where politics, much 'like the network of signifying relations that form the Lacanian Symbolic—the register of the subject and the order of the law', function 'as the framework within which we experience social reality' in the form of a fantasy: 'the fantasy, precisely, of form as such, of an order, an organization, that assures the stability of our identities as subjects and the coherence of the Imaginary totalizations through which those identities

appear to us in recognizable form' (2004, p. 7). As subjects of the signifier, through which we always already inhabit the order of the Other, we
are called into meaning by the signifier itself, through the process of subjectivation, by being endowed with a 'promissory identity', with which we
can, however, never coincide as it is impossible to identify with something
outside ourselves. Politics, thus, names the space where such Imaginary
relations 'compete for Symbolic fulfillment'; it is nothing less than 'the
struggle to effect a fantasmatic order of reality in which the subject's alienation would vanish into the seamlessness of identity' (2004, p. 8). The
ceaseless conflict between the social visions of opposing political perspectives however conceals, as Edelman argues, 'their common will to install,
and to install as reality itself, one libidinally subtended fantasy or another
intended to screen out the emptiness that the signifier embeds at the core
of the Symbolic' (2004, p. 8). Caught up in a chain of ceaseless deferrals,
politics, then constitutes 'the temporalization of desire, its translation into
a narrative, its teleological determination' (2004, p. 9), offering history
as the continuous staging, the fantasmatic narrative of desire's movement
across the endless reconstruction of what we construe as reality.

At the same time, this fantasy is constantly threatened by the relentless
and unpredictable invasion of the drive, which queerness itself is called on
to represent. Architecture critic Aaron Betsky's account of queer space as
'a useless, amoral, and sensual space that lives only in and for experience',
effectively marks out that space, and therefore queerness itself, as a met-
onym of the drive (1997, p. 5). As he contends, queer space 'is a space of
spectacle, consumption, dance and obscenity. It is a misuse or deformation of a place, an appropriation of the buildings and codes of the city for
perverse purposes' (1997, p. 5). In this way, Betsky's account anticipates,
although in phenomenological rather than psychoanalytic terms, the anti-
social thesis which, as we will further examine below, does indeed read
queerness as a non-teleological negativity associated with the death drive,
because its adherence to sexuality and the pleasure principle obliterates
any political aspirations (Edelman, 2004; de Lauretis, 2011). In this sense,
Iliades's camera can be seen as mapping the perennial psychoanalytic oscillation between desire and the drive, navigating the viewer through spaces
that invoke both Ingram's destabilizing yet, potentially, political account of
queer space (what Edelman might term as a space of desire), and Betsky's
take on queer space as wasted and wasteful (or in Edelman's terms, a space
of the drive). By the same token, as we shall see, the film renegotiates conventional constructions of cinematic time as linear and teleological.

After the introductory prelude described above, the film cuts to a low-angle shot of Nandia struggling to balance her body with her hands pushing against the wall, while she gets slammed from behind by an abusive client. Even though her face is not clearly visible, her crying and quiet sobbing at the end of the intercourse provide evidence of both physical and emotional pain. The bleak and murky hues of the scene's lighting give the impression more of a prison cell rather than a prostitute's room. When the client exits the static frame with an array of foreign words the sound of which implies vituperation, the film cuts to a medium shot of Nandia from the side as she makes an effort to compose herself. The audience is then introduced to the brothel, the recurring place of reference at least of the first half of the film, with a tracking shot of Nandia as she walks through the building's corridors to the reception area. On the soundtrack Martha's voice-over continues: 'Nandia appeared all of a sudden in a place we considered our own. It wasn't a plain cafeteria. It was our home.' Playful youngsters then appear in the margins of the moving frame, as well as video game and vending machines and a bar. Iliades then presents us with a three-shot of two rent-boys, Argyris and Miltos and, of course, Martha, who cannot take her eyes off Nandia. 'Our boss had gathered us here from newspapers ads, but he was so much more than just an employer [...].'

Our guided tour of the brothel continues a few minutes later into the film, with a left-to-right pan across an array of young male and female prostitutes waiting for the boss to give them one of the colorful post-its with which he manages the house's clientele. The camera stops and fixes on a three-shot of Zois, the prostitutes' bodyguard, and a couple of young twins sitting at the bar. Behind the girls a TV suggestively plays, glorifying images of the Greek flag, paradoxically accompanied by the European Union's anthem rather than the Greek national one. The irony of this juxtaposition is further enhanced by Martha's voice-over as she explains how the boss takes special care of all of his boys and girls by having Zois protect them and Sfiriktras, a dealer, provide them with drugs. One wonders what this grotesque juxtaposition is really about. Is it a provocation to draw parallels between the 'over-protective and caring family' of the whorehouse and that of the EU? Is it an insinuation that the country's accession to the European 'family' and the monetary union constitutes nothing less than a form of subjugation, metonymically rendered *in* and *by* the film as prostitution? And how ironically relevant does this juxtaposition turn out to be in the age of the so-called 'debtocracy'?[3] How much does the governmentality of the crisis, in its blind and vicious capitalist negotiation between human bodies and fiscal figures, really seem to differ from the pimp's colorful post-its and bargains?

Shortly after this, Martha and Miltos are shown sharing some 'liquid lady' (cocaine dissolved in water) poured on a biscuit by Sfiriktras. Soft piano notes start filling the soundtrack signaling the beginning of Martha's hallucinatory journey. The camera zooms in to an extreme close-up of her eye and then the film dissolves to another zoom shot of a washing machine drum whose faded coloring helps it masquerade as an eye itself, but a spinning eye that washes together random images from memories, dreams and nightmares. A black-and-white clip shows a father playing with his young daughter; an old blue frame features a barely discernible figure of a young girl sleeping; a close-up of a humongous black dildo in the hands of a naked man; an animated shot foregrounds a red heart growing bigger and bigger; an unsteady shot of a Catholic statue of Mother Mary; a poorly lit long shot of Martha sitting naked on a bed in an empty deserted room; a clip from children's cartoons; and, finally, another zoom shot of Martha lying among a gang of naked tattooed men. With this montage of video, animation and photography, Iliades manages to create a highly evocative juxtaposition between happy childhood memories and traumatic images from both the past and the present, all of which inhabit the tragic psyche of the young prostitute. Hopes and dreams emerge as remnants of a lost soul. A nostalgic will to return to a fantasmatic age of innocence is precisely highlighted as a fantasy, underpinned by mythical religious and familial narratives that prove to be no more real than fairy tales themselves. The destructive force of the drive incarnated in Martha's promiscuous and 'perverse' sexual activity, which is here highlighted as indeed a 'painful enjoyment', subverts any fantasy and undermines any dream.

But it is not only drug use that gives Iliades the excuse to throw dreamlike and fantasy sequences in the narrative. On many occasions dream and fantasy interject in their own right and the only narrative element that seems to tie them into the film's story is Martha's voice-over. After witnessing Nandia and Argyris making out in the toilets, Martha finds Miltos stoned and starts kissing and caressing him. On the soundtrack her voice-over returns:

MARTHA   […] our job is misunderstood. It's either shown on the news with strings playing on the soundtrack or perceived as the easiest thing on earth. But fucking three or four people every day is killing you. And everybody looks down on you. It is impossible to date a stranger. He wouldn't understand. Therefore, we started dating each other. Just like in 'Beverly Hills'!

Close-ups of the youths suddenly give way to an unexpected musical number, which features the four young protagonists of the film (Martha, Nandia, Argyris and Miltos) playing, dancing and posing for the camera against a white backdrop, strongly reminiscent of the title sequence of the popular 1990s American TV show (Fig. 2.2). An abrupt change of set and costumes reveals the four characters as burlesque dancers, sporting flashy costumes and heavy make-up and dancing in strictly choreographed moves against a black backdrop. The camera slowly zooms out and the stage is shown to be resting on giant glowing multicolored letters that spell the word 'Happy'. Iliades offers some loving close-ups of his actors here, which show them smiling and enjoying the number. But Martha soon loses her smile as she becomes aware of the presence of their boss, Manos, in the fantasy, who is performing his own show at the bottom of the stage, in front of the big letters. The orchestral non-diegetic music is pushed to the background and Martha's voice-over once again interrupts the flow of the images: 'Nandia was looking at me strangely. She knew I was jealous of her because of Argyris, that I was generally jealous of her. But even though Argyris seemed to fall madly in love with her, she got more and more attached to me.' An exchange of smiles between the two girls then follows, which marks the beginning of their special relationship.

Fig. 2.2 'Just like in "Beverly Hills"!'

The brothel is evidently foregrounded as a place of abuse and oppression, a strictly controlled community, which is governed by the paternalistic figure of the ostensibly benevolent, yet vicious pimp, who ensures
the maintenance of his improvised social order by means of violence
and intoxication. Most of the prostitutes, as Martha states in one of her
numerous voice-overs, are runaway teenagers who sought not a better life,
but a life away 'from their boring and oppressive parents', who, nonetheless, eventually become entangled in a relentless game of sex, violence and
drugs, which is often hard to escape. In the shadow of this vicious circle,
however, an alternative community surfaces among the young prostitutes;
indeed, a marginalized community with its own rules, alliances, aspirations
and fantasies. The brothel thus emerges as a contradictory space. On the
one hand, it is the unproductive locus of violence and sexual insatiability,
a 'useless, amoral and sensual place' to invoke Betsky's words, indeed,
the locus of the drive. On the other hand, it simultaneously emerges as
a productive space where the processes of marginalization and alienation
that frame the everyday reality of queerness and prostitution, as Ingram
has astutely pointed out, provide a platform for the formation of alternative relationships, framed within an economy of desire. And it is these
alternative relationships that underlie the ignition and perpetuation of fantasy, which filmically blurs with the characters' reality, thus preserving the
consistency of their Imaginary identifications; in Martha's case as 'family
material'.

Arguably, this nuanced representation of queer space in *Hardcore* is
not only staged through the complicated treatment of the brothel as an
example *par excellence* of the contradictions that define queer spatiality,
but also through the film's more general ambivalent preoccupation with
the notions of 'home' and 'family'. Unsurprisingly, it is again the brothel
that originally lends itself, as already noted, as an equivocal alternative
familial choice. Indeed, where Martha's (im)passive personality at the
beginning of the film seems largely to invest in the possibility of replacing the parental home with the brothel, the assertive Nandia refuses to
consider it as other than a stepping-stone in her adventurous path to fame
and seeks 'home' in more intimate spaces that she can share with Martha.
As the story unfolds 'home' and 'family', more than mere objects of trivial
chatting between the two girls that happen to come up in passing, emerge
as central concepts among the film's visual and thematic preoccupations.

As revealed in the passages analysed above, an Imaginary version of the
quintessential symbolic figure of the father insistently haunts Martha's lab-

yrinthine hallucinations, thus underpinning her metonymic investments in the brothel as an-other home and Manos as an-other father. However, as the film develops, more conventional notions of familial space and time appear to pervade Martha's desires and compete with her inherent lack of agency as well as with the invincible force of her queer drive. The film's staging of this impossible wavering between longing and living is utterly fascinating. After Manos offers Martha and Nandia a 'mauve appointment' (the highest in his twisted post-it hierarchy) for a posh orgy party, the girls are dismissed in order to prepare sufficiently for the big job. Martha flees to her own 'cuckoo's nest', seeking the illusive relief of Sfiriktras's pills. Iliades then takes the opportunity to offer to us another dark glimpse into the elusive world of intoxication, this time not with a montage of hallucinatory images but with Martha's subtle verbalization of her inmost fantasy. Between a series of murky, heavily shadowed, red-color-infused shots framing Martha and Miltos taking drugs under the inconspicuous, yet enigmatic gaze of Sfiriktras, Martha confesses to Miltos her wish to have a proper relationship with him 'just like the rest of the world'. 'We are not like the rest of the world', Miltos replies and Martha immediately responds, 'Don't you want to make a family?' She then quickly turns her head to Sfiriktras, who purses his mouth in a sardonic smirk. Miltos gives her a quick kiss and lies on her shoulder wishing her good luck at her mauve appointment. Martha exits the frame.

A few minutes later in the film the subtleties of desire give way to the assertiveness of the drive. Nandia and Martha, dressed to the nines, enter a luxurious apartment for their mauve appointment. Iliades's ever-roaming camera traverses the corridors to find the living room, where a large group of well-dressed men and women await the girls under the subtle light of an elaborate crystal chandelier—a scene that has been compared to Kubrick's famous orgy sequence in *Eyes Wide Shut* (Raffel, 2004). The sequence that follows consists of a series of Martha's point-of-view shots, as she scans the room to find Nandia, who is either snorting cocaine or pleasing the clients, juxtaposed with her own close-ups. The latter shots foreground her inner struggle to balance herself between the carnal masochistic pleasure produced by her sexual exploitation by the numerous lascivious aristocrats who slip into the margins of the frame, and a kind of emotional confrontation with her own desires and dreams that takes over the soundtrack in the form of the now familiar narrative motif of her deadpan voice-over (Fig. 2.3). 'Nandia is right. I'm a whore and I enjoy it. I really enjoy being paid and fucked. Tonight Martha has an identity; name: whore,

Fig. 2.3 'Tonight Martha has an identity; name: whore, surname: whore, address: whore'

surname: whore, address: whore. Martha's high tonight. Martha belongs to you. She'll make you proud with a crazy orgy.' However, all of a sudden the voice-over turns into a diegetic verbal attack against Nandia—or is it against herself? 'Nandia, go fuck yourself! I'm not going anywhere! This is not a stepping-stone for me. I like it here. This is where I want to be. Nowhere else.' Everybody freezes. The party is over. Martha's voice-over emerges here as an intrusion of the Real, undermining the consistency of her fantasies. Martha unapologetically suspends her idealized dreams of family-making and pronounces her absolute submission to the painful and self-destructive 'enjoyments' of prostitution, which emerge here, indeed, as an embodiment of *jouissance*, the drive's only destiny and destination.

In effect, *Hardcore*'s overall deployment of voice-over is crucially implicated in the film's preoccupations with the existential contradictions between queer experience, longing and nostalgia. More than a mere narrative device in support of characterization or causality that will fill in the gaps of the filmic rendition of Laskou's novel, Iliades's use of voice-over recalls Chinese director Wong Kar-Wai's characteristic deployment of the device, which Jean-Marc Lalanne has theorized as an eloquent form for expressing the 'fundamental solitude and existential void in which the modern individual makes his way' (1997, p. 24). As Lalanne notes, 'when interior monologue takes the place of dialogue, it is because communication is no longer self-evident'; the monologues 'detach [the characters] from experiencing the present', they become 'spectators of their own existence' and thus are ultimately associated with nostalgia, as a 'melancholic awareness that the present is always what is in the process of coming apart, of ceasing to exist' (1997, p. 24). Indeed, as is already evident in the sequences analyzed above, Martha's voice-over often departs from the expected narration of the story, weaving in confessions, fears and desires that disclose her status as a melancholic spectator of her ephemeral existence, at times resorting to the comforting utopias of her fantasies and at others withdrawing to an impassive surrender to the drive.

The next shot frames the two girls behind the closed doors of the elevator. As they go down, the film cuts to a shot of the city center that showcases the sacred rock of the Acropolis, glorified by the dazzling rays of the morning sunlight, right in the middle of a massive and chaotic bunch of buildings above which lurk some thick grey clouds. Back to the two girls, and the film shows Nandia suggesting to Martha that they move together into a new flat and 'start over, like a family'. The pace with which Iliades throws contradictory images and words into the film is frenetic, creating a feeling of disorientation, enhanced by the heavy rock sounds of One Finger Music's guitars on the soundtrack, thus ultimately undermining the agonizing optimism which might occasionally pop up either in the shiny interstices of the frame or the brief hopeful moments of the characters.

After confronting Manos, who is upset with them for messing up the posh party, in a sequence that once again fluctuates between physical violence and sexual abuse, *Hardcore* cuts to a static shot of what looks like a small, kitsch, yet lovingly decorated dining room, with plastic fruits and flowers on the table, dolls and soft toys on the furniture, photographs and paintings on the walls (Fig. 2.4). This shot is intercut twice with a close-up of Martha, which shows her lying in bed and watching Nandia sleeping. Cutting back to the shot of the dining room, the furniture, the decoration and even the chandelier start disappearing from the frame one by one, thus eventually leaving the room dark and empty. In their place, a couple of chairs and a cardboard box appear instead. The camera then starts moving towards the door, exiting the room and turning to the right to reveal the two girls in the bathroom tidying up, while Nandia suggests that they should go on holiday to avoid further trouble now that things

Fig. 2.4 An ordinary home 'just like the rest of the world'

are getting harder for them. Martha's desire to have an 'ordinary' life 'just like the rest of the world' once more fails her, for their lives are inescapably entangled in the vicious circle of prostitution and violence, which alternately constitutes them as both victims and perpetrators, as we will see below. Indeed, the empty, gloomy rooms of the flat never really fill up with the necessary furniture or decoration that would make them feel like a home, one that could accommodate their dream to live as a family. When the boys visit them in a subsequent scene, visibly intoxicated and carrying guns and drugs, the flat emerges as nothing less than a negative queer place of sexual obscenity and drug consumption, a queer deformation of the patriarchal notion of the family home; it emerges, indeed, as the home of what Edelman has coined as *sinthomosexuals*.

Fighting against teleological accounts of queer temporality and historicism, but most importantly against the quintessential North American homophobic discourse framed around the fantasy politics of what he terms 'reproductive futurism', Edelman introduces the *sinthomosexual* as the figure that embodies queerness's radical anti-sociality. For Edelman (2004, pp. 2–3), reproductive futurism is not simply another political framework but the very foundation of Western civilization, the pivotal 'ideological limit' that infuses all discourse on the contemporary Anglo-

American political stage. Valorizing the institution of reproduction, through which hetero-sex is sanctified, reproductive futurism establishes the figure of the Child as the 'perpetual horizon of every acknowledged politics, the fantasmatic beneficiary of every political intervention' (2004, p. 3).

Evidently, such a political framework not only excludes but must also dispose of those who do not reproduce, as they constitute the materialized gap in its ideological structure, one that will constantly and consistently undermine the axis of this ideology by defying the meaning with which it substantiates its 'fantasy', and which is consummated, as Edelman insists, through the figure of the perennial Child. Edelman's *sinthomosexuality* is a neologism that fuses the 'sterile' homosexual with the Lacanian *sinthome*, the singular way by which 'each subject manages to knot together the orders of the Symbolic, the Imaginary, and the Real', but a singularity which is, however, untranslatable into the realm of the Symbolic (2004, p. 35). As Edelman explains, the *sinthome*, in its refusal of meaning, constitutes 'the template of a given subject's access to *jouissance*', this excess of pleasure that he associates with the death drive (2004, p. 35). Hence, Edelman claims, 'in a political field whose limit and horizon is reproductive futurism, queerness embodies this death drive, this intransigent *jouissance*, by figuring sexuality's implication in the senseless pulsions of that drive' (2004, p. 27).

For Edelman, there can be no such thing as 'queer vision', for queerness cannot be associated with any sense of community, or a transformative future, as it 'marks the excess of something always unassimilable that troubles the relentlessly totalizing impulse informing normativity' (Dinshaw et al., 2007, p. 189). Caught up in a structural repetition haunted by the death drive, it cannot, within such a non-teleological structure, do otherwise than refuse not only the consolations provided by 'futurism's redemptive temporality gussied up with a rainbow flag'—this 'fantasy of a viable "alternative" to normativity's domination', as he calls any aspirations for 'a queer utopia'—but also 'the purposive, productive uses that would turn it into a "good"' (Dinshaw et al., 2007, p. 195). In Edelman's thinking, queerness's drive cannot be conducive to any 'good' and he concludes, 'that's what makes queerness intolerable, even to those who call themselves queer: a non-teleological negativity that refuses the leavening of piety and with it the dollop of sweetness afforded by messianic hope' (Dinshaw et al., 2007, p. 195). Hope is, indeed, exhaustively thwarted in Edelman's conceptualization of queerness; the figure of the *sinthomosexual* is instead assertively projected as the one that not only dismantles individual and collective fantasies but also imposes radical nihilism in their place.

Self-consciously registered and colored as such, fantasy emerges as one of *Hardcore*'s central formal and thematic elements, rather than an inter-luding narrative motif; both a place of arrival and a place of departure, if not queerness's ultimate point of rupture. As witnessed in the scenes analysed above, the film's magnificent dramatization of the oscillation between desire and the drive relies precisely on the persistent infiltration of the negativity of queer experience with either normative fantasies of (patriarchal) family-making or the queer 'fantasy of a viable alternative'. Nevertheless, as the film unfolds, fantasy is devastatingly overcome by queerness's insatiable negativity. Indeed, halfway through the film, the girls' fate takes an unpredictable turn, which arguably constitutes them as female versions of *sinthomosexuality*, each in her own manner emerges as a meaningless force of nature, subjected only to the self-destructive lures of the drive, and unapologetically violating the fantasies that safeguard the coherence of subjectivity, be it familial or national.

Nandia decides to take revenge on Manos by setting up a bloody raid with Argyris, in which the violent procurer, his bodyguard and two pros-titutes are killed. She then kills Argyris as well so that she can shift the blame for the murders exclusively onto him. Suddenly, she and Martha become the nation's favorites after spreading the word, with the help of massive sensationalist media coverage, of a tragic tale that presents them as victims of an abusive prostitution circuit. But the image of Nandia's blood-spattered face gazing directly to the camera as she exits the room of the murders will haunt the rest of the film. Instantly invoking popular cinematic intertexts, such as the films of Lynch and Tarantino, the twist in the narrative provocatively transposes dystopian American fairy tales to contemporary Greece, by metamorphosing the queer victims—or, better put, the victimized queers—into violent perpetrators who take the law into their own hands in order to take revenge against patriarchal violence, as it is trenchantly staged through Manos's oppressive regime. And what is dystopian about this is precisely the fact that the queer revenge does not engender the establishment of a new (queer) order. Rather than unfolding a queer utopian fantasy, the film's trajectory dissolves into the absolute repudiation of futurity.

Indeed, the black shot that follows is nothing less than a mockery of any sense of futurity; both of that which pertains to the normative fan-tasmatic core of reproductive futurism, namely the 'family vision', and of what Edelman scorns as the 'queer vision'. For more than 20 seconds the film goes completely black and Martha's voice-over takes over once again in a tragic, grotesque prattle:

MARTHA   1, 2, 3, 1, 2, 3, 1, 2, 3. The worst is the best. Nandia and I will make a family no matter what. I will stop thinking like Nandia; I have stopped thinking. 3, 4, 5, 3, 4, 5. I don't want to know. I want somebody else to know. The worst is the best. We deserve the best. We will be just fine. Someone knows, I don't. He said that the best is yet to come. We will be just fine.

Family becomes here a stubborn fairy tale, the ultimate fantasy, haunted by 'the emptiness that the signifier embeds at the core of the Symbolic' (Edelman, 2004, p. 8), literally materialized here in the blackened emptiness of the frame. It is explicitly addressed and ridiculed as the compulsive locus of desire that directs Martha's personal fantasmatic narrative (and, in effect, her own illusive teleological ontology); not only a kind of fantasmatic nostalgia for an unlived past, not only the ever-returning point of her longings, but a distorted experience *of* and *in* the present.

Martha's ironic temporal compulsions are further accentuated in another sequence towards the end of the film where Nandia and Martha have breakfast at their new luxurious apartment, which Nandia has bought after her notorious rise to stardom; arguably, yet another ambivalent locus of both desire and the drive. The sequence comprises a three-shot of Nandia, Argyris and Miltos in front of a lavish table, intercut with a medium shot of Martha at the head of the table, all laughing, enjoying the breakfast and making plans for a trip to Rome. Miltos for the first time appears sporting a shirt and tie, and neat hairstyle and asks the other couple whether they could take care of their children while he and Martha will be abroad. Miltos extends his hand to Martha, but as the film cuts to her, his hand is drawn away and Martha's smile fades. She then turns to Nandia asking her whether she would like to have a family or a child. Back to the first set-up the boys are no longer there, nor the elaborate food arrangement; only Nandia, squeezed in the right margin of the frame, dismissing Martha's questions and sarcastically asking her if she is getting old.

The fusion of fantasy and reality in the above scenes serves a double cause: on the one hand, it verifies Nandia's status as an unapologetic *sinthomosexual*, who not only dismisses her own trajectory towards reproductive futurity but also disparages Martha's respective fantasy; on the other hand, it surprisingly elevates Martha into the status of the *sinthomosexual* herself, for her perseverance with the fantasy of reproductive futurity juxtaposed with her pathetic passivity and lack of agency, eventually result in no less than a mockery, a parody, and, thus, an even greater exposure of the fantasy as such.[4]

However, ultimately, in the face of its bloodied *sinthomosexuals*, *Hardcore* not only disturbs the fantasy that sustains the consistency of the Symbolic Order, by attacking the politics of reproductive futurism and exposing the relentless negativity of the drive, but also attempts to penetrate a broader spectrum of fantasy; one that is not strictly delimited by the subject's and the society's Imaginary negotiations between their reproductive desires and nihilistic drives, but rather one that traverses the fantasmatic ideological and self-representational imagery of the nation. Nandia's new-found notoriety, along with her manipulative erotic attachments to high-profile publishers, win her a magazine cover, a music TV show and a leading part in a Christmas stage play that is featured twice towards the end of the film. In the first instance, the play is introduced with a shot of sparks from a gas welder fixing the set, thus notifying us we are about to watch the play's rehearsal, while the excruciating sound that the welder makes cross-fades with a war march. As the camera tilts up Nandia appears standing in the middle of the stage, dressed as a mythical Nymph, sporting a short grey chiton with golden trimmings, Cleopatra-like make-up and neat hairstyle. The film then cuts to a medium shot of Nandia that allows us to notice her rather weary mood as she raises her hands to perform her act. Another cut frames Nandia again in medium shot, this time in front of an array of spotlights. As the camera slowly zooms out a group of dancers, dressed as Ancient Greek warriors, enter the frame helping Nandia walk down some enormous white steps in a series of strictly choreographed, yet clumsily executed moves, and through a rain of confetti. The film then cuts to a shot of a photograph of Nandia as a young ballerina posing for the camera at a beach against the blue waters of the sea. We are obviously back at the girls' new apartment, with Martha lying in bed and staring at the photo and Nandia sitting next to her and saying, 'I'm knackered. The play opens in a week. Are you coming to see me? ... Ok it's nothing special.' 'Nothing special? But isn't this your dream?' asks indifferent Martha. After a long pause Nandia asks Martha, 'Do you love me? ... Are you happy?' to receive no reply but only a hesitant nod. A long shot of the two girls in bed reveals that they are by now not only physically but also emotionally distant from each other. The silence is broken by some sweet notes from a music box on the soundtrack, leading to a dreamy wide-angle shot of the Athens, decorated for Christmas, that frames the huge Christmas tree in the city center in the middle, while computer-generated snowflakes blend with the frame's soft edges. 'And thus arrived Christmas, the season of love, but I didn't know how much love I was left with. Nandia looked all the more distant. Perhaps it was my fault as well', Martha confesses in her voice-over, while shots of the dressing rooms show young Nymphs and Santa Clauses getting dressed and fixing their make-up. 'I need to go to the toilet', says Nandia and the camera follows her as she walks along the theatre's corridors among hurrying actors and extras to find Sfiriktras, who is waiting for her with a sardonic smile, a mysterious paper bag and an obscure forecast of her horoscope.

The pompous sounds of the war march interrupt the slow quiet pace of Sfiriktras's horoscope forecast and the film abruptly cuts once again to a series of spotlights that turn on simultaneously for the camera, thus recalling the opening sequence of the film. Extravagantly dressed as Ancient Greek warriors, the male dancers are once more depicted extending their hands to the sky, thus giving the cue for to Nandia's entrance onto the stage. Her arrival is momentarily suspended with an inserted unsteady shot of the audience, which creates a sort of ambivalent anticipation. A cut back to the stage offers a closer view of the point of the star's arrival, tightly framed by the warriors/dancers. The lights become brighter and Nandia gets on stage, devoid, however, of any of the glamour that characterizes the rest of the set, costumes and overall feel of the play; visibly worn out, with messy hair and make-up, she defies the rehearsed choreography and walks clumsily down the steps amidst the confetti and the confused dancers. A cut to a long shot shows her struggling to balance so as not to fall over, but also gives us a more general view of the set that features a series of Greek columns, Corinthian, Ionian and even a Caryatid in the foreground. Nandia's frenzied behavior is highlighted by a slow-motion pan to the right and an unsteady close-up from behind that places her face to face with the shadowed audience, both intercut with Martha's reaction shots that reveal her nervousness. Back on the stage, Nandia sets fire to the elaborate helmet of a by-standing warrior, while the audience, ironically, starts applauding her incomprehensible gesture, presumably thinking this is part of the show. A long shot of the stage reveals the entire set, in all its kitsch grandeur, with scattered Greek statues and columns, decorated with golden Christmas trimmings and ribbons, a row

Fig. 2.5 National campiness

of girls dancing gauchely, a woman holding a torch and a man next to her holding a sword (Fig. 2.5). Suddenly the flaming warrior starts running frenetically across the stage and the film then follows a fast-paced editing of long shots, medium shots and unsteady tracking shots that frame the chaotic atmosphere that Nandia has created, while Santa Clauses and Greek warriors run on the stage attempting to put out the fire with extinguishers. A Santa then quickly takes Nandia on his shoulders and runs off with her. The film cuts to the girls' flat with Martha sitting nervously in the living room. The war march has already given way to heavy rock guitar chords, which, along with low-key lighting, enhance the fretful feeling of this new scene, where Martha witnesses Santa (who suggestively still has his costume on) penetrating Nandia in the adjoining room. When Santa leaves Nandia naked and exhausted in bed, Martha goes to the bedroom and suffocates her lover to death with her childhood pillow. The heavy rock soundtrack stops abruptly and a soft lullaby accompanies Martha's sobbing which is foregrounded both visually and aurally. Black.

Only a few moments before the end of the film, Iliades invokes the performative nature of the fantasy that frames the national and religious imagery of contemporary Greece while also foregrounding the destructive threat which the queer subject poses to it. The deployment of camp aesthetics is not accidental. Fabio Cleto (1999) draws on Susan Sontag's distinction between 'naïve' and 'deliberate' camp to argue that camp can be both perceived as a 'failed seriousness' as well as an intentional acknowledgement of the unnatural, 'inessential' and contingent 'essence' of performance that privileges form and style over message or content. However, aspiring to complicate this distinction Cleto explains that a reading of camp as always already queer might at once challenge and invoke such binary oppositions, while also exposing how 'both modes are indeed presided over by the artificial character of all social interaction, and by the theatricality of being, with doing as *acting*' (1999, p. 24). As he explains:

> depth-anchored subjectivity is dissolved and replaced by the mask as paradoxical essence, or depthless foundation of subjectivity as actor (in itself, nonexistent without an audience) on the world as stage. And as an object of a camp decoding, the actor exists only through its in(de)finite performing roles, the ideal sum of which correspond to his own performative 'identity'. (1999, p. 25)

By invoking quintessential markers from the Greek national and religious representational lexicon gussied up in absolute campiness, *Hardcore* arguably suggests that, much like camp, these sacred cores of Greekness cannot conceal their '*collective, ritual and performative existence*' (Cleto, 1999, p. 25). The performative character of the national that is invoked here conjures up Homi Bhabha's prominent distinction of the double time of the nation. According to Bhabha, 'in the production of the nation as narration there is a split between the continuist, accumulative temporality of the pedagogical, and the repetitious, recursive strategy of the performative' (2000, p. 297). Through its double time, the nation goes through the process of perpetually being narrated and renarrated, with the performative, as a series of acts and 'rhetorical figures' (flags, salutes, racial characteristics and so on), being the force of repetitive re-enactment of the official national history and identity, established by the pedagogical. Nevertheless, invoking Benedict Anderson's famous conceptualization of the nation as an 'imagined community', marked by 'temporal coincidence, and measured by clock and calendar' (Anderson cited in Bhabha, 2000, p. 297), Bhabha asserts that this 'homogenous empty time' of the nation, which links together diverse actors and actions on the national stage in a form of 'civil contemporaneity realized in the fullness of time', is contested by the emergence of differential temporalities, marked by class, ethnicity, gender and race (2000, p. 297)—and why not add sexuality?

Arguably, *Hardcore* effectively deploys the 'citational, ironic and theatrical character of camp' (Cleto, 1999, p. 25) to invoke the queer character of the nation's 'campiness', which can be identified in a series of performative rituals, from military parades, liturgies and national celebrations, to the extravagant Athens Olympic Games as well as to filmic productions, such as the Greek 'blockbusters' mentioned in Chap. 1. In this way, the film effectively demystifies the nation's artificiality that passes for 'natural' by exposing its self-representation (sarcastically evoked here by the unexpected amalgamation of Ancient Greek iconography with contemporary Western metonymies of the quintessential Christian festival of Christmas) as precisely a fantasy itself. At the same time that the nation's fantasy becomes the object of camp demystification, it also emerges as the focus of the queer subject's final attack. Hence *Hardcore* ultimately introduces a filmic rendition of what we could call 'national *sinthomosexuality*', for, as witnessed in the above sequence, the film effectively foregrounds the queer subject as an embodiment of the meaningless intransigent drive that constantly threatens to demolish the fantasmatic national spatiotemporal structure at every turn.

Indeed, right before the end of the film, Nandia, as pure incarnation of the drive, commits the meaningless, the unjustified, the unintelligible. Unable to verbalize any explanations for her actions she finally succumbs to *jouissance* as the excess of pleasure that is associated with both *Eros* and *Thanatos*, for the bed that accommodates her indifferent penetration by the Santa (indeed, one cannot even regard it as sexual intercourse as she shows no sign of reaction or pleasure) also eventually becomes her death-bed. In this way, Iliades's *sinthomosexual* not only ruins the party/ fantasy that sustains the consistency of the nation through its pedagogical and performative historicity, but also drives the film itself towards a representational void through a frenzied editing of zoom shots, slow-motion pans, unsteady shots and eclectic use of music that alternates between opera, heavy rock and sentimental melodrama, which are only faithful to the frenetic trajectory of the *sinthomosexual* rather than the production of meaning.

Time itself, ultimately, emerges as an ambivalent concept in Iliades's film. On the one hand, the film's temporal structure initially emerges as teleological, for the opening sequence delineates a *telos*, even if an obscure one, which is anticipated throughout the film, while teleology is transparently invoked as such by the inclusion in the narrative of a character who speaks only in horoscopes (Sfiriktras). On the other hand, the film's denouement suggests the opposite, namely an open-ended temporality, as it does not offer a closure for Martha's trajectory, neither does it ever reveal from what position she is narrating. Finally, and perhaps most interestingly, time in the film emerges also as circular, for, rather than agents of change and generators of meaning, fantasy, dream and memory constitute nothing more than mere disruptions of the otherwise futile trajectories of the characters, which revolve around repetitive and unproductive vicious circles, spattered with gore, semen and white 'stardust'. Ironically, the Digital Vault blogger identifies *Hardcore*'s ambivalent narrative structure as 'the film's biggest problem' (2008). For him, the film:

> lacks substance. There are beautiful scenes and there are extraordinarily ugly scenes in this film, but they do not mesh together well enough to give the film the depth that it is striving for. What we end up with is a very well-made, well-acted movie about pretty people doing ugly things that leaves you cold. (2008)

However, what if the film self-consciously defies 'depth' and 'substance'? What if the relentless negativity that it stages and its disruptive mode of representing the queer subject and the spaces that, in their turn, disrupts point exactly towards an ultimate disruption, a distraction from or even destruction of meaning? One that queers have effectively and consistently been accused of representing, as Edelman has suggested? In effect, if there is a meaning, a moral in the film, it is, arguably, none other than its own destruction, its ultimate repudiation. At least insofar as 'meaning' is still appropriated as the singular privilege of the familiar familial and national narratives, which are themselves always already invested in the omnipotent ideological horizon of 'reproductive futurism';[5] and insofar as these narratives still claim to enjoy an exclusive—if not transcendental—access to it, precisely because and by means of such ideological investments.

Nevertheless, before rushing to salute the triumph of the anti-social in *Hardcore*'s spatiotemporal structure, it is important and useful to address Tim Dean's astute critique of Edelman's work, which, much like *Hardcore*, renegotiates Edelman's argument by questioning *sinthomosexuality*'s privileged association with the death drive, as well as by elucidating another perspective on the death drive, which Edelman discards in his work. Dean suggests that what Edelman fails to acknowledge is the fact that the drive is both constant and partial, and it is this partiality that makes it impossible to embrace or reject. As Dean explains, 'a drive can never become an object of consciousness, [thus] can never be embraced or deployed for political purposes' (2008, p. 131). However, it is the unconscious's 'limitless capacity for displacement and condensation', its incapacity 'for synthesis or any grasp of finitude', and thus its 'refusal of totalizing narratives' that renders the ideology of reproductive futurism impossible as totalitarian (2008, p. 134). Following Dean's argument, Lisa Downing suggests that 'the ideology of reproductive futuri[sm], should be analyzed as carrying within it its own points of disruption, its own death drive' (2010, p. 142). As she clarifies, in Lacanian psychoanalysis there is a place for the future, one that is not teleological, but 'infinitely riven with doubling, returns, regression and interruptions' (2010, p. 141). Reaching beyond the pleasure principle and towards *jouissance,* the death drive seeks absolute negation, but this does not necessarily point towards a pull against the movement of the life drive, but rather an exaggeration of it; 'it does not oppose it […] rather it *outstrips* it' (2010, p. 137). The death drive's movement, Downing explains, more than a simple negation of the future, is rather a gesture 'beyond—and in excess of—simple linear ideas of futurity', more than a mere embodiment of nihilism it is also a possibility of creativity and potentiality (2010, p. 138). On this she cites Lacan's own clarification that what should be articulated 'as a destruction drive, given that it challenges everything that exists', should also be regarded as 'a will to create from zero, a will to begin again' (2010, p. 138).

In the film's last sequence, Martha escapes along with Mr Softie, Nandia's most faithful john, heading to the sea. A series of shots foregrounds Martha's face, as the air blows her hair in the convertible car, sporting an enigmatic smile of redemption (bear in mind the audience has just witnessed her killing Nandia) after noticing some children in a passing car. The series of Martha's close-ups gives way to the returning image of the little ballerina in the sea. The child in the picture comes to life, and we can clearly discern now some scattered rubble framing her small figure and the sea behind her (Fig. 2.6). The girl looks directly to the camera for a bit and then slowly exits the frame. Fade to black. Iliades clearly ends his film with a question mark. A question mark that re-addresses fantasy as the pivotal generator of the narratives of the past—that is, if we take the picture that comes to life as a representation of the nostalgia of a fantasmatic past rather than an index of a joyful past reality—as well as the generator of the narratives of the future, incarnated in the image of the child, that perennial embodiment of reproductive futurism, which not coincidentally, eventually grows to become the embodiment of its own nega-

Fig. 2.6   The returning image of the child

tion, that is a *sinthomosexual*. Downing concludes that film and Lacanian psychoanalysis can help us imagine the future as 'plural, disruptive and creative' rather than linear, normative and reproductive; as she proposes, film and psychoanalysis can become 'modes of resistance to, and re-imaginings of, simple conceptions of temporality and the too-simple modes of subjectivity and relationality that appear to accompany them' (2010, p. 145). Indeed, the elemental becomes temporal in *Hardcore*'s final shot, as the remnants of fantasy are pushed to the margins of the frame, outstripped by the ever-moving, ever-changing and ever-returning sea-waves that take over the frame. Water is ultimately foregrounded; this perennial incarnation of the circle of life and life *as* circle whose ceaseless circular movement asks us to reimagine the movement of history itself as an oscillation between fantasy-driven desires (individual, collective, national) and the partially destructive, partially creative tensions of the drive.

NOTES

1. All translations from Greek in the book are made by the author.
2. Aleka Laskou is in fact the pen name of a pair of female authors working in collaboration.

3. The term 'debtocracy' first appears in the 2011 eponymous Greek documentary film by Katerina Kitidi and Aris Chatzistefanou (Greek title: *Hreokratia*). It is derived from the words 'debt' and '*kratos*' (Greek for 'state') and describes the condition by which Greece is not only entrapped within but significantly ruled by the terms that manage the country's sovereign debt, as prescribed by the so-called 'Memorandums of Understanding' between the Greek state and its creditors.

4. Edelman observes that *sinthomosexuality* in traditional cultural imagery is embodied by machine-like men or even by sexless machines, 'who stand outside the "natural" order of sexual repro-duction', ascribing this prevalence of male *sinthomosexuals* in cul-tural representation, to a 'gender bias', as he explains, 'that continues to view women as "naturally" bound more closely to sociality, repro-duction and domesticating emotion' (2004, p. 165). Iliades argu-ably plays with this gender bias of conventional cultural production, through the complicated staging of the oscillation between queer longing and queer doing, especially as incarnated in Martha, who is both female and 'bound to domesticating emotion'. However, as is already evident, *Hardcore* ultimately subverts this gender bias in the most triumphant way, hence verifying Edelman's insight that 'the *sinthomosexual* has [indeed] no privileged relation to any sex or sex-uality' (2004, p. 165).

5. Indeed, the ideology of 'reproductive futurism' infuses the political discourse of both the Greek Orthodox Church and the Greek far right, who deploy the 'divine sanctification' of marriage and the Greek family, as well as the image of the Child, as their primary weapons in their hateful polemic against Greek LGBT activism's demand for the expansion of civil rights to include gay marriage and adoption.

BIBLIOGRAPHY

Anderson, Benedict (2006 [1983]) *Imagined Communities* (London & New York: Verso).

Betsky, Aaron (1997) *Queer Space: Architecture and Same-Sex Desire* (New York: William Morrow).

Bhabha, Homi K. (2000 [1990]) 'Dissemination: Time, Narrative and the Margins of the Modern Nation', in Homi K. Bhabha (ed.) *Nation and Narration* (London: Routledge), pp. 291–322.

Cleto, Fabio (1999) 'Introduction: Queering the Camp', in Fabio Cleto (ed.) *Camp: Queer Aesthetics and the Performing Subject, A Reader* (Edinburgh: Edinburgh University Press), pp. 1–42.

de Lauretis, Teresa (2011) 'Queer Texts, Bad Habits, and the Issue of a Future', *GLQ: A Journal of Lesbian and Gay Studies*, 17, 243–263.

Dean, Tim (2008) 'An Impossible Embrace: Queerness, Futurity and the Death-Drive', in James Bono, Tim Dean and Eva Plonowska Ziarek (eds.) *A Time for the Humanities: Futurity and the Limits of Autonomy* (New York: Fordham University Press), pp. 112–140.

Digital Vault (2008) *Hardcore (2004)* at http://digitalvaultdvd.blogspot.co.uk/2008/12/director-dennis-illadis-starring.html, date accessed 22 April 2016.

Dinshaw, Carolyn, Roderick A. Ferguson, Annamarie Jagose and Tan Hoang Nguyen (2007) 'Theorizing Queer Temporalities: A Roundtable Discussion', *GLQ: A Journal of Lesbian and Gay Studies*, 13, 177–195.

Downing, Lisa (2010) 'The Cinematic Ethics of Psychoanalysis: Futurity, Death Drive, Desire', in Lisa Downing and Libby Saxton, *Film and Ethics: Foreclosed Encounters* (Oxon: Routledge), pp. 134–146.

Edelman, Lee (2004) *No Future: Queer Theory and the Death Drive* (Durham and London: Duke University Press).

Ingram, Gordon Brent (1997) 'Marginality and the Landscapes of Erotic Alien(n)ations', in Gordon Brent Ingram, Anne-Marie Bouthillette and Yolanda Retter (eds.) *Queers in Space: Communities, Public Spaces, Sites of Resistance* (Washington: Bay Press), pp. 27–52.

Jane, Iak (2005) 'Hardcore', *dvdtalk.com*, http://www.dvdtalk.com/reviews/17052/hardcore/, date accessed 22 April 2016.

Lacan, Jacques (1992) *The Seminar of Jacques Lacan, Book VII: The Ethics of Psychoanalysis, 1959–1960*, ed. Jacques-Alain Miller, trans. Dennis Potter (New York: Norton).

Lalanne, Jean-Marc, David Martinez, Ackbar Abbas and Jimmy Ngai (1997) *Wong Kar-Wai* (Paris: Editions Dis Voir).

Raffel, Lawrence P. (2004) 'Hardcore (2004)', *monstersatplay.com*, http://www.monstersatplay.com/review/dvd/h/hardcore.php, date accessed 22 April 2016.

Zervopoulos, Yorgos (2004) 'Hardcore (2004)', *cine.gr*, http://www.cine.gr/film.asp?id=70439l&page=4, date accessed 22 April 2016.

Žižek, Slavoj (1995 [1991]) *Looking Awry: An Introduction to Jacques Lacan through Popular Culture* (London: The MIT Press).

CHAPTER 3

Dogtooth: Of Narrativity

An old-fashioned cassette player appears on screen. An anonymous hand inserts a tape in the player and pushes the play button. We hear:

'The new words for today are the following: *thalassa* [sea], *aftokinitodromos* [motorway], *ekdromi* [trip], *karampina* [carbine]. The "sea" is a kind of leather armchair with wooden arms, like the one we have in the living room; "motorway" is the very strong wind; "trip" is a very tough material that we use to make floors and "carbine" is a very beautiful white bird.'

While the voice explains the meaning of these new words, offering examples of how to use them in a sentence, the close-up of the cassette player gives way to three consecutive medium shots, each framing a different person, in turn a young man and two young girls in their late teens, listening rather nervously to the player and located in a cold white room, which is gradually revealed to be a bathroom. When the recorded 'lecture' finishes, the youngest girl suggests that they play a game of endurance. There follows a rather unrehearsed, improvised dialogue with the three actors often interrupting or complementing each other, using a language full of ellipses, gaps, silences, overlaps.

This is the opening sequence of Yorgos Lanthimos's *Dogtooth* (2009), the film that arguably put Greece back in the cinematic map after a long period of failed attempts by the country's cinema to produce filmic works that would be technically and artistically interesting enough to help the country escape its cinematic isolation at a transnational level. Indeed, Lanthimos's

© The Author(s) 2016
M. Psaras, *The Queer Greek Weird Wave*,
DOI 10.1007/978-3-319-40310-6_3

63

breakthrough film turned international audiences' and critics' attention to the independent cinematic production of a country, which at the time was 'enjoying' the spotlight of international political and economic disgrace, as a result of the wholesale collapse of its economic-political establishment; not necessarily a coincidence, as suggested in the Introduction.

Winning a series of awards at several film festivals around the world, including the prestigious Prix Un Certain Regard at the 2009 Cannes Film Festival and a nomination for Best Foreign Language Film at the 83rd Academy Awards, *Dogtooth* was warmly welcomed by critics, who described it as 'pure and singular' (Olsen, 2011) and even as 'pretty much one of a kind' (Romney, 2010). The critics praised the film's 'exemplary cinematography' (Orndorf, 2010), its 'excellent performances' (Turner, 2010), the 'deadpan, elegant compositions, and intentionally skewed framings' (Bradshaw, 2010), and generally the director's 'complete command of visuals and performances' (Ebert, 2010). Lanthimos himself was, indeed, hailed as 'a bold new voice on the world cinema scene, someone who might soon be elevated to a similar position as those twin pillars of Euro provocation: Lars von Trier and Michael Haneke' (Harkness, 2010). Nevertheless, despite the almost unanimous praise for the film's stylistic 'unaffected simplicity' (Olsen, 2011), *Dogtooth*'s distinctive narrative structure and thematic approach produced a kind of unease among the critics. Dustin Jansick (2011), of *waytooindie.com*, begins by describing *Dogtooth* as a 'disturbing anti-social satire' but goes on to conclude that, ultimately, the film 'leaves most of the interpretations up to the viewer', since it 'could easily be a direct shot towards parents that over-protect their children to the point of inhuman standards and extreme anti-social practices' or 'it could be a political allegory'. Along similar lines, Olsen (2011) sees *Dogtooth* as 'part enigma, part allegory and even part sci-fi in its creation of a completely alternate reality.' Admittedly, the reading of the film as a multi-layered allegory has been very popular among the critics both at home and abroad (Turner, 2010; Orndorf, 2010; Raouzaios, 2009). However, the predominant response to the film's idiosyncratic take on its pivotal themes of kinship and home-schooling was, not surprisingly, more of a surrender to its radical openness of meaning or, indeed, its radical formal and thematic meaninglessness, which in this book acquires particular resonance: '[s]ex seems to have no meaning, not even when incest is suggested. The sickness of this family surpasses all understanding' (Ebert, 2010); '[w]hat prevents this highly original work from being a masterpiece is its lack of narrative drive and character development. After the first 30 minutes, the set pieces become repetitious, they get increasingly shocking' (David Lewis, 2010); '*Dogtooth* is a litmus test for not just your patience but how much de-glamorized sex and violence you can handle, and whether or not you want to be assaulted by a sea of nothingness' (Lippe, 2010); 'Lanthimos keeps us guessing and explains virtually nothing. He also provokes with an edge of queasy sexiness that's all the more unsettling for being utterly perverse and downright awkward' (Romney, 2010); 'Lanthimos leaves the reasons behind the parents' dictatorial behavior up in the air' in 'these snippets of the kids' lives', which seem to be 'part of a cyclical, never-ending story of boredom, half-truths and disturbing behavior' (van Hoeij, 2009). Last but not least, A.O. Scott of the *New York Times* (2010) calls the film 'a conversation piece. Though the conversation may ... be more along the lines of: "What was that?" "I don't know. Weird." "Yeah." [shudder]. "Weird".'

In effect, 'weird', as already discussed, eventually came to be the word that would signify the entire new Greek cinematic movement that *Dogtooth* initiated. Weird as in idiosyncratic or merely incomprehensible, Lanthimos's film is definitely a distinctive dramatization of the quotidian time and space of a Greek family. However, its uniqueness lies not so much in the film's representation of an unconventional Greek family but in its relentless interrogation of the familiar familial and national narratives and, most importantly, in its unconventional mode of dismantling them. *Dogtooth* is no more than a fragmentary narration of the everyday routine of three youngsters, in their late teens or early 20s, who are confined by their parents to the family's luxurious yet isolated rural estate. The youngsters' quotidian time is characterized by boredom and repetition, comprising listening to homemade tapes, which misinform them about the outside world, watching themselves in past home-videos, inventing their own games and participating in family feasts, in which they are assigned to entertain the family by playing music or dancing rather gauchely. The house's strict codes of conduct are introduced quite early in the film, as well as the means by which the parents enforce them in order to preserve the state of things. However, equally early in the film Lanthimos also introduces us to one of the two potential threats to this awkwardly balanced familial time and space, that is Christina, a security guard at the father's work and the only permitted 'intruder' in the family's estate, whom the father pays in order to satisfy the son's sexual 'urges'—the second threat being the children themselves as will be revealed later in the film.

Indeed, from its earliest sequences *Dogtooth*'s familial construct is established as a highly regulatory, rigid and oppressive regime, secluded from the rest of the world, and impregnated with incoherence and permeability. After the opening sequence, which, effectively establishes the—both formally and thematically—eccentric universe of *Dogtooth*, the film cuts to a medium shot of blindfolded Christina, who is being driven by the father to the family's home. For quite a while, the camera fixes on this static, yet at the same time, travelling shot, which offers us the opportunity to look outside the car windows at the 'real' world with its buildings and cars and gas stations, while we hear (but never see) the father asking Christina questions about music as well as whether she has had a bath. We then have a cut to a long shot of the father's car as it turns onto a dirt road. In the following shot, the car stops and the father gets out in order to close behind them a chain gate that bears a no-entry sign. Finally, another shot shows the car entering the estate, revealing the high fences behind which the villa is secluded from the rest of the world. It is by now clear that the family's eccentric microcosm is not placed in some parallel universe, as might have been implied in generic categorizations of the film as 'part sci-fi' (Olsen, 2011). Far away and isolated from the rest of the world, which, nevertheless, is still out there and of which we are offered glimpses quite a few times in the film, *Dogtooth*'s twisted universe is claiming realism, not least in terms of sets, props and lighting. Indeed, in the numerous bright wide-angle shots of the family estate's exteriors and interiors, the villa features as spacious, modern, clean, with big gardens and a swimming pool, as cozy and inviting as in most mainstream visual representations of the 'ideal home'. However, as the film unfolds, the action persistently and unapologetically undermines the familiar familial space and with it the place itself of the ideal home, thus ultimately damaging both the affective as well as the representational value of the family home. As this chapter argues, in *Dogtooth* the family home emerges as a hostile and unproductive place for the subject, and family itself as an oppressive space replete with internal contradictions.

Dogtooth's cynical treatment of sex and caustic invocation of the patriarchal manipulation of sexual difference are perhaps among the most vivid examples of the film's remarkably transgressive rhetoric. After the father's car enters the estate, a cut to the son's bedroom shows him working out, while sitting in the right corner of the wide-angle frame with his back to the camera. The father enters the frame from the right and asks him whether he is ready to accept Christina. The son stands up and Christina enters the room. The father makes the bed and then reaches for his son, ¬obably to fix his hair. As the three characters line up in front of the angled camera, their heads are bizarrely cut off from the fixed frame. ¬he father exits the room, closing the door behind him, Christina

Fig. 3.1   Sex as a mechanism

and the son sit on the bed. Christina first gives the boy a hand-job and then lies back so that the boy can penetrate her. The film cuts (crucially, the first and only cut in the entire scene) to a medium shot of Christina as she supports her body by holding on to the headboard. Ironically, the only thing that actually draws the viewer's attention in this shot is the large number of stickers on the headboard (Fig. 3.1). Lanthimos, emphatically denies offering to his audience any of the usual glamorized sex scenes found in mainstream cinema; his take on a sex scene is pointedly stripped of music, low-key lighting, fetishizing shots of specific body parts, dialogue, emotions. Sex is presented as being as mechanical as driving the car to the family's house, and the scene itself is as boring and annoying as the squeaks of the bed that dominate the soundtrack.

A bit later in the film, a suggestive shot establishes the family dinner's seating arrangements from the perspective of the father, as the camera places the patriarch's back in the center of the frame, crucially leaving the rest of family (and of the frame) out of focus. In this shot we see that the two parents are sitting at the table's two heads, the son on the right-hand side of the father and the two daughters on the left-hand side (Fig. 3.2). During this scene we learn that the younger daughter is the house's first aider, the mother is responsible for the house's supplies which the father, the only one allowed to exit the estate, must provide, the son is painting the father's portrait and 'telephone' is the saltshaker! We also find out that the children are competing against each other in different tasks and are rewarded with stickers. But the girls seem unable to catch up with the son's success, who is once again crowned winner and thus chooses the

Fig. 3.2   The dominant perspective of the patriarch

night's entertainment: video. However, 'video' does not stand for typical family movies but rather for the family's own home-videos, which the children, apparently, must have seen enough times for the younger daughter to have memorized all of the words.

Evidently, *Dogtooth* frames its idiosyncratic familial space within a political economy that is structured around a clearly delineated distribution of gender and sexual roles that, above all else, secures its own perpetuation. Lanthimos foregrounds the centrality of sex in this power system, as the primary constitutive mechanism for the formation of the gender hierarchies that govern the house. Through utterly deglamorized scenes sex is, indeed, foregrounded as a mechanism; thus deconstructed and demystified, it becomes no longer the effect of desire but of patriarchal authority, it emerges as the means by which particular models of sexual identity, framed within the heterosexual matrix, are concretized, ultimately securing patriarchy's own auto-naturalization and temporal existence. Family, accordingly, is portrayed as the spatial and temporal site where these auto-naturalized systems of compulsory heterosexuality and phallocracy are produced, sanctified and thus maintained precisely through the deployment and regulation of sex and sexual difference.

Meg Wesling contends that this concretization and regulation of sex and sexual difference is bound up in the way capital produces subjects accommodated to its own needst (2011, p. 107). As Janet R. Jakobsen explains, in her investigation of the relationship between kinship systems and capitalism, the institutionalization and regulation of sexuality through marriage has essentially produced 'the autonomous individual not just literally but as a form of human subjectivity, the basis for any kind of social relation, including family, the community and the nation-state; a tradition, which, according to Jakobsen, has diachronically infused US politics (2011, p. 27). The production of this form of subjectivity adheres 'not only [to] the value of capital but also [to] the moral value of freedom as synonymous with autonomy' (2011, p. 27). As she elucidates, 'autonomous individuals understand themselves to be free' and the organization of their lives 'in familial units enable[s] their existence in various ways: providing domestic labor, sharing wages, and/or accumulating capital' (2011, p. 27). In this way, sex becomes the raw material for the production of value (either this is the value of freedom or the value of capital) by associating 'a particular subjectivity to economic and moral values' (2011, p. 27). But, '[t]he autonomous individual as the subject of freedom is also the subject of modern justice' (2011, p. 27). Indeed, as Jakobsen explains, autonomy becomes 'not only the ideology of subjectivity under capitalism but the ascription of both value and citizenship to that subject under the law, including (or perhaps especially) the law of the sovereign nation' (2011, p. 26).[1]

Clearly, the above Anglo-Saxon model might provide a useful analytical framework to illuminate the deployment and regulation of sexuality within the operations of capitalism and nationalism in modern Greece, however without obliterating the particular social, political and economic conditions within which the modern Greek family evolved. As demonstrated in the Introduction, the emergence and evolution of the modern Greek family has occurred within a culturally diverse and economically and politically complex national space, which testifies to the fact that the nation has never fully reconciled the contradictions that abound at the core of its foundations. Indeed, on the one hand, following the Western paradigm, the regulation of sex and its deployment for the organization of power relations in modern Greece were, indeed, intimately implicated with the operations of capital and the ascription of value and citizenship under the law of the newly established Greek state, after the nation's independence from the Ottomans. On the other hand, however, these discourses were not necessarily bounded by the ideology of individual autonomy or the production of the respective form of human subjectivity. As discussed in the Introduction, the same patriarchal affective and political structures that pertained to the paternalistic kinship systems of the extended family and the village, dating back to the Ottoman and Byzantine eras, continued to prevail, even after the predominance of the *nikokirei* model in the late nineteenth and early twentieth century, which privileged the nuclear family over the extended one (Cassia and Bada, 2006). Augmented by the perennial demand of the Orthodox Church for a rigid regulation of sexual relations and gender hierarchies as crucial for the nation's survival as well as blossoming, such authoritarian versions of patriarchal ideology favored kinship and familial bonds over the individual to the extent of the latter's unconditional subjection to the former. As Cassia's study reveals, the different familial economic systems that emerged after the massive internal migration waves did not abandon but rather reinforced the role of kinship and patriarchy as economically, socially and politically pivotal. In this way, the formation of power relations within the Greek state was channeled through the nation's fundamental structural core, which was none other than the nuclear family, nonetheless invested in a dated version of patriarchal ideology that has been inextricably linked to the nation-state's fatal trajectory of corruption and, ultimately, of economic, political and ideological bankruptcy.

The secluded microcosm of *Dogtooth*'s familial space clearly reverberates with the rigid affective structure of the sexual relations, kinship systems and their respective hierarchies, which have both regulated and blurred the spaces of the familial, the social and the political in modern Greece. The film thematizes the loss of individual autonomy within the traditional patriarchal familial space and highly problematizes the demand for unconditional submission to the patriarch. In this way, it effectively projects a problematic version of a form of familial subjectivity, in which such values as autonomy and freedom dissolve in the face of the communal familial good, and where the individual's own material and emotional survival is always already negotiable and subjected to the given familial political economy. Nevertheless, what is even more fascinating is the way *Dogtooth* foregrounds kinship and patriarchy as primarily invested in narrativity for both their production and auto-naturalization. Ultimately, I would argue, in *Dogtooth* the family *in* the narrative exposes family *as* a narrative, indeed a myth in itself, and through this discourse the national is, arguably, also contested.

In effect, if the children's loss of individual autonomy, pointedly staged by their asphyxiating state of confinement to the estate, is spatially framed by the villa's high fences, it is temporally sustained by the power of narrativity, which Teresa de Lauretis defines so attentively as 'the generic pressure of all narrative toward closure and fulfillment of meaning' (2011, p. 244). The parents, indeed, maintain a terrorizing atmosphere that secures the children's confinement by deploying two myths: the myth that the children will be able to venture into the outside world once they have lost a dogtooth, and the associated, supporting myth of the lost brother, who supposedly abandoned the house before his time and now wanders about the mysterious universe behind the estate's high fences lost, hungry and unprotected. But, as *Dogtooth* will remind us once again, narrativity is always already caught up in an unpredictable vicious circle of self-production and self-mutation.

Quite early in the film we see the son washing his father's car. After he finishes, we are offered a beautiful long shot that shows him standing in front of the high fences, his back turned to the camera. The film then cuts to a close-up that features his face in profile in the middle leaving the rest of the frame out of focus. The son starts talking to an imaginary person behind the fences, explaining how meticulously he cleans the car in comparison with the imaginary person, whose cleaning skills, as we presume from the dialogue, were quite mediocre. The film intercuts with a shot of the parents, who are in their bedroom getting dressed. The mother says, 'He is at the fences again.' The film returns to the long shot of the son, who is now seen throwing stones over the fences. In the next scene, the son is being punished for his behavior. In the scene's first shot, a plastic bottle with mouthwash is foregrounded, leaving out of focus the headless torso of the son, who is sitting behind it. 'He started throwing stones at me', says the son, and the mother replies, 'Your brother would never throw stones at you.' The son puts some of the liquid in his mouth, which, as we realize, he has to hold inside for a certain period of time. In the next couple of shots we are offered a clearer view of the punishment procedure, which, as we see, takes place in the kitchen and is witnessed by the whole family. Apparently, the film underscores here the way narratives become not only the effect, but most importantly the means for the production of the particular familial universe. As the story unfolds, narrativity emerges as a pivotal factor in the production and sustainability of particular systems of hierarchical power relations, at the same time, however, underscoring the contingency with which the temporality of their discursive existence is impregnated. Ironically, behind the story, this contingency is also suggested by the film's own idiosyncratic formal structure.

Indeed, the myth of the lost brother takes an unpredictable twist after the son kills a cat that has, to its misfortune, entered the family's premises. After the disturbing scene of the cat slaughter, the film cuts to a long shot of the father, who is standing in the middle of the factory where he works, struggling to talk on the mobile phone with the mother over the heavy factory noise that dominates the soundtrack. 'How did it happen? What did you tell them? Good. I'll tell them too. Yes, it's a good opportunity …' The soundtrack continues with the father's voice and the factory's noise, but the film visually cuts back to the house, where we see the son looking at the slaughtered animal. 'Yes, the temperature will rise and there will be strong winds, five to six degrees …', the father's voice continues. The film cuts to a medium shot of the father (however, medium here unconventionally translates to … waist down!) who is shown standing next to his car, in the middle of a dirt road, cutting his clothes with scissors. 'This story must end. It has become tiring for everyone. I agree. You are absolutely right.' In the next shot, audiovisual synchronization returns to the film, and the father is shown in a (proper this time!) medium shot, painting his clothes with fake blood. This cinematic conventionality will not last long, as once again the film cuts to the headless torso of the father. 'Your brother is dead. A creature like the one that has invaded our garden today has dismembered him. The film then cuts to a medium shot of the father, the red in his bloody hands, face and clothes that are foregrounded making a remarkable visual contrast with the green of the rich vegetation and the blue of the swimming pool's waters behind him (Fig. 3.3). Arguably, the affective ambivalence that is produced by the visual antithesis between the partly disturbing, partly grotesque image of the father and the all-embracing, warm and inviting scenery of the estate, encapsulates the rhetoric of the whole film; partly disturbing, partly grotesque, the film runs against the grain of the conventional narratives of the 'all-embracing, warm and inviting' space of the family home.

Fig. 3.3   The grotesque, yet terrorizing space of the family home

The father continues, 'On the one hand, his mistake of leaving when he was not ready was enormous. On the other hand, he was my son and I feel sorry for him.' In a reverse shot, behind the father's shoulder, we see the rest of the family listening to him in shock. The film then cuts to another medium shot of the father, this time neatly dressed and preaching to his family in the garden:

FATHER   The animal that threatens us is called a 'cat'. It is the most dangerous animal that exists. It feeds on human flesh, and specifically that of young people. With its claws it rips the skin of its victims and, subsequently, with its sharp teeth it eats the face and then the whole body. As long as you are inside you are not in danger. You are protected. Nevertheless, we have to be prepared in case something again invades the house or the garden.

He then suddenly starts barking loudly at his family. In the shot that follows all three children and the mother are shown on all fours barking back at the father (Fig. 3.4). The yap exchange lasts long enough to create a very disturbing effect, and then gives way to the late brother's funeral. We are only offered two brief shots of the family standing in dark-colored formal attire in front of the fence and throwing over little yellow flowers. On the soundtrack we hear the siblings' eulogy speeches; however, Lanthimos decides to cut to images from their swimming games of endurance. The film's audio-video desynchronization will last until the

Fig. 3.4 'We have to be prepared … '

elder daughter's speech finishes. We then return to diegetic sound so that we can hear the younger daughter giving instructions to her siblings on how to give artificial respiration. However, after the girl's instructions the sound is surprisingly completely removed. Before we can get a grasp on the events Lanthimos rushes to nullify their meaning and render them redundant, dispensable, obsolete; cinematic time is, accordingly, rendered elastic, manipulable, conditional, even catachrestic. Time and again disturbing events yield to the quotidian, the narrative loops between the hectic and the uneventful. Under the glaring Greek sun everything looks and sounds disturbingly quiet in the end. Indeed, the dissonance between sound and image only exacerbates the audience's frustrating efforts to pick up the pieces of this awkward universe and put them together. Much as the family's offspring is permitted at best limited access to the outside world, so the audience is denied much exposition; we are, indeed, abandoned by the camera itself, which more often than not gives the impression that it has been forgotten by its operators at an oblique position with the record button on.

This is precisely the point where *Dogtooth* emerges as a poignant amalgamation of form and content. Indeed, the unapologetic perseverance of the film's form in disturbing the conventional effect of cinematic illusionism in almost every frame and every cut resonates exceptionally with the way the film's thematics engage in a forceful critique of myth making. Much as the film persistently decapitates its characters, so it incessantly attacks and mutilates religious and national narrativity. From the prominent Christian parables of the prodigal son and the stoning of the adulterous woman that are suggestively alluded to in the sequences described above, to Greek mythology and the ancient drama that are gloriously evoked in the sequences discussed below, Lanthimos seems to engage in a vigorous dialogue with the unfathomable national narrative repository and at times he does not even hesitate to 'cast the first stone' against the perils of narrativity itself.

After the sequence of the lost brother's funeral, the film cuts to yet another awkward composition of a shot that features, in the far right of the frame, a TV showing hardcore porn images; specifically, one can clearly notice a woman performing fellatio on a man. The rest of the frame is out of focus and one can only presume that we are in the house's living room. The film then cuts to a shot of the parents who are sitting on the sofa half-naked. The topless mother rests her head on the father's naked lap. The father, who wears a shirt and tie but no underwear, caresses her. 'I am pregnant.

Twins', says the mother. 'Two boys?' asks the father. 'No, one boy one girl.'
'Are you sure?' 'Yes.' 'Triplets?' 'That's an exaggeration!' 'You are right.
Twins.' The film cuts back to a long shot of the swimming pool where the
children engage in further water activities. The father enters the shot but
the camera cannot bother to tilt up a bit in order to include his upper body
in the frame. The children dive into the water and the father starts counting the time. Lanthimos offers us here some beautiful underwater shots of
the children to the sounds of a simple melody played on the piano. The
piano melody gradually yields to the father's voice, which takes over the
soundtrack; the underwater images still continue.

FATHER   Your mother will soon give birth to two children and a dog.
          I know that some of you may be annoyed because they will
          have to share their rooms, their clothes and even their toys
          with their new siblings. But I want you to see the bright side.
          You will have new people to support you and the family will
          grow. Hence, I want us all to applaud your mother for this
          gift.

The film then cuts to a shot of the family in the living room; the brother
at the top right angle sitting behind the piano, the father on the right end
of the frame resting in an armchair and the three females on the left half
sharing the sofa. After the applause, the son continues his piano playing
while the two sisters express their discontent about having to share their
rooms. The parents reply that if they are well behaved they may not have
to. The film visually returns to the swimming pool and the father, who
is counting up the time with his stopwatch as the children play another
game of endurance. On the soundtrack, however, we hear the mother
continuing the previous conversation, 'If your behavior and performance
improve, I may not have to give birth. However, if things don't change I
have no other choice. But I won't hear a thing about the dog. He will be
born as soon as possible.'

Dogtooth clearly underscores the unapologetically arbitrary nature of
narratives, but most importantly the way they can be deployed to support
specific normative structures that regulate the production of particular subjectivities and forms of identity. As the parents indulge in porn watching
and myth making, the children fall deeper and deeper into a convoluted
labyrinth of narratives that grow all the more absurd, all the more inconsistent, literally converting them into barking toy soldiers; ironically, none of

them seems able to escape this nonsensical construction, not even the parents themselves. Accordingly, the audience soon realizes that there is no point in trying to stitch together the non-matching pieces of this incomprehensible puzzle. As the audience slumps into the abyss of meaninglessness, as we surrender to the excitements and perils of irony, narrativity, this incessant pursuit and ultimate realm of meaning production, is, unequivocally, both thematically and formally dismantled. For, much as the family and the nation are foregrounded and exposed as archetypal narratives, so the medium itself is unapologetically attacked through the film's formal defiance of conventional cinematic narrativity.

Indeed, in the above sequences narratives emerge as the primary means for the production, legitimization and perpetuation of this twisted familial microcosm. Narratives are relentlessly produced and invoked in the service of an ambivalent affective structure, both caring and abusive, both rewarding and punitive, that regulates the everyday reality of the children, while at the same time securing and perpetuating itself. As mentioned above, the authoritarian resonances of *Dogtooth*'s unquestionably oppressive familial structure legitimized readings of the film as an allegory for dictatorial regimes, and, particularly, as an allegory for the nation's former dictatorial past.[2] Nevertheless, more than a mere allegory for dictatorial regimes, Greek or foreign, the film's foregrounding of the ambivalent and sinister nature of narrativity invites a more complicated exploration of the way *Dogtooth* engages with both the familial and the national. For if family is offered as an unapologetically constructed authoritarian regime grounded on relentless processes of myth making, then the nation-state, for which the family has served as favorite narrative, metaphor and quintessential structural core, is accordingly questioned and exposed as, perhaps, the archetypal narrative, the ultimate myth.

Arguably, the most extreme invocation of the family as a metaphor for the nation has, indeed, occurred within authoritarian political regimes. However, despite deploying family as their favorite narrative, these regimes' materialized family politics do not necessarily reveal a sincere support for kinship bonds as such. Historian Paul Ginsborg, in his discussion of the family politics of the great dictators (namely, Hitler, Stalin, Mussolini and Franco), argues that the proper way to look into the relationship between the national, the political and the familial is through 'a wider consideration of the relations between individuals, families, civil society and the state', which understands that 'families are not simply on the receiving end of political power, but are themselves actors in the historical process (2003,

p. 174). As he notes, none of the above dictators, with the possible exception of Franco, paid much attention to the family as such, their family
politics being 'more implicit than explicit, rhetorical than realistic, the sum
of other policies as they came to affect families' (2003, p. 175). However,
all of these regimes 'shared fundamental similarities in their visions of the
relationship between the state and the family, of individuals having ties of
responsibility to their families, and of the way in which families were to
relate to a regimented and controlled civil society' (2003, p. 174).

Imbued with a traditional patriarchal ideology, these regimes' family
politics, as Ginsborg explains, privileged male authority and authoritarianism within the family, as well as the role of the man as warrior in the service
of the nation (the greater world), while condemning the women to isolation from the public sphere, particularly after their marriage, and favoring
motherhood and housekeeping (the smaller world) as the woman's biological and social destiny. Family was, thus, seen as 'organically' linked to
the state, the 'basic "cell" from which the authoritarian state could grow,
and upon which it depended' (2003, p. 180).

Clearly, the dictatorships' system of power relations depended upon
a fierce polemics 'against individualism, conceived of in a classic liberal
sense and as the unwelcome heritage of the French Revolution', thus
reinserting the individual 'into two social entities of prime importance:
one was the family, and the other was a homogeneous and revitalized
national community' (2003, p. 195). Nevertheless, the tension between
the simultaneous summoning of the individual to both the family and the
nation-state exposes the regimes' fundamental internal contradictions, for
the dissolution of individualism into the institutions and ideologies of the
national community often translated into a relentless sucking out of family
members from their homes, and thus a significant submission/dissolution
of family time into the national one. Hence, where the families 'were to
form the constituent parts of an ordered, regimented, healthy, even joyous society', their relationship with the respective society was clearly not
as organic as was suggested, for their subordination to the wider national
community at times rendered them redundant and even hostile. Ginsborg
invokes Ferdinand Mount's argument that families are subversive 'not
in the sense of organizing actively against the regimes, but in the sense
of having codes, cultures, and strategies that are specific to themselves'
(2003, p. 197). In this way, Ginsborg's historical analysis of the family
politics of Europe's most influential dictatorial regimes of the twentieth
century ultimately demonstrates that the appropriation of the institution

of family by the regimes was more symbolic rather than structural. With family being a metaphor, 'a model and archetype for the nation', to use Franco's own words (cited in Ginsborg, 2003, p. 180), a constituent part not so much of the 'joyous society' itself as of its 'joyous' nationalist narrative, the internal contradictions of the dictatorships' paradigm come to the surface, thus denaturalizing and exposing the association between the national and the familial as the effect of discursive practices that are perilous for the individual subject, and as another elusive effect of language.

This precisely sinister character of narrativity, one which elusively objectifies its receivers and mercilessly turns them against themselves, is, arguably, *Dogtooth*'s primary focus of attack. Lanthimos's film magnificently stages the perilous mechanisms of the familiar familial, patriarchal and, concomitantly, national narratives, unearthing not only their internal contradictions but, most importantly, their ambivalent ethical status and function.

In another 'weird' moment in the film, the family is having one of its regular dinners when suddenly the father asks the children whether they would like to listen to their grandfather singing. He then reaches for the turntable and puts on a vinyl record. As the song starts playing, the father sits next to the record-player and translates the English lyrics of the song into Greek. Ironically, Bart Howard's iconic 'Fly Me to the Moon' takes an unpredictable interpretation:

FATHER   Dad loves us, Mum loves us. Do we love them? Yes, we do! I love my siblings, because they love me back. And the spring fills my home. The spring floods my little heart. My parents are proud of me because I do my best. But I'm always trying to do better. My home, you are beautiful and I love you. And I will never abandon you.

Halfway through the song the film has already cut to a shot of the rest of the family, sitting in the living room, the three children in the foreground listening to the father with religious reverence, while occasionally smiling at each other, and the mother behind them looking at them and making sure that the 'sermon' is delivered befittingly. To the sounds of the song's bridge the family stands up and starts dancing, with the camera once more being indifferent to the occasional beheading of the characters. The religious connotations of the scene abound. The preacher is spatially distinguished from the pilgrims, who silently attend the 'liturgy' and only actively participate when called upon. And the preacher repeats the same old story of the loving society, which is governed by a superior power that the members of society must keep faithful to so that the society (but not necessarily the individual) can flourish and blossom; indeed, the same old narrative that is also featured in various nationalist discourses, which, unsurprisingly, capitalize on both the religious and familial sentiment.

But *Dogtooth* goes a step further and investigates the extreme limits of the patriarchal narrative, thus exposing its inherent contradictions and interrogating its ambivalent ethics. In perhaps the most shocking sequence in the film, Lanthimos dares to probe the contentious borders of incest, thus provocatively stretching the limits of the demand by the rigidly patriarchal (and compulsorily heterosexual) traditional familial power system for the subject's unconditional submission. And he does so with an excruciating tranquility that makes the sequence all the more disturbing.

When the father discovers that Christina has 'contaminated' one of his innocent offspring, that is the elder daughter, by introducing her to the mainstream popular culture of the 'outside world' and specifically to Hollywood films, he decides to take drastic measures in order to eliminate the possibility of any further menacing intrusions into his rigidly structured familial construct. He thus announces to his wife that Christina must be replaced and that he is thinking of 'handing the task' to one of the daughters as they cannot trust anyone from outside the house any more. In the scene that follows the boy gets to choose which of the two girls he prefers to engage in sexual intercourse with. The scene begins with a three-shot of the siblings in the bathtub, the boy in the middle and the two girls around him. Having his eyes closed, the boy touches the breasts and bottoms first of the elder sister and then of the younger one. Lanthimos does not hesitate to offer a closer view of this awkward examination with two respective close-ups. The film then cuts to the elder daughter's bedroom where we see the mother combing her daughter's hair, the girl looking at the mirror, silent and deadpan. Another cut shows the mother opening the boy's bedroom door and letting the daughter in. As the door closes behind the mother, the film invites us into the boy's bedroom in order to witness the incestuous coitus. The siblings undress and the boy takes his sister's hand and puts it on his penis so that she helps him get aroused with a hand-job. Lanthimos frames the characters' bodies in such a way that the boy's erect penis is clearly exposed, although once again the heads are cut off. During the penetration a medium shot of the girl shows her closing her eyes and clenching her teeth in a hopeless effort

Fig. 3.5   Beyond desire: sex as an act of kinship

to endure both the physical and emotional pain. In the background of this shot a mirror behind the girl suggestively bears the reflection of her brother's face (Fig. 3.5). At the end of the intercourse a shot from above features the siblings' faces as they lean against the headboard. The girl, visibly exhausted, channels her distress through an astonishing recitation of a line from one of the Hollywood films that Christina had given her, 'If you do it again, I'll gut you, you bitch. I swear on my daughter's life that you and your gang will soon flee the neighborhood.' The young man looks at her puzzled, mirroring the viewers' response to the scene they have just witnessed.

Here, *Dogtooth* arguably reverses the case regarding incest that Butler makes in *Antigone's Claim* (2000). In Butler's reading of the Sophoclean tragedy, Antigone's claim to and act of burying Polyneices against Creon's edict originates in a latent incestuous love for her brother, for the sake of which she is determined even to bury herself alive. Antigone's renegotiation of the law of structuralist kinship, which, as Butler explains, frames what Lacan terms the Symbolic Order, effectively establishes the final act of Sophocles' Oedipal trilogy as the basis for a post-Oedipal psychoanalytic approach. For Antigone's real law-breaking does not pertain to the law of Creon, the law of the state, but to the law of the Father, which has essentially constituted itself through the incest taboo. 'The abiding assumption of the symbolic that stable kinship norms support our abiding sense of culture's intelligibility', Butler argues, has produced 'that moralized sexual horror that is perhaps most fundamentally associated with incest' and which establishes certain forms of kinship and kin relations 'as the only intelligible

and livable ones' (2000, pp. 70–71). As she explains, 'the incest taboo legit-
imates and normalizes kinship [and kin positions] based in biological production and the heterosexualization of the family' (2000, p. 66). However,
she admits 'normalization is invariably disrupted and foiled by what cannot be ordered by regulatory norms', thus revealing that 'the incest taboo
contains its infraction within itself' (2000, p. 66). In this way, the incest
taboo 'does not simply prohibit incest but rather sustains and cultivates
incest as a necessary specter of social dissolution, a specter without which
social bonds cannot emerge' (2000, p. 67). It is not useful, however, to
claim that Antigone represents a mere perversion of the law in a way that
establishes perversion as a structural necessity for the law itself to be constituted and maintained; this 'does not help make possible […] other forms of
social life, inadvertent possibilities produced by the prohibition that come
to undermine the conclusion that an invariant social organization of sexuality follows of necessity from the prohibitive law' (2000, p. 68). For, in this
line of thought, the perverse remains entombed in a form of negative dialectics, as the essential and negative feature of the norm, which, nonetheless, denies any rearticulation of the norm itself. Butler does not, of course,
argue for incestuous relations here; she rather wonders whether the incest
taboo could 'become the basis for a socially survivable aberration of kinship
in which the norms that govern legitimate and illegitimate modes of kin
association might be more radically redrawn' (2000, p. 67), hence, ultimately, paving the way to rethink kinship, kin positions and blood relations
per se. For 'the kinship trouble at the heart of Sophocles' underscores incest
as precisely the effect of language, a normative and normalizing structure,
which organizes kin relations as well as the actors, positions and places of
normative family, while simultaneously establishing them 'at the level of
the symbolic [as] a necessary psychic support against an engorgement by
the Real' (2000, p. 70). In effect, kinship itself emerges as the effect of
language.

Clearly, Butler's queer reading of *Antigone* as a renegotiation of the
incest taboo that illuminates the discursive production of biological kinship
could easily apply to the transgressive narrative of Panos Koutras's *Strella*,
the film addressed in Chap. 4, where the dramatization of a romantic relationship between a father and his transgender child creates a queer utopian aesthetic space to radically reframe and reimagine kinship and blood
relations. Ironically, though reversing both *Antigone*'s and *Strella*'s paradigms, by offering incest as the effect of patriarchal authoritarianism rather
than of aberrant desire, the incest scene in *Dogtooth* ultimately produces

the same effect, which is none other than the denaturalization of the famil-iar familial bonds. The violation of the quintessential kin relations is para-doxically ordered in *Dogtooth* by the father himself while supported and facilitated by the mother. The father makes the decision to 'hand the task' to the daughter but it is the mother who undertakes the preparation of the 'illicit bride' and escorts her to the 'bridal bed'. The scene is certainly laden with multi-layered and caustic insinuations against ideologies of sexual dif-ference; from the capitalization and splitting of the female body to the collusion of the mother in the discourses of patriarchy. Indeed, in only a few minutes Lanthimos manages to sum up the split that, as Luce Irigaray argues, in patriarchal capitalism produces three bodies for 'woman': the wife/mother (use-value, private property), the daughter (commodity/exchange-value), and the whore (use-value and exchange-value) (1985, pp. 185–186). Ironically, the mother here emerges as a pivotal agent of patriarchy, which exceeds the use-value that Irigaray ascribes to her, while the daughter's kin position is set aside—if not utterly obliterated—and her body arguably assumes the role of the whore.

One may wonder whether the incest scene in *Dogtooth* translates into yet another renegotiation of the law of the Father, this time by the very figure who assumes the pivotal patriarchal symbolic position, that is, the father himself. Indeed, is it possible to consider that *Dogtooth* provides the basis here for a subversive restructuring of the Symbolic, a radical resolu-tion to the Oedipal complex akin to Butler's post-structuralist reading of *Antigone*, by way of introducing an alternative organization of kin posi-tions and relations that defies the incest taboo and allows brothers and sisters engage in sexual intercourse? Alas, no. With desire being uncondi-tionally silenced or indeed radically silent in the entire film, the transgres-sive violation of the normative kin relations is paradoxically foregrounded here as the effect of an unprecedented patriarchal demand. Nevertheless, despite not providing the basis for 'a socially survivable aberration of kin-ship', this paradoxical demand by the patriarch, which unapologetically renders the incest taboo redundant, ultimately results in a poignant dis-articulation of patriarchy itself. For the patriarch's defiance of the incest taboo, which, as Butler argues above, constitutes the structural core of patriarchal kinship, is essentially the defiance of patriarchy itself. Patriarchy is, indeed, exposed as an incoherent and contingent structure, whose tem-poral existence relies on arbitrary and inconsistent narratives. And as such a contingent structure it necessarily depends on performativity for both its production and proliferation.

Butler uses the paradigm of *Antigone* to highlight precisely the performative character of kinship:

> Antigone is caught in a web of relations that produce no coherent position within kinship. She is not, strictly speaking, outside kinship or, indeed, unintelligible. Her situation can be understood, but only with a certain amount of horror. Kinship is not simply a situation she is in but a set of practices that she also performs, relations that are reinstituted in time precisely through the practice of their repetition [...] her action is the action of kinship. (2000, pp. 57–58)

It is remarkable how Butler's analysis of Antigone resonates with the siblings' precarious familial positioning in *Dogtooth*, thus shedding light on the way the film exposes the internal contradictions at the heart of patriarchal kinship. In effect, Antigone could easily be substituted for the two siblings (or even all three of them) in the above passage. For *Dogtooth*'s disturbing[3] scene of compulsory non-consensual incest is, in many respects, featured as having a kind of ritualistic character, which, despite producing a 'certain amount of horror' in its unapologetic defiance of the patriarchal structure, effectively exposes kinship as 'a set of practices' that the children have to perform; indeed 'relations that are reinstituted in time precisely through the practice of their repetition'. The youngsters' act emerges exactly as yet another act of kinship, even if it is one that violates the quintessential structural kin positions and relations, which, as Butler illuminates, constitute the symbolic and with it the totality of cultural intelligibility. Not that *Dogtooth* proposes new modes of kin association. On the contrary, the act's performative character, underscored by the film's both narrative and formal deglamorization of sex, as well as the characters' mechanical response to their experience (suggestively channeled through filmic references in the case of the sister), precisely underscores the internal contradictions at the heart of the structure as well as the contingency of its discursive nature. And sex is once more foregrounded as a regulatory mechanism for the preservation of the gender and sexual hierarchies of the house, through which the parents guarantee the perpetuation of the familial structure. Yet, this time the parents effectively bring its very form to crisis; for in order to annihilate the possibility of the structure's permeability they appear willing to render it elastic. Patriarchy itself, hence, emerges as an incoherent narrative subjected to the contingencies of its own fantasmatic teleological temporality; indeed, a vicious circle that keeps its subjects entrapped in a precarious existence, while at the same time ironically promising them stability and 'blossoming'.

Unsurprisingly, national narrativity relies heavily on patriarchy's temporal structure and its promise of growth and reproduction through the strict
allocation of gender roles and the even stricter regulation of sexual practices. However, the dissolution of individual autonomy, managed through
the symbolic appropriation of authoritarian patriarchal kinship bonds, is
not exclusive to nationalist dictatorial regimes. Individual autonomy often
emerges as yet another subplot on the side of the established nationalist
narratives of the modern liberal nation-state, whose primary aim becomes,
indeed, the nation-state's own preservation and expansion, most of the
time at the expense of the individual. As we have seen in the Introduction,
Peter Bien (2005) illuminates how 'Greece' and 'Greekness' have come
about through a distinct process of aestheticization that has relied on the
paradoxical amalgamation of such incongruous relational structures as
family, religion and the nation, perhaps best encapsulated in the infamous
slogan 'Fatherland, Religion, Family'. In this process, both the Orthodox
Church and traditional patriarchal familial bonds have been intimately tied
up with the way nationalism and capitalism emerged as dominating forces
on the self-representational stage of the modern Greek state. Indeed, the
Greek paradigm exemplifies precisely the way nationalism's domination of
the metaphysics of modernity has been invested not only in the subordination of the religious element to the state but, most importantly, in the
dissolution of the traditional extended family ties of the Greek village into
a modern, urbanized and capitalist-oriented kinship system that privileged
the nuclear family while still heavily relying on the patriarchal regulation
of gender and sex. Hence, the reformed patriarchal Greek family served
as a metaphor, a metonymy for and narrative of Greece and Greekness,
and as a vehicle for their construction as narratives; in other words, family
emerges as both the nation's aesthetic manifestation (nation as a 'family')
and the quintessential means for its own aestheticization, its own coming
to aesthetic—if not ontological—being (family as the core of the 'nation').
In these terms, Greece's process of aestheticization eventually exposes
Greece as a metaphor itself rather than the actualized space (and place)
of a homogeneous and revitalized national community. However, such a
process of aestheticization requires the recursive strategy of performativity that will preserve and reproduce the national narrative over time, and,
ultimately, congeal its status as, indeed, historical, rather than discursive.
This process is precisely what Homi Bhabha (2000) has named as the
double time of the nation; an argument already examined in the previous
chapter, which claims that the continuist, accumulative temporality of the

'pedagogical' requires its constant repetition through the 'performative', namely the sum of national rituals, parades, liturgies, celebrations, and aesthetic re-enactments (through literature, film, theatre, etc.).

Dogtooth's resonances with the above discourses of the nation's narrativity, performativity and modes of self-representation are, indeed, fascinating. More than a mere allegory of the nation and its authoritarian regimes, Lanthimos's film arguably engages in a deeper interrogation of the way the nation's self-representation emerges and replicates itself, thus ultimately questioning and renegotiating our very means of conceptualizing the family, the nation, the medium itself. For, as the textual analysis that follows reveals, the existence and perpetuation of the familial structure in *Dogtooth* depends on the exact same terms of temporalization that characterize the double time of the nation, that is on a temporal organization that is not merely invented as continuist and accumulative but also one that requires its constant repetition. Ironically, through this dramatization the film also interrogates the medium's own collusion in the construction and repetition of familial (and, by implication, national) time. Indeed, alongside its mythical narratives explored above, which construct a particular continuist time that, much like Greece's, must be constantly reinvented, the family's idiosyncratic temporality is also eminently invested in a mediated repetition of the quotidian that borders on fetishization, as the family's quotidian time, strictly organized around particular activities, while excluding others, is consistently recorded and reconsumed for entertainment.

Back in the first scenes of the film, and just after the awkward sex scene between Christina and the son described earlier, Christina joins the rest of the family in the living room for a glass of fresh juice. The scene begins with a wide-angle shot of Christina and the elder daughter sitting on the sofa. The younger daughter enters the frame from the right side (her head cut off), holding a glass of juice, which she offers to Christina, and then goes and sits next to her sister. As Christina drinks up her juice, we hear the voice of the mother coming from off-screen, 'I've put some apple juice in it, too.' 'It's very nice' says Christina and continues, 'Unfortunately, I must go.' The film cuts to a 'reverse shot', which frames in the center the three girls from behind, leaving the mother and the father in the two corners. The father asks, 'Could we shoot a video together?' 'Yes, we don't have one with Christina', says the mother and asks Christina, 'You don't mind shooting a video together, do you?' 'Not at all', replies Christina. The father then takes the camera, stands up and starts shooting the girls

Fig. 3.6   Producing and performing familial time

(Fig. 3.6). The film cuts back to the original set-up of the scene, which features the two daughters smiling and posing for the camera, whereas Christina looks visibly discomfited. The younger daughter asks, 'Dad, can I also sit next to Christina?' 'Yes my love', the father replies. The girls swap positions and then the son enters the frame from the right running to sit on the sofa along with the girls. 'Christina can you smile a bit more?' the father asks again. Christina then makes an effort to smile for the camera in contrast to the three siblings, who seem quite at ease with the peculiar arrangement.

The home-videos theme in *Dogtooth* arguably reverberates with Julianne Pidduck's argument about 'the constitutive relationship between kinship and audiovisual form', which capitalizes 'the tremendous power of visual culture generally, and audiovisual texts specifically, as a special kind of kinship practice' (2009, p. 464), while foregrounding, at the same time, performativity as an integral and constitutive part of (familial) narrativity. Indeed, unlike Christina, the children seem at ease with the video shooting, thus highlighting it as precisely a repetitive act in the construction and organization of familial time. But *Dogtooth* deploys the theme of the family home-videos not only to point out the way 'kinship is mediated across time through the commemorative and generative processes of visual media', as Pidduck puts it (2009, p. 462), but through this to make strange the familiar familial imagery and narrativity. Home-video making in *Dogtooth* does not necessarily pertain to the recording of exceptional, memorable instances from the familial calendar, namely birthdays, anniversaries, parties, but extends (or is rather limited) to indifferent, quotidian familial time, which is both produced and consumed/experienced as an effect of the medium itself. Arguably, this doubling of familial temporality emerges as both formative and fetishizing; the children pose and smile for the camera as if posing for random family photographs, and then gather around the television to consume these indifferent quotidian moving images as an entertainment option, or, even more so, as a form of family ritual. The medium is reduced to the transient, the ephemeral, which is thus fetishized. In this way, *Dogtooth* ultimately undermines conventional home-video making and with it any practice of narrating the family by highlighting both as the effect of an ambivalent process of temporal construction and temporal elision. Through this, familial narrativity is denaturalized and exposed as an equally ambivalent process, aimed at an imaginary space that relies on both a cyclical/performative and a teleological conceptualization and construction of time; the time that has to be invented and the time that has to be performed. Arguably, the resonances of *Dogtooth*'s familial spatiotemporal construction with the discourses on national narrativity and the Greek paradigm, discussed previously, resurface more clearly than ever here.

However, at the same time, *Dogtooth* attacks the very means of narrativity and, generally, signification, through a fierce interrogation of both human and filmic language and the way they are intimately implicated in the formation of familial (and, concomitantly, the national) subjectivity. As evident in the very first scene of the film analyzed at the beginning of this chapter, the film's parental regime relies on a strict manipulation of language that regulates signification and with it the constitution of the familial subject. A Lacanian reading of *Dogtooth*'s familial structure would not be irrelevant here, as the film illuminates the process of subjectivation through the submission of the child to the Other, despite (or perhaps precisely because of) the construction of an alternative Symbolic Order. For Lacan, the constitution of the subject is in effect an alienating process, in which the formation of subjectivity emerges as the effect of the alien signifier, after the child's entry into the Symbolic Order and the Law of the Father through the acquisition of Language. As Ben Tyrer observes, in *Dogtooth*'s parental regime the formation of the familial subject takes place through a meticulous linguistic project that depends on a double process: 'a reactive re-signification and a proactive dictation of signifieds' (2012). Indeed, the house's construction of an alternative Symbolic Order relies on an assignment of radically different signifieds to already recognized signifiers, so that any threat to the perpetuation of the parental regime, coming usually from outside, is eliminated. Hence, names acquire new meanings ('zombies' are small yellow flowers), and things new names (the vagina is called 'keyboard') or new functions (the television is only used for watching home-videos). Strikingly enough, *Dogtooth*'s manipulation and appropriation of language as essential for the process of constructing familial subjectivity (and, in tandem, of narrativity) reminds us here of Koraïs's linguistic project of *katharevousa*, which, as we have seen in the Introduction, at the time was considered vital for the construction of a continuist Greek national time and identity.

However, what emerges as even more fascinating from such a Lacanian reading of *Dogtooth* is the way the film offers the relationship between signification and subjectivity as an inescapable vicious circle, thus ultimately dismantling our very means of conceptualizing the family, the nation and the medium itself. Indeed, the film clearly suggests that much as the medium can be deployed in the service of familial (or national) temporalization, it also encompasses the means of its dismantling. When Christina introduces the elder daughter to Hollywood videos in exchange for sexual favors, the unsuspecting offspring enters a whole new universe, in which the parental construct of the strict regulation of the relation between signifiers and signifieds collapses and the familial subject is both exposed and rearticulated. The lack of sexual signification within the familial construct prevents the elder daughter from translating accordingly Christina's advances, who asks her to 'come closer and lick' her between the legs in exchange for cheap accessories. However, when instead of accessories the elder daughter asks Christina for the two rental videotapes she has in her bag, the house's signifying system comes under threat and, ultimately, is exposed as inherently contradictory and permeable. From the recitation of lines from the Hollywood films, witnessed in the incestuous sex scene above, to even more physical re-enactments, in the form of shark attacks or boxing matches,[4] the elder daughter's Hollywood acculturation seems to provide her with new signifiers through which she channels her emotional permutations. But the more the elder daughter immerses herself in the foreign narratives the more she departs from her familiar familial subjectivity, a movement that culminates in her very renaming. After the father punishes the daughter with some blows on the head with the videotapes she watched, the film cuts to a medium shot of the two sisters in bed, the younger daughter massaging her sister's head. 'I want you to call me Bruce', says the elder daughter. 'What is Bruce?' 'A name. Every time you say Bruce I'll turn.' The younger daughter then starts calling 'Bruce' and her sister changes positions in the room, every time turning her head to her sister's call. As Tyrer (2012) again points out, in this fascinating dramatization of the process of interpellation, in which the subject is called into being by the signifier itself, the film not only highlights that the signifier is the cause *of* and *for* the subject, but, most importantly, that the subject as such is always already trapped within signification, even if it wants to substitute one narrative for another, one Symbolic Order for another.

In conclusion, subjectivity emerges as always already caught up in signification, with narrativity being the quintessential element of its formation. Narratives are what essentially help us come into being. Without them, any sense of identity falls apart and loses itself in the abyss of meaninglessness. Yet this is the abyss that *Dogtooth* proposes as an ethical gesture against another more perilous one, namely the abyss of narrativity that has historically instituted multiple oppressive regimes of subjectivation, be they patriarchal, familial, national. Through this abyss of meaninglessness *Dogtooth* ultimately exposes the medium as yet another signifying system with its own interpellating logics and modes of subjectivation. However, elusive and uncanny as this project may be, it is, ultimately, queer. Edelman reminds us, 'The narrative that raises meaninglessness as a possibility, after all, necessarily bestows a particular meaning on such meaninglessness itself' (2004, p. 120). Following Edelman's axiom, I would argue that the film's controversial meaninglessness is, indeed, nothing less than an unapologetic refusal and denunciation of a particular set of meanings, immanent in the discourses that *Dogtooth* so beautifully and, at the same time, so disturbingly invokes, attacks and dismantles: namely, nationalism, patriarchy, heteronormativity. Ultimately, *Dogtooth*'s formal defiance and thematic subversiveness is an invitation to explore film's ethical potential as a queer medium; one which foregrounds irreducible difference as an essential precondition in articulating discourses of the self and the other. Indeed, perhaps, much as our genitals become 'keyboards' that rewrite ourselves time and again, the medium becomes a platform for queerness to rewrite relationality.

NOTES

1. Surprisingly, this is the same economic-political model that homonormative accounts of gay identity ascribe to their same-sex marriage claims, invoking the neoliberal nation-state's constitutional rights of autonomy and freedom to act. Indeed, contemporary gay activism showcases the married same-sex couple as the idealization of the sovereign nation's recognition of human rights, as well as an effective materialization of its neoliberal capitalist agenda by the for-

mation of a familial unit that is productive for the nation-state. Ironically, this results in the sanctification of marriage and family by those very subjects that both institutions have historically rendered unintelligible or even unlivable.

2. In its modern history Greece has experienced two dictatorial regimes, the Metaxas regime, under the leadership of General Ioannis Metaxas, which ruled Greece from 1936 to 1941, and the Greek military Junta of 1967 to 1974, alternatively known as the Regime of the Colonels.

3. The scene is, indeed, profoundly disturbing not so much because of the incest subtext as for its twisted rape undertones, something which is suggested by both film form and performance.

4. *Dogtooth* references directly such big Hollywood blockbusters as the *Jaws* and *Rocky* franchises, also pointing out the massive impact of mainstream popular culture on the formation of subjectivity.

BIBLIOGRAPHY

Bhabha, Homi K. (2000 [1990]) 'Dissemination: Time, Narrative and the Margins of the Modern Nation', in Homi K. Bhabha (ed.) *Nation and Narration* (London: Routledge), pp. 291–322.

Bien, Peter (2005) 'Inventing Greece', *Journal of Modern Greek Studies*, 23/2, 217–234.

Bradshaw, Peter (2010) 'Dogtooth', *The Guardian*, http://www.theguardian.com/film/2010/apr/22/dogtooth-review, date accessed 22 April 2016.

Butler, Judith (2000) *Antigone's Claim: Kinship Between Life and Death* (New York: Columbia University Press).

Cassia, Paul Sant, with contributions by Constantina Bada (2006) *The Making of the Modern Greek Family: Marriage and Exchange in Nineteenth-century Athens* (Cambridge: Cambridge University Press).

de Lauretis, Teresa (2011) 'Queer Texts, Bad Habits, and the Issue of a Future', *GLQ: A Journal of Lesbian and Gay Studies*, 17, 243–263.

Ebert, Roger. (2010). 'Dogtooth', *Chicago Sun-Times*, http://www.rogerebert.com/reviews/dogtooth-2010, date accessed 22 April 2016.

Edelman, Lee (2004) *No Future: Queer Theory and the Death Drive* (Durham and London: Duke University Press).

Ginsborg, Paul (2003) 'The Family Politics of the Great Dictators', in David I. Kertzer and Marzio Barbagli (eds.) *The History of the European Family. Vol. 3, Family Life in the Twentieth Century* (New Haven: Yale University Press), pp. 174–197.

Harkness, Alistair (2010) 'Film Review: Dogtooth', *The Scotsman*, http://www. scotsman.com/news/film-review-dogtooth-1-800939, date accessed 22 April 2016.

Irigaray, Luce (1985) *This Sex Which is Not One* (New York: Cornell University Press).

Jakobsen, Janet R. (2011) 'Perverse Justice', *GLQ: A Journal of Lesbian and Gay Studies*, 18, 19–45.

Jansick, Dustin (2011) 'Dogtooth', *Way Too Indie: Independent Film and Music Reviews*, http://waytooindie.com/review/movie/dogtooth/, date accessed 22 April 2016.

Lewis, David (2010) 'Review: In "Dogtooth" House, Sanity is Relative', *San Francisco Chronicle*, http://www.sfgate.com/movies/article/Review-In-Dogtooth-house-sanity-is-relative-3176134.php, date accessed 22 April 2016.

Lippe, Adam (2010) 'Dogtooth', *A Regrettable Moment of Sincerity*, http://regrettablesincerity.com/?p=5320, date accessed 22 April 2016.

Olsen, Mark (2011) 'Movie Review: "Dogtooth"', *Los Angeles Times*, http://articles.latimes.com/2011/jan/07/entertainment/la-et-capsules-20110107, date accessed 22 April 2016.

Orndorf, Brian (2010) 'Dogtooth', *dvdtalk.com*, http://www.dvdtalk.com/reviews/44386/dogtooth/, date accessed 22 April 2016.

Pidduck, Julianne (2009) 'Queer Kinship and Ambivalence: Video Autoethnographies by Jean Carlomusto and Richard Fung', *GLQ: A Journal of Lesbian and Gay Studies*, 15/3, 441–468.

Raouzaios, Yiannis (2009) 'Ο Κυνόδοντας (Dogtooth)', *myfilm.gr*, http://www. myfilm.gr/4788.html#reviews, date accessed 22 April 2016.

Romney, Jonathan (2010) 'Dogtooth, Giorgos Lanthimos, 96 mins, (18) Life During Wartime, Todd Solondz, 96 mins, (15)', *The Independent*, http://www.independent.co.uk/arts-entertainment/films/reviews/dogtooth-giorgos-lanthimos-96-mins-18brlife-during-wartime-todd-solondz-96-mins-15-1953388.html, date accessed 22 April 2016.

Scott, A.O. (2010) 'Dogtooth: A Sanctuary and a Prison', *New York Times*, http://www.nytimes.com/2010/06/25/movies/25dog.html?_r=2&, date accessed 22 April 2016.

Turner, Matthew (2010) 'Dogtooth (Kynodontas)', *viewlondon.co.uk*, http://www.viewlondon.co.uk/films/dogtooth-kynodontas-film-review-30069.html, date accessed 22 April 2016.

Tyrer, Ben (2012) 'This Tongue Is Not My Own: *Dogtooth*, Phobia and the Paternal Metaphor', posted in *academia.edu*, https://kcl.academia.edu/BenTyrer, date accessed 22 April 2016.

van Hoeij, Boyd (2009) 'Review: Dogtooth', *Variety*, http://variety.com/2009/film/reviews/dogtooth-1200474781/, date accessed 22 April 2016.

Wesling, Meg (2011) 'Queer Value', *GLQ: A Journal of Lesbian and Gay Studies*, 18, 107–125.

CHAPTER 4

Strella: Of Queer Utopias

In Panos Koutras's *Strella/A Woman's Way* (2009), the eponymous protagonist's final confrontation with her ex-lover Yorgos (Yannis Kokiasmenos) is marked by the latter's confession that she had made him love her in every possible way a father could have loved his child. Their meeting ends in a kind of silent, yet salient reconciliation. Devastated, but redeemed, Strella (Mina Orphanou) leaves the luxurious hotel and wanders about the festively decorated streets of Athens at Christmas to the sounds of *Tosca* as uniquely performed by the iconic symbol of Greek femininity Maria Callas. There then follows a series of medium shots of Strella walking past the Christmas lights on the lampposts, with cars passing, and even a garbage truck, while Strella casts blurred, 'out of focus' glances at the nocturnal, busy streets of the Greek capital, and tears draw bifurcated streams on her androgynous face (Fig. 4.1). Through a series of close-ups and medium shots, the camera is, evidently, fixed and fixated, in this sequence, on Strella's/Mina Orphanou's face; that exotic queer face with the strong features, the long nose, the succulent lips, the high cheekbones, and the big wet almond eyes, reflections of the inherently traumatic past of this and every transgender body; for there is always some sort of pain behind thick eyeliner and pink glitter. A need to cover and cover up, to pass and pass off. But also an irony, a self-irony that is always caught up in the excess of both appearance and character.

Significantly, especially as captured in this short scene, Strella/Orphanou's face remarkably resembles Callas's own dramatic one—particularly as it appears in her interpretation of *Vissi d'arte*, in her performance

© The Author(s) 2016

M. Psaras, *The Queer Greek Weird Wave*,

DOI 10.1007/978-3-319-40310-6_4

Fig. 4.1   Glamorizing the transgender face

at the Royal Opera House in 1964.[1] Hence, Strella/Orphanou's trans-gender face, much like her body, both so lavishly portrayed by Koutras's camera throughout the film, instantly emerge as texts in themselves, or hypertexts to be more precise, palimpsests with residues of a series of references and discourses: namely, patriarchy, femininity, queerness, Greekness, family, and cinema itself, all of which are addressed, re-enacted and/or renegotiated in Koutras's film.

Indeed, this short, yet heavily charged, scene functions as a sort of recapitulation, a somewhat dramatic epilogue, centered on Strella's wet, silent face, while the fade to black that follows the final shot of Strella walking away from the camera, her body merging with the city, momentarily gives the impression of a lead-in to the film's end credits. And yet Koutras decides to delay the film's ending slightly, offering yet another final sequence to his audience in what seems like a generous, campy, cheerful postscript. Indeed, this last sequence not only does justice to the overall queer feeling and aesthetics of the film, but also arguably establishes the film among what José Esteban Muñoz (2009) describes as 'aesthetic queer utopias'.

Strella is the third feature film by Panos H. Koutras, a filmmaker whose name has been associated with Greek postmodernism and New Queer Cinema, after the release of his first feature *The Attack of the Giant*

Moussaka in 1999. This carnivalesque critique of contemporary Greek society, with its campy kitsch aesthetics, the light-hearted treatment of its themes, as well as the parodic performance style of the numerous transgender and queer characters/actors that literally parade in the streets of Athens, established Koutras as the Greek Almodóvar. Ten years later, and amid the first signs of the imminent financial crisis, Koutras released the heretical *Strella*, which he co-produced with the Greek Film Centre.

Strella did quite well on its national theatrical release, but was much more successful in its transnational journey across international film festivals, especially those with a particular focus on LGBT themes, from Berlin to Osaka, Chicago, Paris and London. The marketing of the film as a Greek drama whose story revolves around the unique relationship of a 45-year-old ex-convict with a 25-year-old transgender woman, however, revealed little about the density and complexity of both the film's themes and narrative, or about its aesthetic values and the way it reconfigures both postmodern filmmaking in general and New Queer Cinema in particular. With *Strella* Koutras self-consciously strips off the surface of the 'Homo-pomo' style[2] and mercilessly excoriates its skin to reveal the inmost fears, passions and dreams of queerness, its fantasies and nightmares. *Strella* is definitely not just another example of queer/postmodern filmmaking; there is something more to it, a surplus, which is affective, aesthetic and philosophical, and which, surprisingly, can only be grasped through a queer idealist hermeneutics. Hence, this chapter reads *Strella* through such a methodology, and specifically through the conceptual lenses of José Esteban Muñoz's queer utopian project, as introduced in his book *Cruising Utopia: The Then and There of Queer Futurity* (2009). My aim is to shed light on the way the film renegotiates long-established national narratives offering, at the same time, alternative ways of conceptualizing the national, familial and sexual self.

After 15 years of incarceration for a murder he committed in his home village, Yorgos is released and spends his first night out at a cheap hotel in Athens, where he meets Strella, a young pre-op trans prostitute. The two soon develop a close relationship and fall in love. Determined to start over, Yorgos decides to go back to his village in order to sell all of his property there and also search for his son, Leonidas. At the village he finds out that his son was seen working as a prostitute in Athens. He then quickly returns to the capital and confronts Strella, demanding to know all about her past. Strella confesses that she had left her village for Athens some years after her father was imprisoned for killing the man who tried

to rape her. Yorgos realizes that Strella is his lost son but, more shockingly, he discovers that Strella already knew all about everything the whole
time. The shock is followed by violence and then distance before the odd
couple ultimately reconciles. Indeed, the film's denouement conforms to
what seems like a queer version of mainstream cinema's worn strategy of
the 'happy ending', or even to Pedro Almodóvar's favorite way of resolv-
ing his plots through the redeeming framing of alternative queer families.

In the film's final sequence, we are invited into Strella's apartment, where
preparations are taking place for the New Year's party. Strella and her best
'girl', Alex, are cooking the turkey, while Yorgos and Alex's baby sister are
putting the final touches to the already extravagant Christmas decorations
of the small flat, and all this to the sounds of *skyladika*.[3] Guests arrive, that
is 'Yorgos's guy' as Strella calls him, and Yuri, his Ukrainian friend, who
instantly becomes Strella and Alex's attraction of the day. What follows
looks much like the usual festivities of an archetypal family celebrating the
New Year, having dinner and drinks, dancing and cutting the cake, around
the Christmas tree. However, queerness is unapologetically ubiquitous,
visible in the campy decorations and the flamboyant costumes of Strella
and Alex, 'haunting' the small flat of this surviving neoclassical building
through the vagueness of the relationships among the members of this
newly created—newly reassembled—family, thus, ultimately, disturbing
the conventionality of such a familial representation.

In the film's last shot, we see Yorgos opening a window to look outside
at Athens, which—as we presume from the sounds of fireworks on the
soundtrack—is also celebrating. However, Koutras refuses to offer to the
audience any skyline shots of the city or even a shot of the landmark hill of
the Acropolis. Much as we never learn what year the people are celebrating, we are equally denied a reminder of the geographical location of the
action. The spatial and temporal ambiguity is not without meaning. The
here-and-now is displaced by a then-and-there, or anyplace anytime; the
episode we have just watched is not claiming to be the record of an event,
let alone of a real event, as its representation is denied a spatiotemporal frame that would help it assume verisimilitude. The scene is arguably
framed within the realm of the imaginary, it is highlighted as fantasy, as
utopia, a concrete queer utopia, as Muñoz would call it, characterized by
optimism and signifying the potentiality that imbues the very existence of
queer subjects and queer relationality, despite the difficult circumstances
of their everyday lives. Koutras's camera zooms out to include in the frame
a window on the left of Yorgos through which we can discern his new

queer family. The camera lingers on that frame for a while, until the electric guitars of the hard rock theme of the end credits start strumming, signaling the end of the film.

As Dimitris Papanikolaou notes in his introduction to the published version of the film's screenplay, surprisingly, some viewers/critics found the film's denouement less scandalous than they would have wanted (2010, p. 18). In addition, he says, some reviews in fact criticized the whole film for being almost conservative on the basis of two arguments. The first relies on the idea that, especially with such an ending, the film re-establishes a version of the 'immortal Greek family', which, despite its transgressive nature, has Yorgos and Strella re-enacting traditional patriarchal gender roles, as happy father and daughter. The second argument accuses the film of lacking a clear political position, as it obliterates a contextualization of the story and the characters' trajectories within the oppressive social structure that actually dominates their everyday reality. The first accusation is answered by Koutras himself, as Papanikolaou explains, in an interview at the London Lesbian and Gay Film Festival; as Koutras admits, 'Greeks wanted a tragic end—perhaps having the lead character committing suicide or something like that. But my goal was exactly to avoid such a thing' (in Papanikolaou 2010, p. 18).

As for the second argument, Papanikolaou thinks that it fails to understand and appreciate the film's introspective nature, in the sense that *Strella* is more concerned with an ethics and aesthetics of the self rather than with the broader social and political concerns of queer activism. Such sociopolitical contextualization, he argues, is something the audience must do (2010, pp. 18–19). Indeed, the film seems to want to break with the tragic and phobic discourse of the canonical representation of sexual difference that has prevailed in Greece in recent decades, of which Papanikolaou offers a short, yet illuminating account (2010, p. 19). Papanikolaou locates the first rainbow flags in the Greek sky in the provocative, yet politically conscious and progressive texts of queer magazines, such as *Amphi*, *Kraximo* and *Lavris*, whose discourse was not limited to a cartography of sexual difference, but sought to investigate the intersections of desire with systems of power and identity (2010, p. 20).

However, according to Papanikolaou, the dominance of socialist party PASOK in the 1980s, with its so-called 'populist' agenda, generated a mass culture with phobic syndromes against homosexuality, culturally translated into tragic representations and narratives of same-sex desire that could generically be listed as melodramas of social critique with a hint of

pornography (2010, p. 21). George Katakouzinos's *Angel* (1982) constitutes a landmark of the representation of the queer body as (both social
and biological/physical) pathology; a film which showcases the body of
the transvestite as both repulsive and desired, thus confirming the pho-
bias of an AIDS-panicked society, which seeks to analyze, control and—
if possible—eliminate the 'perverse' and, hence, 'cursed' queer subject
(2010, p. 22). Unfortunately, Papanikolaou laments, the visibility offered
to queer people by private television in the 1990s, and the proliferation
of public discourse on same-sex desire have served merely to reaffirm the
homophobic rhetorics of the 1980s, as they consolidated a very particular and reductive visual identity for the homosexual in the face of the
campy—yet compulsively closeted—gossip 'queen' of the afternoon TV
panels (2010, p. 23).

   If nothing else, Papanikolaou's brief yet astute remarks on the representation of homosexuality in Greece in the past few decades help to pin down
the political and aesthetic space within which mainstream representations
and accounts of queerness have been constructed, thus correspondingly
elucidating the spectrum of its own politics. What emerges as highly problematic in these accounts is not so much the reductive representation of
same-sex desire in the figure of the TV gossip queen but the poor queen's
misery at having to officially remain in the closet in order to be able to
gossip, despite his ostensible campy behavior and costume. Clearly the
paradox of the gossip queen's glass closet reveals Greek society's inherent
hypocrisy, which has historically striven to draw strong lines between the
private and public spheres, particularly with regards to issues of gender
and sexuality. In this shadow, and with homophobia still being considered
the default and morally legitimate mode for addressing sexual difference in
the Greek social space, queerness in Greece signifies not only resistance to
monolithic representations of sexual difference, and/or opposition to the
homogenizing nature of identity politics, but also resistance to the more
fundamental phobic representation of sexual difference as pathology.

   Such phobic discourses and representations of sexual difference are
prominently addressed and critiqued through *Strella*'s radical reframing of
the familiar familial and national space. As this chapter argues, the film crucially marks out a horizon where such oppressive ideological structures and
their representational strategies fall apart and queer subjects are allowed
to dream and live their dreams, even if only within the realm of the aesthetic. This ever-expanding aesthetic horizon is precisely the locus where
Strella intersects with contemporary queer theory and, more specifically,

with Muñoz's work. 'Queerness is not yet here. Queerness is an ideality', says Muñoz at the start of his book, highlighting from the very beginning the optimism which imbues his queer theoretical project (2009, p. 1). Arguing against those who claim that 'all we have are the pleasures of this moment', Muñoz suggests that 'we must dream and enact new and better pleasures, other ways of being in the world, and ultimately new worlds. Queerness is a longing that propels us onward, beyond romances of the negative and toiling in the present' (2009, p. 1). These new worlds proposed and promised by queerness can often be glimpsed, in his view, 'in the realm of the aesthetic, especially the queer aesthetic, which 'frequently contains blueprints and schemata of a forward-dawning futurity' (2009, p. 1). However, as he explains, this turn towards the aesthetic does not mark an 'escape from the social realm, insofar as queer aesthetics map future social relations' (2009, p. 1).

Muñoz draws on Ernst Bloch's theorization of 'educated hope' as the basis for a concrete form of utopia, which, unlike ahistorical abstract utopias, pertains to the hopes of a collective, emergent group; hope here understood as an anticipatory affective structure that is simultaneously critical affect and methodology. In this way, Muñoz turns to a kind of critical idealism, which he considers particularly useful for a queer hermeneutics, and especially necessary given the current dominance of the anti-utopian, pragmatic discourse of queerness as a death drive. In selected works by seminal artists and writers, such as Andy Warhol, LeRoi Jones, Frank O'Hara, Samuel Delany, as well as by contemporary performance and visual artists like Dynasty Handbag, My Barbarian and Kevin McCarty, Muñoz tracks the 'anticipatory illumination of art', a surplus of both affect and meaning, which helps us experience the utopian feeling of what he calls 'the not-yet-conscious' (2009, p. 3).

Muñoz's utopian feeling, this affective surplus, is more of a mode of exhilaration in which one glimpses the potential of a restructured society, an opening, which, though it might possibly engender disappointment, is 'indispensable to the act of imaging transformation' (2009, p. 9). In Muñoz's view, it is necessary to risk such a disappointment, if we are to overcome the impasses of the current disabling political pessimism that prevails in contemporary queer discourse.[4] Muñoz suggests that disparagements of queer relationality aim to privilege sexuality, as a singular trope of difference within queer theory, and to disregard other 'contaminating' analytical forces such as race, gender or other particularities. He also recognizes that the anti-utopianism that is inherent in these projects, 'has a well-worn war chest of post-structuralist pieties', critically power-ful enough to render any social theory that invokes the concept of utopia 'vulnerable to charges of naïveté, impracticality or lack of rigor' (2009, p. 10).

However, Muñoz's utopian project is not only a polemic against the anti-relational strands of queer theory, which he calls 'romances of the negative, wishful thinking, and investments in deferring various dreams of difference', but also a critique of 'ontological certitude [...] partnered with the politics of presentist and pragmatic contemporary gay identity' (2009, p. 11). For Muñoz, the homonormative and assimilationist politi-cal agenda of contemporary LGBT activism in North America, with its adherence to the institutions of marriage and the army, in which it wishes to integrate its subjects, is anything but utopian in the sense that it not only sanctifies traditional straight relationality by aiming at the naturaliza-tion of the 'flawed and toxic ideological formation known as marriage', but also fails to address those queer subjects that do not fall into its rigid categories (2009, p. 21).

Drawing on German idealist practices of thought, and particularly on Bloch's critical notion of utopia, Muñoz's queer utopian project also con-stitutes a critique of 'straight time', this 'autonaturalizing temporality', which promises as the only futurity that of reproductive majoritarian het-erosexuality. In its place he proposes to install the potential of a queer futurity. 'The point', he explains, 'is to stave off a gay and lesbian anti-utopianism that is very much tainted with a polemics of the pragmatic rights discourse that in and of itself hamstrings not only politics but also desire' (2009, p. 26). For him, queerness is a utopian formation 'based on an economy of desire and desiring,' a desire for another time and place not isolated for the individual, but for a collective futurity that 'functions as a historical materialist critique' (2009, p. 26). On this Muñoz, again follows Bloch's view that the 'essential function of utopia is a critique of what is present. If we had not already gone beyond the barriers, we could not even perceive them as barriers' (Bloch, 1988, p. 12).

Muñoz, however, does not suggest that we should turn away from the present, but that the present should be known 'in relation to the alterna-tive temporal and spatial maps provided by a perception of past and future affective worlds' (2009, p. 27). And the past within the Blochian logic is of course not static or fixed but performative; as Muñoz notes 'the past does things'. At this point, he borrows the Derridean concept of the past as trace, in order to describe the unrealized potential of queerness; for

Muñoz, in the 'ephemeral traces', the 'flickering illuminations from other times and places', one can notice a surplus, which is both cultural and affective. Within these sites, he identifies a 'queer feeling of hope', away from the heteronormative theorizations of temporality (both the politically hopeless presentism, as well as the reductive framing of futurity in the exclusive terms of reproductivity). Muñoz admits that such a conceptualization of hope 'takes on the philosophical contours of idealism' (2009, p. 28). Dismissing pragmatic disavowals of queer futurity, he calls for the potentiality of 'queer relational formations within the social', for an idealist trajectory of queerness, which is, however, '*epistemologically and ontologically humble*', in the sense that it is projected on a 'not-yet-conscious' spatiotemporality; a '*then-and-there*', which has an investment in alternative modes of spatial organization such as the transregional or the global and on temporal diversions from the present towards the past or the future (2009, p. 28). Muñoz's ultimate target is the displacement of the hegemonic '*here-and-now*' of the heteronormative (or homonormative) theorizations and politics of a present framed by the nation-state and driven by corporate interests.

Muñoz positions himself in opposition to Marxist scholars who disparage hard-fought struggles of gender and sexual liberation as merely demands for 'lifestyle diversification', as well as against white gay neoliberals, 'who studiously avoid the question of ethnic, racial, class, ability, or gender difference', and concentrate on sexuality as the queer issue *par excellence*. Instead, he proposes an idealist and, at the same time, rationalist vision of a concrete queer utopia as the only way to overcome the political impasse of pragmatic politics and anti-utopian thought (2009, p. 31). As he insists, 'rationalism need not be given over to gay neoliberals who attempt to sell a cheapened and degraded version of freedom', prescribed in the form of a largely ideological (as well as decayed) institution known as marriage (2009, p. 32). In an appropriation of Heidegger's description of freedom as unboundness, Muñoz counter-proposes that queerness should not bend to the gravitational pull of straight time, but rather, surpass the anti-performative nature of the pragmatic, 'engaging the performative as force of and for futurity' (2009, p. 32).

In this sense, *Strella* may be seen as deploying a rhetoric that restates the performative nature of the past, which Muñoz understands in Derridean terms, by interrogating and destabilizing familiar narratives of Greekness, the Greek national space and the Greek family. At the same time, however, it generates a discourse that allows for queer fantasizing, for imagining new worlds, new horizons beyond the here-and-now, in the direction of unmarked spatiotemporal frameworks. Seen in the light of Muñoz's conceptualization of concrete utopias, *Strella*'s utopian discourse has nothing to do with the film's depiction of abstract gay paradises, but with the fact that through its 'flickering illuminations', and its overall queer and queering spatiotemporal structure, it disturbs and reframes the familiar familial and national space, as well as long-established national myths and narratives, from the archetypal Oedipal myth to that of the sacred nuclear family. Through such reconfigurations the film is thus able to explore alternative ways of thinking about and organizing the social, of restructuring the nation and the family, not only the chosen but, most importantly, the biological one.

It is thus clear that the film's queer explorations are grounded in its postmodern aesthetic. The film effectively deploys the thematic and stylistic repertoire of New Queer Cinema, which by 2009 could already look back over almost two decades of filmic production, but it also alludes to Greek film history through a number of intertextual references, which are significant to both its deconstructive discourse, and its utopian longings. *Strella*'s primary pre-text and point of reference is none other than the internationally celebrated and highly successful 1955 film, *Stella*, directed by Michalis Cacoyannis and featuring the Greek superstar and later Minister of Culture, Melina Mercouri. The titles' resemblance is certainly not a coincidence; when Yorgos asks Strella her name she replies, 'I'm Stella, but my friends call me Strella because I'm a bit jazz [Greek slang for mad, crazy].' But even before that, the very first frame of the film breaks down the film's title in English, explaining that 'Stella' is a feminine first name, while *Trella* is a Greek noun, which means madness, lunacy, extravagance. However, is *Strella* just *Stella* with a queer twist? Is Koutras's film nothing more than a queer version of *Stella*?

The parallels between the two films are numerous, as Koutras does not hesitate to make direct references to Cacoyannis's classic text; Melina Mercouri's songs hold a significant place in *Strella*'s soundtrack, while a drag queen's impersonation of Mercouri as Stella is foregrounded at least twice in the film (Fig. 4.2). However, what is most striking, and useful to us here is the way both films, each in its own particular context of production and reception, mark a turning point in the way the national space is represented, challenged and renegotiated, deconstructed and/or projected as a fantasy on screen. *Stella* is the story of an emancipated *bouzoukia* singer who falls in love with hyper-masculine footballer Miltos. Miltos keeps

Fig. 4.2 Mania Lempesi impersonating Melina Mercouri as Stella

insisting on her marrying him, but Stella, who is unashamedly against marriage, jilts him at the altar, something that provokes Miltos's rage, and leads to his finally killing her. As Achilleas Hadjikyriacou observes, Cacoyannis's film challenged traditional gender spheres and hierarchies, offering alternatives to patriarchy and initiated controversial debates both at home and abroad regarding issues of gender representation (2012,p. 187). Stella's assertively emancipated lifestyle, which comprises 'premarital sexual activity, selection and change of sexual partners, provocation of the male sexual gaze, sexual aggressiveness, living and working in the public sphere and, most importantly, being in charge of herself', constitutes, Hadjikyriacou claims, 'the code of practice that makes Stella an anomaly for the predominant "pink and blue" social system' (2012, p. 189).

Indeed, Stella aggressively invades the public space and transforms it into a stage where the renegotiation of gender roles and overt defiance of patriarchy are foregrounded and highlighted. Significantly, this takes place in the symbolic space of Stella's workplace, the live music tavern Paradisos (Paradise). Robert S. Peckham and Pantelis Michelakis, using Mikhail Bakhtin's terminology, describe Paradisos as a 'chronotope', that is a site of contestation where 'the dynamics of assimilation and resistance […] are articulated' (2000, p. 68). As they explain, '*Paradise* is dramatized as an antisocial space which challenges conventional identities'; it 'is pitted against the established social order', representing 'a potential threat' to the 'respectable society' of the Athenian bourgeoisie (2000, p. 69). This is further highlighted by the fact that Paradisos is consistently identified in the film with Stella, the 'star' of Paradisos, who, as we have seen, constantly challenges both established patriarchal gender norms, and her own performative position as an object of scopophilic male desire. Nevertheless, *Stella* ultimately restores the canonical cinematic sexual balance by punishing its eponymous protagonist for claiming control of the gaze, which, as Laura Mulvey argues, 'belongs' to the male character (and spectator).[5] In the film's final scene, Stella is stabbed to death by her 'castrated' lover, Miltos, in an open space right in front of the closed doors of Paradisos and in the presence of an anonymous crowd, thus highlighting 'the presence of the patriarchal society and its role in the crime', as Hadjikyriacou astutely observes (2012, p. 194).

Despite the almost explicit correlation,[6] the drag queen bar Koukles (Dolls) in *Strella* does not share the narrative and symbolic function of Paradisos. More than a site of contestation which ultimately succumbs to the patriarchal teleology, Koukles emerges, as I argue in this chapter, as a productive space for the queer subject and, even more so, as a utopian queer horizon. This narrative function of Koukles is bound up with the way in which Koutras's film critically reworks the classical realist narrative film format, subverting the normative patriarchal course in both spatial and temporal terms. For *Strella* not only reframes the traditionally patriarchal representational spaces of Greece, Greekness and the Greek family but also installs a queer utopian vision that is both a critique of the patriarchal present and an optimistic horizon for queer futurity.

This is, arguably, the point where Koutras's film diverges from its intertextual ancestor, intersecting rather with the more recent tradition of the New Queer Cinema. Papanikolaou observes that the film is replete with references to the particular cinematic movement:

> from Todd Haynes to François Ozon, to Ferzan Özpetek and Greg Araki; and from Jenny Livingstone's documentary *Paris is Burning* (which features the emblematic figure of the 'Mother-Trans') to Sebastien Lifshitz's *Wild Side* (where the transsexual's return to her motherland, childhood, the desires and traumas of the past, takes place through the present of a new queer family). (2010, p. 10)

At the same time, Papanikolaou identifies Almodóvar's influences on Koutras's film: 'much like many films by the Spanish director (*Law of Desire*, *Bad Education*), *Strella* is also concerned with the heavy body of memory, particularly that of abuse and desire, which though it lies heavy on everyone, is primarily imprinted on the freed (but not necessarily liberated) transgender body' (2010, p. 10). But there is clearly more in *Strella*, and in the other films mentioned than the way the transgender body is afflicted by memory. Much like the films of Lifshitz and Almodóvar, *Strella* highlights the way memory is interrelated with space, thus invoking and, at the same time, elucidating the spatial and temporal dimensions of Muñoz's project. Indeed, Koutras's film showcases how the performative nature of the past is intertwined with spatial narratives, that is, narratives related to the way the Greek national space has been imagined, produced and thus experienced, and whose repercussions construct a given present for the queer subject. At the same time, however, *Strella* accommodates 'flickering illuminations' of 'alternative temporal and spatial maps', which can help us through the impasses of pragmatic discourses of the present and allow us to reconfigure it. These utopian explorations are, arguably, played out in the film through a direct and unapologetic spatial contradistinction between the village and the capital city, a contradistinction that is clearly highlighted as physical, representational and ideological.

The representational antithesis between the village and the city dates back to classical Greek cinema's melodramas and the so-called *fustanella* dramas. These genres, each with its own formal and narrative devices, consistently and invariably staged the contrast between the vices of urbanization and the lost purity evoked by the Greek countryside. As Vrasidas Karalis notes, 'after the Second World War and the Greek Civil War, mass migration towards urban centers completely transformed the demography of cities, thus creating the conditions for an urban and industrial culture' (2012, p. xi). The anxieties of modernity were addressed much the same way as in the rest of the Western world, by its favorite medium, the cinema, which, however, only tried to contain them by confirming 'conservative values and practices, legitimizing them as modern and acceptable' (2012, p. 87). Indeed, the *fustanella* genre offered idealized depictions of the village as the locus of a 'lost innocence',[7] while the image of the innocent villager who goes to the city and deals with the intricacies, contradictions, and pretensions of the new urban culture became the dominant theme in most comedies of the period. Urban dramas, such as for example Yorgas Tzavellas's melodramas, were also very popular—something which Karalis describes as a 'reflection of a deep empathy for the lonely individual in the urban reality of anonymity and depersonalization' (2012, p. 65). Anthropologist James Faubion offers a description of the spatial loss and fantasmatic nostalgia of the émigré that could work well to explain this fetishization of the village in the imagery of the Greek proto-urban cinematic culture, whose impact has been so vast that it essentially dominates the visual representation of the Greek countryside to date. According to Faubion:

> the émigré's catastrophic realization of the impossibility of perfect reunion [...] renders the lost parent, the lost *oikos*, the lost *polis* and the lost *ethnos* sentimental transformations, each of the other. They are alike traumas of delocalization, of the abjection of homelessness. They are alike traumas of deprivation, of the diminishing or retraction of the plenitude of the self. Yet, because they are all traumas, they can themselves directly be generative only of *Träume*, of dreams, of 'memories' that distort and disguise their actual referent and of memories that can consequently only be simulacra, presumptive copies that lack any genuine original. (2006, p. 186)

Arguably, cinema offered the most effective platform for containing this modern trauma of delocalization through the manufacture of its own *Träume*, its own distortions and disguises, that is—literally—its own simulacra, distant themselves from the actual lost *oikos*. In this way, classical Greek cinema's idealization of the village as the locus where archetypal Greek values, such as hospitality, religion, family and patriarchy still abide, has cinematically elevated it to the status of the perennial refuge of the alienated subject seeking to abandon the big city, as well as the place where that subject can achieve a 'transforming redemption through interaction with the purity of natural life' (Karalis, 2012, p. 262).

In contrast, according to Karalis, mainstream cinematic representations of Athens may be seen as constituting an aesthetic materialization of a negative discourse about the capital city which Faubion terms as the 'Athenian negative', and in which the Greek capital emerges as a '"negative" place of "civic alienation"' (Karalis, 2012, p. 249). This discourse, as Karalis suggests, 'dominates the mythography of the new filmmakers who frame urban reality as a space of dramatic re-enactment of the ongoing conflicts without redemption or catharsis' (2012, p. 249). However, it is important to note that Karalis's invocation of the 'Athenian negative' ironically overlooks the

affective ambivalence that is immanent in the particular discourse as construed by Faubion.

Faubion observes that contemporary Athenians' alienation is verbal-
ized in the very common Greek saying, *'Edho einai Valkania, dhen einai
paixe-yelase'*, which he translates 'It's the Balkans here, not a cakewalk.'
(2006, p. 189) For Faubion the irony that is inherent in this idiom surpasses the limits of a mere humorous simile; it evokes *agon* and struggle
but also hope (2006, p. 189). As he explains, these people 'hope for better
from one another', despite seeing their hopes 'all too often thwarted', and
they also 'expect better of themselves' without disregarding their dependence on the other, the significance of having to coexist (2006, p. 189).
In this way, the 'Athenian negative' is a discourse that acknowledges both
the victimization of the subject by a corrupted system—reflected in the
palimpsestic scenery of Athens, which juxtaposes the marble remnants
of a glorious past with the 'white elephants' of an infamous and much
contested present, the opulent villas of the suburbs with the miserable
apartment buildings of the center—as well as that subject's potential for
agency in the service of the 'common good'. Thus seen, it is ultimately
an affectively and ethically ambivalent discourse, a mixture of both disappointment and determination, of anger, frustration yet, simultaneously, of
a grounded hope.

This ambivalence is precisely reflected throughout *Strella*, for unlike
Karalis's account of other contemporary Greek films, there is a kind of
resolution, of catharsis in the way Koutras's film frames contemporary
Athens, which is organically related to the film's overall queer utopian
ethics and aesthetics. The film does not demonize nor glorify the Greek
capital; it foregrounds it as a space of contradictions, where human existence tests its limits, confronts its worst nightmares while at the same time
indulging in its most extreme fantasies and dreams of a better collective
future. The film does not turn a blind eye to the 'Athenian negative', as it
clearly includes in its frames the malaises of the chaotic Greek capital, such
as traffic, overpopulation, illegal trading. But, in a way these are pushed
to the margins of the frame. It seems as though the film prefers to foreground not necessarily the bright side of the city, but at least some of the
city's brighter corners, especially those pertaining to its queer subjects;
Koukles and Strella's flat emerge as precisely such an example. As I argue
below, *Strella* clearly privileges the Greek capital over the countryside, the
village, reversing the canonical representations of these two perennially
oppositional national spaces.

After Yorgos is released from prison, he tries to piece himself together and plan his next moves in such a way that he can rebuild his life. Unsurprisingly, his first plans for the future have to do with sorting out the haunting remnants of the past: first, to find his missing son and, second, to sell his property in the village and use the money to build a new life in Athens. In Yorgos's first visit to the village, which happens quite early in the film, the village is clearly highlighted as the symbolic realm of the past, which the protagonist seeks to break with in order to be able to construct his future. However, as the narrative progresses, in Yorgos's two subsequent visits to the village, more than just a host to and signifier of a haunting past, the village is established as an equally haunting ideological space that encompasses multiple regimes of oppression for the queer subject as well as the origin and measure of the queer subject's failures.

The village is introduced with wide open shots of a vast landscape with green fields and great mountains in the background, accompanied by dramatic non-diegetic music, which blends in with occasional sounds of birds and dogs in the background. But soon the overwhelming landscape shots give way to a brief sequence of unsteady tracking shots intercut with Yorgos's tight close-up frames as he walks through the village; a formal antithesis that instantly turns the village into a claustrophobic place, with narrow empty lifeless streets and a decaying rural architecture. This brief sequence creates an effect of disorientation and unrest that reflects both Yorgos's emotional state and the film's overall treatment of the physical and symbolic space of the village. In the scene that follows, Yorgos meets with the owner of a local bar who appears to be an old friend. Yorgos reveals his intentions to sell his house and asks questions about his lost son. The bar owner seems reluctant to offer any information about Leonidas but is willing to help Yorgos with the selling of his house by bringing him into contact with an ex-police officer who is interested in buying property in the village.

If Yorgos's first visit to the village is concerned with taking forward his plans for the future, his second visit is more of a confrontation with the present. Halfway through the film Yorgos again visits the village to meet the ex-police officer and finalize the deal, selling his property to him. Interestingly, the ex-officer is featured as a supporter of the country's past dictatorship regime, which was infamous for its hyper-masculinist, rigidly patriarchal and extreme nationalist agenda. Quite distant both stylistically and aesthetically from the rest of the film, with hard lighting creating sharp contrasts and cold colors throughout, this scene apparently creates

Fig. 4.3 'You know what they are called … transvestites'

for Koutras the appropriate atmosphere to introduce the film's thorniest issue (Fig. 4.3). Closing the deal by making a toast with a shot of *tsipouro* the ex-policeman drinks to Yorgos's 'new life', but also takes the opportunity to inform Yorgos about his son's true whereabouts: 'Rumor has it he's been seen in Syngrou [Athens' infamous cruising area] … that he's not a man anymore … You know what they are called … transvestites.' Yorgos abruptly stands up, pays the bill and, profoundly upset, exits the bar. The camera follows him as he departs from the village in a brief series of unsteady tracking shots and jump cuts. The village instantly emerges not only as the bearer of the haunting secrets of the past (up to this moment it has not yet been revealed why he was imprisoned) but also as the ubiquitous surveillant of the present, the quintessential locus of patriarchy and the heteronormative authorities that constantly generate the shame that haunts the here-and-now of the queer subject.

Yorgos immediately returns to Athens and confronts Strella, who does not seem reluctant to reveal details of her past to him, thus indirectly, yet clearly, confessing that she is his missing son. What follows is a series of sequences that frame the protagonists' struggle to come into terms with their 'hubris' in engaging in the ultimate taboo of incest. In the dialogues that follow what was thus far only insinuated in the film is now made explicit. What was a mere allusion to the Oedipal drama constitutes now an explicit reference that is invoked, foregrounded and renegotiated. As Papanikolaou explains, in *Strella* the archetypal Oedipal complex is not only reversed, but 'cannibalized', as Strella, the son who becomes trans, sleeps with her father and 'potentially forms with him a new queer family' (2010, p. 98). The discourse on incest allows for a direct confrontation between queerness and tradition, between contemporary Greekness and the nation's ideological origins, particularly those related to the classical Greek tragedy tradition, whose conventions are evident throughout the film not only thematically but also formally, though eventually unapologetically defied and reworked. For, indeed, unlike ancient drama, here recognition never leads to catastrophe.

When Strella confesses her incestuous relationship with her father to 'Mother Trans' Mary, who has been her guardian ever since Strella moved to Athens and she is now dying of cancer, Mary reacts, half melodramatically, half parodically:

MARY   This is hubris!
STRELLA   What?
MARY   Hubris, as our ancient sisters used to say ...
STRELLA   Who?
MARY   Our ancient sisters: Sophocles, Euripides ...
STRELLA   Who are these girls? Trans?
MARY   Don't make fun!

Lying in white silk lingerie, the trans matriarch (performed by the Greek trans legend Betty), between cigarette smoking and morphine patches, offers the audience a wonderful instance of humble yet hopeful, queer thinking:

MARY   What can I say? I hope you'll find your way through this.... If you love each other that much ... this is what matters the most. Of course, it will be something new.... Wow girl, you are completely insane! Oh God, times have changed, but, unfortunately, only *I* will not be able to catch up ...

Evidently, in the queer universe of *Strella* anything seems possible; even a romantic relationship between a father and his transgender child. But where the lead characters seem devastated by their re-enactment of the Oedipal drama, which is explicitly invoked as such in the film, the film itself, far from being judgmental, seems to be willing to offer ways to help them resolve it in far more productive ways than in its original version. Once more, the film's quest for ethical resolution is staged as a spatial antithesis between the village and Athens. This is clearly highlighted by the juxtaposition of two aesthetically distinct, yet thematically interrelated, sequences that run concurrently in the film. Both of these sequences have to do with death, one physical and one metaphorical, the one colorful and celebratory, the other dark, gloomy and excruciating: namely, Mary's funeral and memorial service in the bar Koukles, and Yorgos's own private 'burial' of his childhood memories and his oppressive past in his third and final visit to the village and his paternal home.

The by now familiar travelling shots of the Greek rural landscape introduce Yorgos's third and final visit to the village. Soon after, Yorgos is shown opening the door to a dark, deserted house, with crumbling discolored walls and old rusty furniture, as a series of slow, unsteady pans reveals. Callas's *Tosca* starts playing in the background and the murky and gloomy shades of the village yield to the colorful camp decorations of Mary's funeral. Pink and orange flowers dominate Mary's coffin, and with it the frame, as the camera tilts up to reveal the grieving, yet excessively made up and extravagantly dressed trans and drag queens who attend the ceremony. A cut back to the village shows Yorgos revisiting his previous life through trivial objects he finds scattered around the deserted house. Callas continues singing, but as her song gradually dominates the soundtrack, it simultaneously becomes diegetic as the film cuts to Koukles, where Strella impersonates Callas, dressed as another Tosca. But Strella abruptly abandons her lip-synching, leaving Callas's voice coming naked through the speakers, thus destroying the momentary illusionism of her impersonation. However, while Koutras tips a wink to his audience with this self-reflexive gesture that highlights the parodic nature of drag performances, back in the diegesis Strella lays her wet eyes on Mary's glorious portrait and, subsequently, on her trans sisters who are watching her interrupted act with sympathy. With a slow panning shot that shows both affection and admiration, Koutras's camera follows the individual personal drama of each of the trans and drag queens gathered at Koukles to grieve the death or celebrate the life of their beloved 'Mother'. Behind the excessive make-up, the wigs, the flashy jewelry, or even the fake tears that the 'girls' had to put on for the dramatic purposes of the scene (indeed, most of them are not actors, but real drag performers at Koukles) one can identify the affective surplus that Muñoz invokes in his utopia project. In these flickering illuminations of queerness the girls' trans bodies encompass the

Fig. 4.4   The ephemeral and the utopian

transient, the ephemeral, the unfixed and the superficial that is inherent in the materiality of queer existence, while their eyes reflect the atemporal, the monumental, the utopian of their queer dreams (Fig. 4.4).

Another cut to the village shows Yorgos waking up from a nightmare, still in the deserted house; Yorgos's nightmares are actually a recurrent motif in the film and always feature a squirrel that looks away from the camera to a natural landscape that is in the background, but each time the frame's colors, lighting and action produce a different emotional effect that arguably reflects the protagonist's psychological transitions. This time, the squirrel is absent and it is raining heavily. Yorgos thinks he hears something and starts looking around the house in panic. He then finds a metal stick on the floor, picks it up and starts breaking everything that gets in his way in a very aggressive temper. Much like the previous scenes that take place in the village, this one also constitutes a series of unsteady shots and jump cuts, with low-key lighting and dark, cold colors, thus clearly evoking the feelings of disorientation, agitation and distress that the paternal space engenders for the queer subject. Devastated and exhausted, Yorgos climbs up to the house's attic where he finds several black and white pictures, as well as his favorite childhood toy, an old red View-Master, through which he used to look at cartoon pictures, the protagonist of which was a squirrel; this scene helps us link Yorgos's nightmares to what looks like a traumatic childhood. The subsequent long shot shows Yorgos crossing the river to the other side of the forest before the film fades to black. This is the last shot of the village in the film. Yorgos has now crossed to the other side and nothing will ever bring him back again. The crossing marks the final rupture with the origin of his traumas, the end of his nightmares and the beginning of his new life in the city.

Clearly, where the village and the paternal home emerge as haunting and hostile spaces for the queer subject, back in Athens Koutras's camera foregrounds the productive qualities of both Koukles and Strella's apartment, which are showcased as quintessential queer spaces, not only in terms of decor and aesthetics, but most importantly as spaces of affective resilience. These are the places where the queer characters celebrate life and grieve over death, recount the past, negotiate the present but also dream the future. Strella's apartment is campily decorated with nudes on the walls, animal prints, colorful bead chain curtains, instead of doors, separating the rooms, elaborate chandeliers hanging from the ceiling and Callas's portrait displayed prominently. This is the location for the film's most dramatic scene of confrontation between Strella and Yorgos as well as the film's most erotic scene, where Strella/Orphanou's transgender body is fully unveiled and glorified through the unique erotic atmosphere

Fig. 4.5 Strella impersonating Maria Callas as Tosca

that is created by low-key lighting and the subtle coloring effects of a spinning table light.

Koukles, on the other hand, is not a fictional place, but an existing bar in the center of Athens, which regularly hosts drag shows and which has gained a great deal of popularity, not least because of the publicity conferred on it by the film. Koukles is the place where Strella performs her parodic drag impersonations of Callas (Fig. 4.5), but also the place where she meets her 'sisters' to celebrate *together* their birthdays or to pay tribute to their late 'trans Mother', as noted above. Koukles, much like Strella's apartment, is clearly demarcated in the film as a place of excess, both visual and affective; the trans girls are depicted sporting all the necessary excessive features of a drag performance (make-up, costume, accessories), while also experiencing—and producing—contradictory forms of affect: from cynicism to empathy, from excitement to anguish.

However, Koukles also engenders a unique affective experience for both the queer characters and performers, as well as for the audience: what Muñoz describes as 'astonishment' (2009, p. 5). Again drawing on Bloch, Muñoz explains that astonishment is an important philosophical mode of contemplation. Akin to such an understanding of astonishment are feelings of fun and appreciation, which are thoroughly exemplified in the camp fascination of queer people with celebrity. This fascination, Muñoz argues, offers 'through glamour and astonishment, a kind of transport or a reprieve from what Bloch called the "darkness of the lived instant". Astonishment helps one surpass the limitations of an alienating presentness and allows one to see a different time and place' (2009, p. 5). Arguably, the drag impersonations of great Greek divas, such as Callas and Mercouri, that take place at Koukles, encompass this feeling of reprieve that Muñoz describes. By accommodating such performances, Koukles in turn emerges as 'an urban landscape of astonishment' in which the queer subject can temporarily experience a dream-like state, a momentary utopia, a distance from the darkness of its alienating and devastating presentness. Koukles becomes a place where queer dreams can materialize, even momentarily and with all the self-consciousness of the vanity, triviality and ephemerality that infuses both the dreams and the bar itself. Koukles, thus, as depicted in the film, emerges as an ephemeral trace in itself, as its stage offers the drag queens the space to live their dream, namely to deify their idols and be worshipped by their own audience, even for those few minutes of their acts. At the same time, however, the space offered by the film itself to open up these acts and these dreams to the public domain, to share these flickering illuminations of queerness with broader audiences through the unquestionable power of the film as a mass medium, brings us back to Muñoz's conceptualization of the queer aesthetic as the potential realm for imagining new worlds and thinking about queerness as 'a long-ing that propels us onward, beyond romances of the negative and toiling in the present'(2009, p. 1). Arguably, this is achieved in the film not only by and within the dreamworld of Koukles, but by Koutras's overall treat-ment of queerness; by means of aesthetics, form and narrative, Koutras foregrounds the bright side and sight of the camp world of drag, without, however, turning a blind eye to the dark details of trans lived experience (shadowed by histories of abuse, discrimination, marginalization, neglect). Yet, somehow these details are pushed to the margins of the frame to allow for the queer spaces depicted as well as the overall film itself to emerge as hopeful 'wish-landscapes'; landscapes that, by extending 'into the territory of futurity', ask us to reframe and reclaim the present, denounce the past and reimagine the future.

This is why *Strella* cannot be approached simply as a queer postmodern appropriation of *Stella*, one that merely seeks to uncloset queer versions of Greekness, when seen from the inside, or Greek versions of queerness, when seen from the outside. Koukles is not just a queer Paradisos, the mere locus of gender and sexual subversion, but a space where a whole new ethical conceptualization of the present is made possible. Strella refuses to let herself die in the arms of the Greek patriarch in the manner of her intertextual 'grandmother'. In her determination to find a way through the queerness of her life and feelings, Strella, with her trans 'sisters' and her father-lover in tow, not only breaks with the traditional regimes of her oppression, but also reconfigures the marginal urban spaces she inhabits as subject to potentially new ethical boundaries. Hence, ultimately, Strella and with her *Strella* enter, with all their camp wigs, excessive make-up, expensive boob jobs, their witty lines and their wet eyes, into the realm of aesthetic queer utopias by offering alternative models of being and organizing the social, by pointing towards the potential of a new ethics, located in a then-and-there, humble, yet hopeful.

Returning to the last sequence of the film, named above as the post-script, there are two moments that, perhaps, exemplify the film's status as a queer utopia in the most concise and effective way. These moments are important to pick out and pay attention to, not so much because of their narrative meaning and gravity, but, on the contrary, for the affective sur-plus they produce as their primary effect. The first moment portrays Strella lying on the sofa with a glass of whiskey, her arms touching a photograph, possibly of her beloved 'trans Mother' Mary, who has just died, next to which lies Yorgos's red View-Master. Alongside the diegetic sounds of the popular *bouzouki*-dance hit 'Blame it on Love'/'Ftei o Erotas', smooth non-diegetic piano notes ignite a very brief moment, where action is suspended and the frame is filled with a series of beautiful close-ups of Strella, juxtaposed with her eye-line matching shots, as she glances first at Yorgos, who is repairing the baby girl's toys, then at the baby lying on the carpet, and finally at the Christmas tree, which alongside the traditional flashing lights unashamedly sports obscene hardcore pictures of gay male bodies. Returning to Strella's close-up, we see her smiling in a rather ambivalent manner, which evokes both the irony that imbues her extraordinary life-story and the relief and comfort that characterizes the film's denouement.

The second moment belongs to Yorgos. Just after the turn of the year, Yorgos goes to the bedroom where the baby is sleeping, looks at her and smiles. This is followed by a succession of three shots, all of which share the common characteristic of including a frame within the frame. In the first one we see Strella, Alex and the two guests through an interior window that connects the living room with the bedroom, as they are preparing to cut the New Year's cake, all smiling, laughing and having fun (Fig. 4.6). Yorgos enters the frame from the right and stays on the frame's right

Fig. 4.6   Reframing the familial space

margin turning his head to look through the interior window. We then have a cut to Yorgos's medium shot as he looks at his newly found/created family, with the bead chain curtains on the two sides of the frame held out of focus in the foreground and framing his beautiful low-key-lit portrait, in which he essentially projects his gaze directly to the camera. He turns his face away, and the camera follows him as he walks to the bedroom window. We then have a cut to the film's final shot. The frame is at first divided by the wooden frames of the window, but soon enough Yorgos opens the window and looks outside at the city. The camera then starts zooming out; with Yorgos still framed within the window, we hear the sounds of the city's celebrations and fireworks, which in turn give way to the hard rock theme of the end credits. Yorgos, his new queer family, and the city are finally suddenly double framed by the recurring motif in the film of the View-Master squirrel, this time his leafy frame also decorated with Christmas lights. Cut to black.

Both of these short scenes are moments of suspension, of delay, of con-templation—consistent with a few other similar ones earlier in the film. They are moments of silence, where the unspoken becomes significant, materializes in the image, and then gives way to imagination, dreaming, hope. This 'utopian sensibility' of the film, clearly, distances itself from Richard Dyer's (1981) conceptualization of the medium in terms of escap-ism (1981). Indeed, *Strella* refuses to attest to theorizations that exile film to the realm of the imaginary, to which the alienated subject escapes in order to counter the monotony, boredom, inequality and injustice that pervade his/her quotidian life. As an aesthetic utopia that is concerned with the here-and-now, *Strella* rather reveals the medium's potentiality to emerge as a utopian site of resistance, opposition and political contesta-tion, as an unlimited horizon of imagining and claiming change. After all, as Fredric Jameson warns in his voluminous and multifaceted investigation of the concept of utopia, 'it is a mistake to approach Utopias with positive expectations, as though they offered visions of happy worlds, spaces of ful-fillment and cooperation, representations which correspond generically to the idyll or the pastoral rather than the utopian' (2007, p. 12). 'Utopian form', as he poignantly asserts, 'is itself a representational meditation on radical difference, radical otherness' (2007, p. xii).

Strella is, hence, more resonant with Christopher Pavsek's delineation of the 'utopia of film' as this is evoked, envisioned or even realized in the political cinemas of Godard, Kluge, and Tahimik (2013). Pavsek draws on Alain Badiou's philosophical concept of the event as 'the creation of a new possibility', for it 'changes not only the real, but also the possible' (Badiou, 2009), to make the case for the *event of cinema*, as he calls it (2013, p. 7). As Pavsek proposes, such an idea of cinema encompasses:

> the conviction that cinema has expanded the realm of possibilities for art, that cinema has the possibility of a truly universal vocation or calling, that it cannot be content to exist as a minor art or as a commodity slated for mere consumption by one class so that another might be enriched, but instead that it must engage in the universal project of human emancipation. (2013, p. 8)

In line with Jameson's aforementioned warning, Pavsek does not identify the utopia of film in cinematic depictions of idyllic paradises, but rather in filmic attempts that 'work through the failures of the project of liberation and of cinema as an art form' (2013, p. 11). Explicitly invoking the political aspirations of the left, Pavsek's project invites us to think of cinema 'as a form of thought' (2013, p. 15) that illuminates the 'unfulfilled promises and possibilities that arose in history' and 'calls for their future realization' (2013, p. 22). The works of the above filmmakers, Pavsek contends, prefigure such forms of utopia in the sense that they pave the way for an ideal future through incisive reflections of the imperfect past and the deeply flawed present.

Strella, though clearly not sharing the political vision of either Pavsek or the filmmakers whose work he examines, is nonetheless an equivalently utopian work of reflective engagement with the failures of the past and the flaws of the present. As this chapter demonstrates, Koutras's film is all about framing and reframing past and present discourses, bodies, spaces, realities; and this continuous reframing, underlined in the film not only thematically but also formally, as the last series of shots reveals, is ultimately what constitutes the queerness of this utopia. For though laying claim to a better collective future, *Strella*, like most queer things, is an aesthetic utopia that resists fixity and a clear spatiotemporal framework; it is fragmentary and ever-changing, ever-reshaping, ever-reframing.

In conclusion, *Strella* is clearly infused by this kind of 'grounded, educated hope', which Muñoz (2009) describes in his idealist utopian project on queerness's temporality. Though constricted in narrow corridors of cheap hotels, underground trans clubs and crumbling rural buildings, the characters transform these murky, dark places into productive spaces of confrontation with and rearticulation of the past, the present and the future, into spaces of unapologetic relief of queer incestuous desire, and, ultimately, of a queer refusal of the nation's oppressive ideological regimes; these fantasmatic sites of production of national, gender and sexual identities and histories. Oedipus is redeemed; his primordial sins, incest and patricide, acquire whole new queer meanings. The crumbling walls of Yorgos's parental home point to the collapse of the Law and the Symbolic Order, the agent of prohibition and the quintessential signifier of patriarchal oppression. In the warm living room with the Christmas tree and the laughing infant of the closing sequence a whole new queer order emerges, an alternative site of conceptualizing and 'doing' family, as well as of configuring religion and the homeland. Cinema here invites us not merely to identify with a queer gaze and a queer view of the world; it significantly encourages us to reframe our perceptions of the present through the 'flickering illuminations' of queer moments, of utopian moments, of moments of queer utopias.

NOTES

1. A clip of this performance appears on YouTube at http://www.you-tube.com/watch?v=NLR3lSrqlww
2. A term coined by Ruby Rich to frame New Queer Cinema's aesthetics in her seminal essay 'The New Queer Cinema' (1992).
3. *Skyladika* (etymologically linked to *skylos* [dog]) is a derogatory term that is used to describe modern *bouzouki*-dominated Greek songs associated with low culture.
4. On this, Muñoz refers explicitly to Lee Edelman's and Leo Bersani's anti-relational, anti-social and anti-futurity queer projects, as introduced in their respective books *No Future* (2004) and *Is the Rectum a Grave?* (2010), which locate queerness's anti-sociality in its status as a force of constant resistance to normativity and its favoring of sexuality.
5. Despite being unprecedentedly subversive for its time, Cacoyannis's work was still highly influenced by the narrative strategies of classical Hollywood, whose 'patriarchal unconscious', as Laura Mulvey demonstrates in her seminal essay 'Visual Pleasure and Narrative Cinema', privileged a spatial and temporal continuity that, above all, complied with and perpetuated patriarchal course. As Mulvey argues, for the patriarchal unconscious of traditional narrative film,

'woman as representation signifies castration, inducing voyeuristic or fetishistic mechanisms to circumvent her threat' (1975, p. 756).

6. Koutras chooses to introduce Koukles with an allusion to *Stella*'s first scene at Paradisos, in which Mercouri is dancing as Sara Montiel, while the tavern's waiter is struggling to follow her dance with the spotlight. Similarly, in *Strella*'s first scene at Koukles Strella is trying to fix the spotlight on the stage, where a drag queen (Mania Lempesi) rehearses her impersonation of Melina as Stella.

7. According to Stelios Kymionis the *fustanella* genre (its name deriving from the eponymous traditional knee-length pleated skirt worn by Greek men in pre-modern times) underpinned the symbolic association of the village with the construction of a very specific notion of Greekness and a concomitant mythologization of the nation's past. Set temporally in the past and spatially in the village, and presenting the villagers in traditional folk attire 'the genre of Mountain Films', as Kymionis translates it, valorizes an aspect of Greekness that pertains to 'a respect for tradition and pure community values' and a sense of Greek masculinity as the amalgam of such values as honor, justice, bravery and social militancy (2000, p. 56).

BIBLIOGRAPHY

Badiou, Alain (2009) 'Is the Word "Communism" Forever Doomed?', *www. lacan.com*, http://www.lacan.com/essays/?page_id=323, date accessed 22 April 2016.

Bersani, Leo (2010) *Is the Rectum a Grave?: And Other Essays* (Chicago: University of Chicago Press).

Bloch, Ernst (1988) *The Utopian Function of Art and Literature: Selected Essays*, trans. Jack Zipes and Frank Mecklenburg (Cambridge, MA: MIT Press).

Dyer, Richard (1981) 'Entertainment and Utopia', in Rick Altman (ed.) *Genre: The Musical* (London: Routledge), pp. 176–189.

Edelman, Lee (2004) *No Future: Queer Theory and the Death Drive* (Durham and London: Duke University Press).

Faubion, James (2006) 'Hyperreal Athens: Phantasmatic Memory and the Reproduction of Civic Alienation', in Vrasidas Karalis (ed.) *Culture and Memory*, Special Issue of *Journal of Modern Greek Studies*, 175–190.

Hadjikyriacou, Achilleas (2012) 'Cacoyannis' Stella: Representation and Reception of a Patriarchal Anomaly', in Lydia Papadimitriou and Yannis Tzioumakis (eds.) *Greek Cinema: Texts, Histories, Identities* (Bristol: Intellect).

Jameson, Fredric (2007 [2005]) *Archaeologies of the Future: The Desire Called Utopia and Other Science Fictions* (London: Verso).

Karalis, Vrasidas (2012) *A History of Greek Cinema* (New York: Continuum).

Kymionis, Stelios (2000) 'The Genre of Mountain Film: The Ideological Parameters of Its Subgenres', *Journal of Modern Greek Studies*, 18/1, 53–66.

Mulvey, Laura (1975) 'Visual Pleasure and Narrative Cinema', *Screen*, 16/3, 6–18.

Muñoz, Jose Esteban (2009) *Cruising Utopia: The Then and There of Queer Futurity, Sexual Cultures* (New York: New York University Press).

Papanikolaou, Dimitris (2010) 'Στρέλλα: μια ταινία για όλη την οικογένεια' [*Strella*: A Film for the Whole Family], in Panos H. Koutras and Panayiotis Evangelides, *Strella* (Athens: Polihromos Planitis).

Pavsek, Christopher (2013) *The Utopia of Film: Cinema and its Futures in Godard, Kluge, and Tahimik* (New York: Columbia University Press).

Peckham, Robert Shannan and Pantelis Michelakis (2000) 'Paradise Lost, Paradise Regained: Cacoyannis's Stella', *Journal of Modern Greek Studies*, 18/1, 67–77.

Rich, Ruby (1992) 'The New Queer Cinema', *Sight and Sound*, 2/5, 31–34.

CHAPTER 5

Attenberg: Of (Dis-)Orientation

Halfway through *Attenberg* (Athina Rachel Tsangari, 2010), the director offers a brief yet fascinating sequence of unsteady medium shots and close-ups of the incessantly moving bodies of the film's main female characters Marina (Ariane Labed) and Bella (Evangelia Randou) as they compete against each other in an intense tennis match. The camera at times seems to strive to focus on the ever-moving human body while at others it gives the impression of surrendering itself to it, as that body emerges as an indomitable force of nature. After the match, the film cuts to the locker rooms and the camera pans across the brown tiles of shower cubicles, while the sarcastic tune of Daniel Johnston's 'I Am a Baby in My Universe' starts filling the soundtrack. The camera moves right to left and then forward, in its own right, through the busy locker room where several women of various ages and body types are getting dressed and putting on make-up. The camera then comes to rest, showing in medium shot Marina, who sits on a bench with her head away from the camera, but visibly staring at some women getting changed in the background. The film then cuts to another static medium shot of Marina looking at her naked body in the mirror (Fig. 5.1). The song stops abruptly. Accompanied not by music but only the annoying squeaks of doors closing, without special lighting effects creating an erotic atmosphere, nor lavish decor to accompany the human flesh, but only the dull, neutral-colored lockers that frame Labed's body and the mirror that reflects it, the female figure, which has canonically been glorified and objectified by the medium, stands here naked, but desexualized and de-eroticized.

© The Author(s) 2016
M. Psaras, *The Queer Greek Weird Wave*,
DOI 10.1007/978-3-319-40310-6_5

123

Fig. 5.1   De-eroticizing and reclaiming the naked female body

Arguably, the above sequence showcases the film's formal and thematic axes in the most vivid way. In Tsangari's idiosyncratic cartography
of the human body's exploratory, yet often frustrating, oscillation between
mobility and stasis across the monotonous and oppressive contours of
social life, quasi-experimental unsteady shots alternate with deftly composed lingering ones through an often blunt and unembellished editing,
which cuts together images and bodies that appear and withdraw without
much spatiotemporal coherence or narrative significance. For, as Tsangari
herself admits, she prefers to approach dramatic filmmaking like an anthropologist: 'I don't use psychology [...] I prefer biology or zoology. These
are my tools' (Kauffman, 2011). Indeed, much as Marina examines her
naked body with a deadpan face that creates the effect of ambivalence
and indeterminacy, so the film offers the human body as an object of an
open-ended ethological study and examination rather than an object of
scopophilic or voyeuristic desire, or even a projection of an ego-ideal for
the audience to identify with.

Winner of the Best Actress award (Ariane Labed) at the 67th Venice
International Film Festival, at which it was also nominated for the Golden
Lion, winner of the Silver Alexander at the Thessaloniki International Film
Festival, and an official selection at the most distinguished international
film festivals around the world, including the London BFI, Sundance

and Toronto, *Attenberg* continues the legacy of the 'Greek Weird Wave' initiated by Yorgos Lanthimos's *Dogtooth*. Indeed, Lanthimos actually features in *Attenberg*'s credits as co-producer, as well as one of the four protagonists.

Set in a decaying industrial coastal town, *Attenberg* follows Marina's efforts to work through her sense of being socially dysfunctional and the repulsion she feels towards intimacy, and also to come to terms with the fact that her father Spyros (Vangelis Mourikis) is terminally ill. She spends her days listening to and singing the songs of the band Suicide, taking sex education lessons from her friend Bella, who she later asks to have sex with her father as a last favor for the dying man, and, last but not least, watching with her father the wildlife documentaries of Sir David Attenborough, whose suggestively misspelled/mispronounced name after all provides the film's title. Marina herself discovers sex somewhat awkwardly in the bed of an engineer (Yorgos Lanthimos) passing through her town, for whom she temporarily works as a driver, even though she is visibly more excited when she is in bed with her father mimicking wild animals' behavior. When her father dies, Marina undertakes the gruesome task of sending her father's corpse abroad in order to have him cremated and then receiving his ashes and scattering them into the Greek sea.

In response to the question of what unites Greece's new generation Tsangari observes a common preoccupation with family: 'It's a Greek obsession. The reason our politics and economy is in such trouble is that it's run as a family. It's who you know' (Rose, 2011). Rose comments, 'In a larger sense, young Greeks are up against the tyranny of their ancestry, of Greece's nostalgia for its own history.' In the same interview Tsangari also indicates how the cinema could engage in a productive dialogue with the ongoing economic-political crisis in her home country and its social repercussions. Tsangari says, 'This is the situation and somehow we have to fix it now, and cinema is a great way to do that. I'm not saying I'm going to make a film about the riots—I don't want to be that literal—but Greece is an unknown country, even to its citizens, and I want to discover it for myself' (Rose, 2011).

Indeed, as argued in the previous chapters, cinema emerges as a powerful means for young Greek filmmakers to rediscover Greece, renegotiate its 'nostalgia for its own history' and revolt against 'the tyranny of their ancestry'. Like *Hardcore*, *Strella* and *Dogtooth*, *Attenberg* is a work of defiance and exploration, the pursuit of an alternative gaze that revisits the national space, both the physical and the ideological, as well as the discourses that underlie each of them. As this chapter argues, *Attenberg* reworks and reframes familiar familial and national narratives through its subversive themes, while also investigating alternative ways of registering and editing the body *in* the film and the body *of* the film. The latter is arguably achieved through the film's unconventional form, which, as I examine below, challenges and critiques monolithic and essentialist cinematic representations of the human body/self as always already sexual, productive and sociable.

If *Attenberg* is a work of (re)discovery then this is primarily worked out through an idiosyncratic examination of the way the body moves across (un)familiar familial and national space, an examination which, more than merely ethological, as many critics suggest (Kauffman, 2011; Savage, 2012), is fundamentally phenomenological. For *Attenberg*'s discourse is not invested in character or narrative, thus being consistent with Tsangari's own defiance of psychology and preference for zoology and biology as her major tools. In the film the director's camera is rather fixed and fixated on the often futile task of registering the ever-elusive, ever-moving human body; this body which more often than not slips out of the frame. This body which, through the various forms that it takes in the film (the permanently disoriented body of Marina, the dying body of her father, the hyper-sexualized body of Bella, the unknown body of the visitor), navigates transgressively through the familiar spaces of the home and the homeland only to reclaim them, to proclaim its demand to rediscover them anew. *Attenberg*'s project is, ultimately, effectively queer, as this chapter argues. For the body (*in* the film and *of* the film) emerges here as always already queer. This is not, however, achieved through the film's representation of queer desire or non-normative sexuality. The body rather emerges here as queer precisely in the way it moves across the national space, that other large and largely uncanny body, defamiliarizing and deconstructing its ground, its landscape, its discourses, its language, its fixations, its dreams, its narratives, and unapologetically selling them out in return for a demand for more ethical ways of conceptualizing and shaping them.

This fascinating exploration of the way the body traverses the habitual space of the family and the nation in *Attenberg* arguably reverberates with Sara Ahmed's queer phenomenological project. In her book *Queer Phenomenology: Orientations, Objects, Others* (2006), Ahmed deploys 'queer' in that double sense of the term that will prove to be quite productive for this reading of *Attenberg*. Namely, apart from the term's canonical use as that which registers non-normative sexual practices and the bodies that perform them, Ahmed puts forward 'queer' also as 'a way of describing what is "oblique" or "off line"'; indeed, a way of describing 'bodies out of place [which] can work to make things seem "out of line", and [which] can hence even work to "queer" space' (2006, p. 161). Ahmed proposes that a return to the original meanings of the word 'queer' (i.e. odd, bent, oblique) could help us 'see that the word itself "twists," with a twist that allows us to move between sexual and social registers, without flattening them or reducing them to a single line' (2006, p. 161). And although, as she admits, 'this approach risks losing the specificity of queer as a commitment to a life of sexual deviation, it also sustains the significance of "deviation" in what makes queer lives queer' (2006, p. 161).

In line with Ahmed's argument, *Attenberg* stages deviation as an essentially corporeal act that, indeed, works to 'queer' space. The film is full of such queer moments, particularly between the two female protagonists, that in effect pose the question of (queer) deviation as not only or not necessarily sexual. Such moments frequently emerge in the subversive pedagogical methods of promiscuous Bella as she tries to introduce Marina into the sexual world. The opening scene effectively establishes this 'queerly' queer nature of the film, by featuring what has been described as 'the worst' (Rose, 2011) or 'most awkward' (Felton, 2012) kiss in screen history. The film begins with a shot of a whitewashed wall. Marina enters the frame from the right and Bella from the left. As soon as they reach each other they crane their necks and start kissing in a way that not only lacks any sense of passion but also produces a rather discomforting effect (Fig. 5.2); as Felton observes (2012), 'It is almost as if Marina is trying to eat large segments of birdseed out of Bella's mouth.' Marina pulls back and Bella asks her if she liked it. 'I've never had something wriggling in my mouth before', replies Marina. 'How does my tongue feel?' Bella asks again. 'Like a slug. It's disgusting.' 'You have to breathe, otherwise you'll choke.' Marina takes a deep breath and tries again. While kissing Marina tells Bella she is too much of a dribbler and pulls back again, saying she will throw up. After a short technical discussion, the girls start rubbing their tongues together, but Marina, visibly disgusted, stops for a third time, and asks Bella, 'How do people do it?' 'Don't you want to learn?' 'No.' Bella reaches out to kiss Marina again, but Marina refuses, pushing Bella back. The kissing session then turns into a spitting fight not long before Tsangari cuts to a wide shot which shows the girls getting down on all fours and hissing at each other like wild cats. Cut to the titles.

Fig. 5.2 Revisiting sexuality: perhaps the weirdest kiss in screen history

Attenberg's opening sequence establishes the film's austere aesthetics as magnificently paired with its subversive rhetoric against familiar narratives of the body. Bleak and cold colors, minimal editing, rigorous compositions, lack of music and unrefined diegetic sound frame a human body which clearly refuses to attest to normative or essentialist discourses of sexuality. As in *Dogtooth*, sex in *Attenberg* is thus deglamorized and showcased from the very beginning as unlinked from desire, underscored as a social construct as well as the effect of a series of performative acts that draw particular trajectories for the human body. However, as this chapter argues, in *Attenberg* the human body often defies these trajectories, and with them a series of other fixed lines that the social has drawn for it to follow and which in time congeal into oppressive ethical regimes. The 'queerly' acting body in *Attenberg* quite often reverts to meaningless animalistic behavior, thus breaking with the contours of the social and exploring a pre-discursive landscape, which, akin to the documentaries of Attenborough, interrogates and reclaims the space of the 'natural'. Hence, corporeal deviation ultimately emerges as an ethical act, a queer ethical act.

In Ahmed's queer phenomenology such socially demarcated 'lines' become, indeed, a pivotal analytical tool for an investigation of the way genders, sexualities and races are ascribed to the human body or performed by it. In line with the broader phenomenological turn in cultural studies, Ahmed investigates the intersections between phenomenology and queer theory or, rather, deploys phenomenology to inform queer studies, insofar as the former emphasizes 'the importance of lived experience, the intentionality of consciousness, the significance of nearness or what is ready-to-hand, and the role of repeated and habitual actions in shaping bodies and worlds' (2006, p. 2). Without ignoring theoretical debates on queer politics and the so-called 'anti-social' thesis, Ahmed rather focuses on the spatialization of sexuality through the notion of 'orientation', for, as she proclaims, 'bodies are gendered, sexualized, and raced by how they extend into space'; hence her project pertains precisely to an investigation of 'how bodies become orientated by how they take up time and space' (2006, p. 5). For Ahmed orientation 'involves aligning body and space: we only know which way to turn *once we know which way we are facing*' (2006, p. 7). Her discussion draws on Heidegger's conceptualization of orientation as a matter of familiarity with the world. As Heidegger argues in *Being and Time*, 'I necessarily orient myself both in and from my being already alongside a world which is familiar' (cited in Ahmed, 2006, p. 7). And familiarity, as Ahmed explains, is the effect of inhabitance, as a dynamic extension of the body into space, which affects what comes within reach, what becomes familiar and what remains out of reach or excluded from our homing devices. Hence, she argues, '[t]he question of orientation becomes [...] a question not only about how we "find our way" but how we come to "feel at home"' (2006, p. 7).

However, 'if orientation is making the strange familiar through the extension of bodies into space, then disorientation occurs when that extension fails' (2006, p. 11). Ahmed confesses, '[i]n living a queer life, the act of going home, or going back to the place I was brought up has a certain disorienting effect' (2006, p. 11). As she explains, the family home is full of traces of heterosexual intimacy, in such a manner that it is difficult for the queer body to take up its place without feeling those traces as points of pressure. 'In such moments, when bodies do not extend into space, they might feel "out of place" where they have been given "a place." Such feelings in turn point to other places, even ones that have yet to be inhabited' (2006, p. 12). A queer phenomenology, thus, becomes precisely a project of 'redirecting our attention toward different objects, those that are "less proximate" or even those that deviate or are deviant' (2006, p. 3). This is the point where 'lines' become resonant in this project.

If orientation involves aligning body and space then it also engenders a direction of and for the body; its extension from a given 'here' (understood not only as the location but most importantly the position of the body in space) to a possible 'there'. As Ahmed explains, for Husserl the point of 'here' is 'the zero point of orientation, the point from which the world unfolds and which makes what is "there" over "there"' (p. 8). In this way, orientation is about 'the intimacy of bodies and their dwelling places': 'the "here" of the body and the "where" of its dwelling' (2006, p. 8). Orientation, in effect, becomes a 'here' of bodily dwelling, 'what takes the body outside of itself, as it is affected and shaped by its surroundings' (2006, p. 9). But, 'bodies do not dwell in spaces that are exterior but rather are shaped by their dwellings and take shape by dwelling', for 'spaces are like a second skin that unfolds in the folds of the body' (2006, p. 9). As a result, Ahmed suggests, much as the spaces 'impress' on the body, thus reshaping the body surface, they themselves are reshaped 'by the comings and goings of different bodies' (2006, p. 9). Space, indeed, 'acquires "direction" through how bodies inhabit it', however, not in the sense that space is necessarily dependent on the subject, 'as the container of space rather than contained by space', but in terms of an organization of the social as an 'agreement about how we measure space and time', which, as Ahmed explains, is why we usually experience social conflict as a matter of 'being "out of time" as well as "out of place" with others' (2006, p. 13).

But it is lines that actually matter, the sensation of lines that join two points together (a 'here' and a 'there') that 'give matter form and that create the impression of "surface, boundaries, and fixity"' (Judith Butler, cited in Ahmed, 2006, p. 14). For, to follow a line is to make some things or some people available, reachable and others not. Alignment indeed might mean to be in line with others, facing the direction that is already faced by others, which 'allows bodies to extend into spaces that, as it were, have already taken their shape' (2006, p. 15). And direction, for Ahmed, is not a casual matter, but something that is actually organized:

> We might speak then of collective direction: of ways in which nations or other imagined communities might be 'going in a certain direction,' or facing the same way, such that only some things 'get our attention.' Becoming a member of such a community, then might also mean following this direction, which could be described as the political requirement that we turn some ways and not others. We follow the line that is followed by others: the repetition of the act of following makes the line disappear from view as the point from which 'we' emerge. (2006, p. 15)

Ahmed invokes Butler's notion of performativity at this point, suggesting that the repetition of particular directions has as its effect that 'the bodies [...] acquire the very shape of such direction[s]', for to go directly means to 'follow a line without a detour, without mediation', not to deviate at any point (2006, pp. 15–16). As she elucidates, '[t]he lines that direct us, as lines of thought as well as lines of motion, are in this way performative: they depend on the repetition of norms and conventions, of routes and paths taken, but they are also created as an effect of this repetition' (2006, p. 16).

Ahmed argues that to follow such lines means to commit one's life to a particular way of moving through space and time. It becomes crucially a sort of social investment that assumes 'a specific "take" on the world, a set of views and viewing points, as well as a route through the contours of the world, which gives our world its own contours' (2006, p. 17). Such a commitment is best exemplified in what Ahmed calls the politics of 'lifelines', which pertains to the 'relationship between inheritance (the lines that we are given as our point of arrival into family and social space) and reproduction (the demand that we return the gift of the line by extending that line)' (2006, p. 17). The social pressure that accompanies such lines, which ordain particular modes of living and prescribe their reproduction, might, however, 'feel like a physical "press" on the surface of the body, which creates its own impressions' (2006, p. 17). These lines might, thus, 'gather on the skin' and become 'signs of the past, as well as orientations toward the future, a way of facing and being faced by others' (2006, p. 18). But, much as we might be pressed into such lines, we might also be offered the gift of an unexpected line that gives us the opportunity to escape an impossible world or an unlivable life.

'Some lines', Ahmed proposes, indeed, 'might be marks of the refusal to reproduce: the lines of rebellion and resistance that gather over time to create new impressions on the skin surface or on the skin of the social' (2006, p. 18). But this does not always occur as the effect of an accidental encounter that redirects us and opens up new worlds; it 'can be lived purely as loss' (2006, p. 19). 'After all', as she notices, 'it is often loss that generates a new direction' (2006, p. 19). At this point, Ahmed returns again to the notion of deviation as what 'can help generate alternative lines, which cross the ground in unexpected ways' (2006, p. 20). As she confesses:

Inhabiting a body that is not extended by the skin of the social means the
world acquires a new shape and makes new impressions. […] Becoming
reorientated, which involves the disorientation of encountering the world
differently, made me wonder about orientation and how much 'feeling at
home,' or knowing which way we are facing, is about the making of worlds.
(2006, p. 20)

Attenberg never really creates the conditions for the constantly disoriented bodies of its characters, and particularly of its protagonist Marina,
to reorient, make new worlds or really ever achieve that 'feeling at home'.
Tsangari's film could arguably be considered as more of a repository of
the body's failed attempts to extend into the skin of the social; indeed, a
queer coming-of-age film. Marina's body emerges as an exemplary case
of a queer body; of a body acting queerly in its marking of an unsur-
mountable rupture between the 'here' of its presence and the 'where' of
its dwelling. Marina is foregrounded as being constantly 'out of time' and
'out of place'. However, this is clearly not staged in the film as the effect
of same-sex desire that automatically cancels out the lines that the skin
of the social strives to draw on the skin of the queer body; namely, what
Ahmed frames as the lines of inheritance, and the concomitant lines of
femininity, patriarchy and heteronormativity. *Attenberg*, indeed, does not
offer a crystallized representation of queer desire in the image of Marina.
Following Ahmed, this chapter reads *Attenberg* queerly, through the mesmerizing lenses of a queer phenomenology of the body, which, although
unlinked from same-sex desire, still bears witness to the queer refusal to
reproduce lines of inheritance, and the equivalently defiant impulse to follow, or appropriate, or even generate lines of rebellion and resistance.

Blogger Patrick Felton (2012), of battleshippretension.com, offers an
interesting perspective on *Attenberg*'s remarkable amalgamation of aesthetics and thematics, which we could use as a starting point in this reading of Tsangari's film as a queer transgressive navigation of the body (*in*
and *of* the film) across the familiar familial, national and cinematic space,
which both reverberates with and extends Ahmed's queer phenomenological project. On the one hand, as Felton observes, the 'notable lack
of musical score' 'refocuses our attention towards the diegetic sounds of
the film'—indeed 'the sounds of industrial hell: cars, mopeds, machinery,
air conditioners, all the things that are usually sought to be erased from
the soundtrack' (2012). This excruciating industrial soundscape blends
seamlessly with the film's visuals. As he describes, 'The film is plotted with

numerous static shots lingering over urban landscapes, empty rooms and the plant which dominates the landscape. The film's cold natural light combines with its seaside setting to give it a lonely and isolated feeling' (2012). Felton praises the film's rigorous aesthetics, as they create the perfect set, that is, a 'desolate urban habitat', for Tsangari 'to study the strangest of creatures' (Felton is specifically referring to Marina here, though the human species as a whole might also resonate with his description). As he puts it, 'The film itself is like the Attenborough documentaries, constantly studying and probing the actions and behaviors of its subjects in relationship to their natural habitat. The film's treatment of Marina is anthropological, objective, clinical, and unsentimental' (2012). Nevertheless, much as the film's title poignantly fails to pronounce Attenborough's name correctly, the film itself, even though to a great extent it appropriates the nature documentary's observational style, fails or rather refuses to depict its subjects' particular habitat as 'natural' or even accommodating; it rather obsessively underscores that habitat's uninviting and unproductive qualities.

The urban industrial gloom of Aspra Spitia is, indeed, foregrounded as a hostile and unproductive space for the subject, a place where the body cannot extend. Tsangari's camera time and again follows Marina's silent meanderings along the empty streets of the city, as she rides her bike or drives the company's car. But, though the body is in constant movement when in the film's exterior shots, this movement is not necessarily productive or bounded by causality. Space and time are often rendered fragmentary, looped, catachrestic, excessive, and hence unproductive, always keeping the human body at a distance, indeed, 'out of place', 'out of synch'. In these shots Marina is mostly silent, but only Marina; for the soundtrack is disturbingly dominated, as Felton astutely points out, by those sounds of 'industrial hell' that are usually edited out in mainstream cinema. And, just as the city's excruciating sounds occupy the soundtrack, the city's grim colors haunt the film's visuals. The isolated and—to the mainstream Greek audience—barely identifiable town of Aspra Spitia emerges as a ghost town haunting the nation's self-representation, corroborating instead the failures of the modernist visions of nationalism and capitalism. In a poignant scene halfway through the film, Marina and her dying father, whom Tsangari suggestively makes one of Aspra Spitia's architects, stand on the rooftop of a building that overlooks the meticulously planned and designed town. 'It's as if we were designing ruins,' Spyros grieves, 'as if calculating their eventual collapse with mathemati-

cal precision. Bourgeois arrogance. Especially for a country that skipped the industrial age altogether. [...] We built an industrial colony on top of sheep pens and thought we were making a revolution.'

Unsurprisingly, Spyros's lamentation here echoes the current public sentiment of ideological disenchantment with the nation's modernist visions and narratives, which arguably constitutes the primary affective response to the country's economic-political crisis. But it is also impregnated with the broader denunciation of the familiar familial and national narratives, of the notion of the nation as a family, as well as of the 'sacred' patriarchal family itself as the perennial metaphor for the nation; a denunciation, which is the primary focus not only of *Attenberg*'s rhetoric, but, as this book argues, of the rhetoric of the entire contemporary trend in Greek cinema. Marina unexpectedly responds to her father: 'I like it. It's soothing, all this uniformity.' However, the film's overall portrayal of this 'soothing' and 'uniform' urbanscape as hostile and unproductive for the subject questions the validity of her reaction and envelops it with irony. Indeed, the national space is constantly interrogated in Tsangari's film, not only at the level of representation, which clearly departs from canonical depictions of coastal Greece as a tourist paradise, but also in ideological terms. As Marina travels past the looming backdrop of the industrial plant and the uniformly designed, yet lifeless white houses of this 'perfected' paradigm of modernist architecture,[1] one witnesses the irony implicit in the failure of the nation's dreams, the disillusionment and emptiness that characterizes its present. And the meaninglessness that imbues the quotidian meanderings of the young protagonist ultimately reveals the small town of Aspra Spitia—and by implication, the national space that is encapsulated in it—as Marina's double or even Marina's antagonist.

Aspra Spitia is introduced in *Attenberg* in the film's title sequence, a collage of static shots that show tiny fragments of the small town and in which one admires Tsangari's subtle interplay between mobility and stasis; that same interplay that, as we will see below, underlies the film's overall queer phenomenological discourse. The title sequence begins with a wide shot of a grass lawn that prominently features a rotating water sprinkler, which literally 'sprinkles' with life the otherwise monotonous static shot. As the noise from the sprinkler cross-fades with Suicide's 'Ghost Rider', the film cuts to another static shot that features a different water sprinkler, this time against the backdrop of a big building that looks like a hotel and which has all its curtains shut. In the shot that follows, we see an empty restaurant, probably the one hiding behind the closed curtains of the previous shot, while in the shot's background we can clearly discern two TV sets that are both showing the same football match. The next shot foregrounds some colorful plastic chairs against a high metal fence that separates them from an empty tennis court that occupies the background. This is followed by another wide shot of the (again) empty interiors of a Catholic church, a shot of a narrow street framed by the lavish and meticulously decorated gardens of the town's houses, a shot from above of a large balcony squeezed between blocks of flats and featuring a toy car in the middle, and finally another shot of a water sprinkler framed within rich vegetation and framing the film's title. The town is portrayed as empty, yet not deserted. Life is both present and absent in the above sequence, for though movement is generated by objects, this movement is not delinked from the ever-elusive human body. And it is precisely this very absence of the body in the above frames that highlights it as a necessary condition for movement; the water sprinklers have been programmed by a human hand and are waiting for another to switch them off, the toy car is waiting for a child to ride it, the TV sets for an audience or at least another hand who will turn them off, the narrow street for bodies to traverse it. As if it were a gesture of archaeological excavation the title sequence unravels the long-forgotten thread that binds cinema with the history of art, and particularly the still lifes of pre-cinematic painting, with which film, nonetheless, so zealously sought to break in an effort to capture that intangible wonder of movement. Indeed, in the ubiquitous still and tableaux shots of *Attenberg* one identifies an authorial intervention to rediscover the affective power of filmic space and re-establish it as more than a mere container of action, a backdrop for the narrative, but, primarily, as an affectively resilient landscape produced through the provisional operation of various energies. Reconceptualizing movement beyond its canonical association with action is, of course, a gesture that has analogous temporal repercussions, that demands a rethinking as well as a reconfiguration of cinematic time as neither productive nor teleological; something which, at the level of the film's thematics, reverberates with an equivalent reframing of familial and national time.

Janet Harbord proposes that an 'affectual' understanding of filmic space would require a consideration of space 'as a product of movement, rather than a frame within which action takes place' (2007, p. 164). Harbord follows here Michel Serres' and Bruno Latour's renunciation of the perennial division between the 'neat categories' of time and space and their subsequent invitation to reconnect the two in a way that reveals 'states of movement, process and a constant recombining of elements as forms that resist [such] conventional classification' (2007, p. 163). As Harbord argues:

> Latour's notion of process is significant for the analysis of film, for it shifts attention away from action towards movement as an emotional state. Serres extends this idea of process into the grammatical, identifying the redundancy of thinking with verbs, with actions and activities, suggesting rather that process draws attention to the movement between things, the prepositional terms that situate relations. (2007, p. 164)

Thinking in prepositional terms, which would entail, for example, employing 'intervals (*between*), orientation and directionality (*toward, in front of, behind*), proximity and adherence (*near, on, against, following, touching*), immersion (*among*), [etc.]' (Serres, 1994, p. 71), is to reconceptualize movement within space in the form of mobile relations between things. Such an articulation of spatial relations ultimately 'facilitates a reading of how the particular energies in any context, or text, are operating' and highlights space itself as a 'landscape produced through the relational contracts of things' (Harbord, 2007, p. 164). Nevertheless, relinking space to time through the reconceptualization of movement as a spatial category of relational energies does not necessarily entail an understanding of energy and movement through canonical conceptualizations of either of the two, 'historically embedded in concerns with productivity' (2007, p. 171). In effect, as we have seen in *Attenberg*'s title sequence, filmic space can emerge as a space generative of possibilities, yet rather failed ones, a space of missed encounters, of relational contracts between objects and bodies that are, however, never fulfilled. And as we will see below, this is what the whole film is, ultimately, all about: this state of spatiotemporal excess, of unproductive expenditure, which 'allows us to conceive of the body in motion, and not simply as movement but as an entity through which differential forms of energy flow' (2007, p. 170).

Right after the title sequence the film cuts to a sequence of two tableaux shots of Marina and her father at the hospital. In the first shot the two characters sit on large white chairs in what looks like a waiting area, while in the second shot we are taken into a hospital room, where the father is resting on a bed and Marina is sitting by his side, both silently reading books. Both of these shots are dominated by silence, whiteness (indeed, a blankness reflected in the white of the chairs, the curtains, the bed sheets and the scene's overall lighting) and stillness (of both the objects and the bodies), all of which gesture to an emptiness (of meaning, exposure, emotion) that is only vaguely interrupted by Marina's occasional and very subtle peeks at her father. After these introductory moments of visual and aural suspension, Tsangari cuts to a tracking medium shot of Marina on her bike—the excruciating noise from the motorbike abruptly taking over the soundtrack and marking a strong aural antithesis to the previous scene. We are then offered a long shot of the factory's entrance, at which Marina arrives and parks her bike. She rushes to enter the industrial prem-ises before she is stopped by the factory's security guard, who informs her that she has to work as a driver for an engineer who is visiting the plant. The film then cuts to a travelling medium shot of Marina in the car. Her eyes fixed on the road, she, however, seems to miss the magnificent land-scape, which the audience can enjoy behind the car windows—the sea, the mountains and the little white houses of Aspra Spitia, all lavishly illumi-nated by the blazing morning sun. In the next series of shots Marina drives the engineer to the factory; a travelling shot from inside the car places Marina and the engineer on the two sides of the frame, thus again provid-ing the audience with a view of the coastal town through the windshield, a static long shot shows the car entering the factory premises and another static extreme long shot reveals the plant in all its intimidating magnitude.

Clearly, the film's first sequences give Tsangari the opportunity to pro-vide the audience with geographical information about location, but most importantly reveal *Attenberg*'s pivotal spatiotemporal structure, which arguably relies on a persistent interplay between mobility and stasis. The film oscillates between moments of excessive movement and moments of relentless inertia, between frenzied unsteady shots on the one hand and tedious, monotonous lingering shots or melancholic tableaux on the other, all of which arguably allow us to investigate the 'body in motion' as, indeed, 'an entity through which differential forms of energy flow', to recall Harbord's words. This chapter began with a description of a remark-able example of such an oscillation, staged in the tennis court scene and the subsequent scene in the locker rooms. In that sequence we witness the camera foregrounding both the body in motion and the immobile body. In the first of the two scenes, Marina's frenzied tennis playing perfectly matches the unsteady camerawork and the sharp edits, thus highlighting disorientation and agitation as primary forms of affect that her body expe-riences out in the open social space. In the subsequent scene the film foregrounds the complete blockage of movement, namely inertia, as yet another kind of affective experience, indeed an effect of the body's failure to extend into the skin of the social, in effect to orientate. Ambivalence arguably infuses both Marina's gaze as she examines her naked body, as well as the audience's affective experience of the scene which, as we have seen above, does anything but sexually objectify the female figure.

Discussing the relation between action and space, Ahmed underlines that the question of action is essentially a question of how we inhabit space and how bodies and objects intimately co-dwell. Nevertheless as Henri Lefebvre points out, '[a]ctivity in space is restricted by that space; space "decides" what actually may occur, but even this "decision" has limits placed upon it' (1991, p. 143). For the difference between things and bodies is precisely the fact that bodies inhabit or haunt space much as they are haunted by it. Unlike objects 'the body is not itself an instrument but a form of expression, a making visible of our intentions', as Ahmed clarifies following Merleau-Ponty (2006, p. 53). Hence, just as Harbord argues that filmic space should not be thought of as merely a container of action, Ahmed suggests that space in general should not be considered as a mere container for the body. As she explains:

> [space] does not contain the body as if the body were 'in it.' Rather bodies are submerged, such that they become the space they inhabit; in taking up space, bodies move through space and are affected by the 'where' of that movement. It is through this movement that the surface of spaces as well as bodies takes shape. (2006, p. 53)

As already evident in the sequences discussed above, Marina's movement across the space *of* the film and the space *in* the film is marked by elusiveness. Her body appears unable to extend into the social space and, more often than not, experiences either moments of excessive, unproductive movement, which at times even evade the sight of the camera, or moments of relentless inertia, studiously framed in long and rather tedious static shots. Through this oscillation, which is as much affective as it is corporeal (if one could ever distinguish between the two), the skin of the social (the familial and the national) is arguably accordingly shaped as unproductive and excessive.

Thirty minutes into the film, Spyros asks Marina if she would ever get married. Marina seems quite reluctant to do so and shares with her father her lack so far of desire for men and her uncompromised repulsion towards sex and particularly the idea of being penetrated. In contrast, she admits she finds women more interesting, even though she clearly states that this does not however translate to any kind of physical attraction towards them. 'I want you to start living with other people', says Spyros at the end of their discussion. 'You've never taught me to live like that', replies Marina. Clearly, *Attenberg*'s protagonist here underscores sociality as the effect of habitual action rather than the natural outcome of a kind of transcendental state of things. But the film as a whole takes that line of thought a step further; arguably, the character's overall movement across the time and space of the film ultimately gestures to the performative character of every form of relationality, precisely through its sustained focus on those that are particularly concerned with discourses of gender and sexuality.

Ahmed again argues, 'what bodies "tend to do" are effects of history rather than being originary. We could say that history "happens" in the very repetition of gestures, which is what gives bodies their tendencies' (2006, p. 57). Taking into consideration how the repetition of action takes us in certain directions and not others helps us to understand that it is effectively not neutral work; it, instead, crucially shapes the body in particular ways, 'it orients the body in some ways rather than others' (2006, p. 57). And the bodily horizon of bodies, that is the edge of what a body can reach, is effectively shaped by such histories of action, for '[s]paces are not only inhabited by bodies that "do things", but what bodies "do" leads them to inhabit some spaces more than others' (2006, p. 58). As Ahmed elucidates, echoing Butler, the naturalization of gender as a property of bodies, objects and spaces occurs through the 'loop' of such repetition, which makes the repetitive effort of performing gender appear effortless, slyly pushing it to the background and ultimately making it disappear (2006, pp. 56–58). In this way, '[w]hat we "do do" affects what we "can do"', argues Ahmed suggestively, and continues:

> This is not to argue that 'doing' simply restricts capacities. In contrast, what we 'do do' opens up and expands some capacities, as an 'expansion' in certain directions that in turn might restrict what you can do in others. If gender shapes what we 'do do', then it shapes what we can do. Gender could thus be described as a bodily orientation, a way in which bodies get directed by their actions over time. (2006, p. 60)

Now, when bodies take up spaces that do not extend their shape this results in failed orientations or disorientations, which Ahmed frames 'as the "queer effect" of oblique or diagonal lines, created by bodies out of place' (2006, p. 61). Queer disorientation thus entails the failure to reproduce the straight lines or, indeed, the lines of straightness, and, in effect, brings about an eventual reorientation of the body. This might ultimately cause new lines to emerge, bodies to acquire new shapes and spaces in turn to acquire new bodies, Ahmed concludes (2006, p. 62).

Marina, though making clear her repulsion towards intimacy, nonetheless appears curious enough to investigate the possibility of exploring the lines of femininity and heterosexuality all too readily drawn for her by the skin of the social. And though again she explicitly denies that her repulsion towards sex is attributed to some kind of repressed or latent same-sex desire, her (hetero)sexual journey is marked by a substantial corporeal difficulty in successfully reproducing the aforementioned lines, highlighted precisely as a failed orientation, indeed, a disorientation. Accordingly, through these scenes the film itself gestures to the discursive and performative character of sex and gender, and effectively brings the 'background' of gender and (compulsory hetero)sexuality to the foreground, denaturalizing it and rendering it as, indeed, problematic.

Marina's difficulty in 'incorporating' herself into the 'skin of the social' is, indeed, highlighted in the film as corporeal. When in public spaces and without her father she is seen moving gauchely, fast and rather nervously, or sitting immobile and isolated staring at strangers' bodies—arguably, 'embodying' the film's pseudo-observational style. At one such moment Marina appears playing table football on her own at the hotel restaurant. Tsangari first frames her from behind, only to highlight her clumsy moves as she spins the bars or throws the ball into the table, while her agitated playing is further augmented by the violent sounds of the hits and strikes of the ball that are foregrounded on the soundtrack. The film cuts briefly to a long shot of the engineer, who is also at the restaurant having lunch, and then back to Marina with a medium shot that reveals her uneasy state of mind. The engineer joins in the game and the film cuts to a two-shot that inaugurates the pair's gradual icebreaking. At first, Marina is visibly uncomfortable, but gradually her body seems to channel its emotional tension through the football table's rods and extend into the other side, reaching out to the hands of the engineer (Fig. 5.3). She smiles at him when she scores. Marina literally lines up here with the objects that straight culture makes available, reachable to her as objects that can extend her body into the social space (indeed, the football table as an object that facilitates social interaction and the engineer as a permissible object of desire). And her alignment is underscored as both corporeal and affective.

Fig. 5.3   Aligning the body with permissible objects of desire

A few minutes later in the film, Marina is invited into the engineer's hotel room. In a series of static shots from which the human body often slips away, Tsangari suggestively strives to frame Marina's nervous efforts to put into practice the 'sexual education' she has gained from Bella's lessons. Nevertheless, unlike the body's unpredictable extension beyond the reaches of the filmic frame, its movement across the space of the sexual is marked by a profound failure to productively extend. Marina's grotesque attempts to kiss and caress the engineer as well as her mechanical and utterly de-eroticized stripping off result in a mockery of canonical depictions of (hetero)sex, an ultimate parodic rendition of the naturalizing and normative discourses of sexuality.

However, if in *Dogtooth*, as argued in Chap. 3, sex is staged and underscored as a regulatory mechanism, indispensable for the production and naturalization of the gender and sexual hierarchies of patriarchy, in *Attenberg* sex is foregrounded as a necessary means for the body's alignment with the lines of the social, the space where the subject's consummation of its quintessential relational contract occurs. This is not to annihilate the possibility of desire, however, for Marina explicitly expresses her desire for the engineer to both the engineer and her father. But Tsangari's film crucially foregrounds sex as subjected to a series of conditions that annihilate the possibility of its occurrence in absolutely naturalizing terms;

it effectively foregrounds it as yet another 'effect of history' rather than 'originary', to use Ahmed's words again, a series of corporeal acts, which, through repetition, shape the skin of the social as much as they are shaped by it.

Sexual performativity, or rather the fact that sex and sexuality always already rely on performativity, is further emphasized in the film's central sexual scene, which establishes the space of the sexual as precisely governed by such a series of regulatory corporeal acts which the body needs to perform in order to be able to inhabit it, thus transgressively pushing desire not only to the margins of the frame but, most importantly, to the margins of sexuality itself. The scene begins with a close-up of Marina and the engineer in bed kissing. Foregrounding some slight movements of the characters' heads, lips and tongues, which only accentuate the unbearable stillness of the rest of their bodies, revealed in a subsequent wide shot, the scene definitely disappoints our expectations. For unlike the canonical sex scenes of mainstream cinema, this one lacks not only all the conventional formal characteristics of such a scene (soft and suggestive lighting and coloring, romantic music, embellishing framing of particular body parts) but also in the energy associated with bodies engaged in sexual activity; what is colloquially understood as 'passion'. Marina is instead framed as unable to extend her body into the space canonically considered as the one that facilitates the human body's 'natural orientation'. The 'naturalness' of such an orientation is rather exposed as a fantasy, while performativity is foregrounded as a necessary condition for the re-enactment of such orientations that regulate the extensions of bodies into space; the sexual and—by extension—the wider social.

Marina is not appalled by the engineer—on the contrary, she clearly states that she finds him attractive and that she feels comfortable lying on top of his body. However, what her words propose her actions fail to adhere to. Indeed, although she seems all too eager to put into practice Bella's instructions, her incessant and detailed description of her physical and emotional permutations do not allow for a 'natural' unfolding of sexual activity. The engineer, visibly put off, repeatedly asks her to stop talking: 'Is the interview over? […] Could you do us a favor and stop talking that much? […] Can you stop describing what you are doing?' At some point Marina offers 'to blow' him, she moves down and reaches his limp penis, starts caressing it and gently rests her head on it. 'It's moving a bit. Are you doing this or is it doing it on its own?' The embarrassing effect of the scene yields to what now looks like a parody of mainstream sex scenes. Tsangari ends the scene with a wide shot of the two bodies left naked yet immobile in bed. She will return to the engineer's hotel room a few minutes later in the film. This time, at last, we witness penetration in a sequence of two wide shots that bears all the formal characteristics of the scene described above, while also unapologetically refusing any exposure of a further physical and emotional attachment between the two characters. Tsangari frames the characters' bodies moving like emotionless, indeed passionless, machines and, hence, re-enacting what the medium perhaps most glamorizes of all corporeal practices in an utterly tedious and de-eroticized manner (Fig. 5.4). Thus represented, human sex is stripped of its canonical discourses; it rather becomes the object of clinical observation, indeed, of ethology. Tsangari refuses to provide much information about character development and psychology, just as she admits in her interviews. Behind the incessant interplay between stasis and mobility unfolded in her static frames, Tsangari's pseudo-ethological perspective offers the human body as a space of multiple energies, which, however, are, more often than not, hard to map out, predict or regulate.

Attenberg is ultimately all about the body's journey across, against or in parallel with the lines of the social; the sexual, the familial, the national. Marina at times seems to strive to follow these lines—her struggle posing exactly the question of their 'naturalness' (as in the case of the heterosex-

Fig. 5.4   Reframing sex, formally and thematically

ual lines above)—whereas at others she appears to defy or ignore or even reinvent them. The latter case is what primarily describes her relationship with her father, framed in the film in a series of sequences that are composed by static wide shots and deft tableaux, which again accommodate moments of relentless corporeal stasis or excessive movement.

The conventionality of the father and daughter relationship is challenged quite early in the film. In Marina's very first discussion with her father, framed within the same tableaux with which the film begins and only occasionally intercut with close-ups of the characters, the girl suggestively introduces the fundamental question of the incest taboo. 'Do you ever picture me naked?' she asks. 'No. A father's mind repels such thoughts', replies Spyros and, invoking biological legitimizations of the incest taboo, explains to his daughter that the existence of taboos secures the perpetuation of mammal species without complications and degenerations. Unlike her father, Marina confesses that she has imagined her father naked yet without a penis. She also admits that even though she does indeed find the thought disturbing she, nonetheless, does not repel it. But soon enough their conversation resolves in Marina's rather tragic realization that 'some things should indeed remain taboo'.[2] Ironically, much as Tsangari would like to avoid psychology, she cannot help but have her characters engage in the fundamental psychoanalytic discourse. For Marina underscores here the fact that the formation of a socially intelligible familial subjectivity depends precisely on the disavowal of the phallus insofar as this poses a threat to structural kin relations by signifying the possibility of a sexual relationship among the occupiers of the pivotal symbolic positions. Hence, Spyros's body acquires the symbolic position of the father so long as it is a non-sexualized body, that is, a body without a penis.

Throughout the film the relationship between the daughter and her dying father verges, however, on the uncanny, the elusive, the excessive and the unproductive, staged through sequences that adhere to the film's overall oscillation between stasis and mobility (formal and corporeal). Time and again the familial pair is shown sharing long moments of silence and stillness, framed in rigorously staged tableaux either in the hospital's waiting room or at home in the bedroom motionlessly watching the natural life documentaries of Attenborough. At other times, these moments of stillness might be accompanied by macabre discussions about life and death, or resolve into meaningless rhyming games and corporeal improvisations, in which Marina and her father mimic the movements and sounds of the gorillas, birds and other species featured in their beloved TV series.

Exemplary of the first instance is a scene where Marina, lying in bed next to her father, who is asleep, is watching an episode from Attenborough's documentary about gorillas. The film cuts between a tableau of Marina and her father, both confined to the bed, and a shot of the TV screen, in a way which proposes a poignant juxtaposition between the two screen spaces; namely the filmic space of the home and the televisual space of the jungle. In a shot from the documentary a gorilla is clearly seen moving gently yet confidently through the rich vegetation of the jungle and reaching out to its family. Tsangari cuts momentarily to the immobile Marina and her father. This is ironically done right at the moment when Attenborough explains the remarkable if somewhat uncanny understanding between humans and gorillas. She then cuts back to the TV screen, which showcases the loving relationship between the members of the gorilla family as they extend their bodies towards each other and into the space of the jungle, calmly yet assertively. This juxtaposition, this vacillation between movement, as the effect of intentionality, in the jungle and stasis, as the effect of bodily blockage, in the bedroom, further highlights Marina's state of inertia as the pivotal 'embodiment' of her complicated relationship with the world, her inability to productively accommodate the social space, her visible disaffection from it.

Tsangari's numerous tableaux in the film do nothing less than filmically register precisely this thematic of inertia. Harbord provides an interesting insight into the relationship between such scenes of staged stillness and inertia as affective experience. Drawing on Gilles Deleuze, who argues that the tableau in film is of a different order from the still-life photograph, she explains:

> where photography posits not a stillness but an instant extracted from the flow of time, the stillness of film creates a tension in the discomfort of a lack of movement, of *durée* held in frozen form yet still breathing. It suggests, at the edges of this moment, the possibility that time passes yet nothing has changed. It gestures to an internal world that remains out of sight, unknowable, unreadable. (2007, p. 167)

Indeed, Marina's internal world remains highly uncharted, though not necessarily uninvestigated, throughout the film. With a preference for biology over psychology, Tsangari rather foregrounds the embodied experience of disorientation, pushing to the margin conventional forms of cinematic exposure achieved through narrative exegesis and characterization. In effect, most of the characters' actions remain unexplained, unresolved, unmapped, meaningless. Hence, Tsangari's tableaux, precisely through the effect of the suspension of the time that is 'yet still breathing', emerge as substitutes for such exposure. As Harbord astutely remarks, '[t]he camera's pausing on acts of seeming banality, observing with a meticulously steady eye, provokes this search for reasons, to fill the gaps in the void of explanation' (2007, p. 167). However, where Tsangari refuses to explain, to expand, to conclude, the stillness or the movement of the body foregrounded in her deftly crafted frames, more than mere objects of observation, of ethological analysis, become themselves revelatory of a phenomenological redefinition or even reshaping of the spaces where the body dwells, both the physical spaces and the ideological/representational ones. Indeed, much as we are craftily driven to follow a body that is constantly 'out of place' and 'out of time', we are encouraged to revisit the familiar familial and national space, and reconceptualize it as unproductive, 'unnatural', disorienting.

In this sense, Tsangari's appropriation of Attenborough's observational style is only present through the effect of irony. For contrary to the gorillas' confident extension into their natural dwelling, *Attenberg* underscores the human body's perennial disorientation in the un-natural urban habitat as well as in a space that is pointedly marked as familial. Indeed, the film's sustained formal and thematic conversation with the influential British documentaries ultimately illuminates the film's intention to problematize the 'naturalness' of the familial and national space and unearth, instead, its discursive and performative character, through precisely a phenomenological rhetoric that focuses on the body's failures to extend into it. Marina's body is effectively shown as constantly blocked, confused, disoriented, lost, oscillating itself between dull stillness and agitated, meaningless movement. And this occurs as the effect of a series of failures to extend into the socially demarcated spaces of sexuality, gender and, most significantly, of the family, which here emerges as excessive, sterile, decaying. For Marina's father is a male body without a penis, but it is also a dying body, a body which signifies imminent death; with an already dead mother and a living dead father Marina's familial space is a space of rupture, a dwelling of losses, a fundamentally unproductive locus of perennial defeat.

In one of the last sequences at the hospital, Tsangari offers another interesting tableau in the father's hospital room. On the left side of the frame we have the father who is lying in bed, filling in an application to be

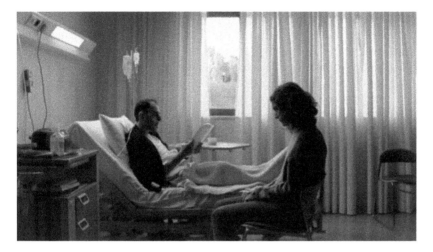

Fig. 5.5   Between life and death: confined to a decaying familial space

cremated. On the right side Marina is again sitting motionless on a chair by her father's side. A gap between the curtains behind them lets the sunlight enter the room, while also giving the frame a suggestive texture by filling the gap between the two bodies with a narrow strip of green (from the garden outside) (Fig. 5.5). The juxtaposition between the bright and colorful setting outside and the monotonous and gloomy hospital room inside gestures to a juxtaposition between life and death which further accentuates Marina's asphyxiating confinement to a decaying familial space. Not that her love for her father is at any time questioned. On the contrary, Tsangari is careful to highlight Marina's uncontested love and care for her father; we, indeed, witness her at times washing Spyros's hair, applying *aloe vera* to his hands or even asking Bella to have sex with him as a last favor for the dying man.

But the symbolic space of the family is ultimately underscored as a space of loss and defeat. After the long wide shot in the hospital room, the film cuts to a series of tracking shots that follow Marina from behind as she pushes Spyros in a wheelchair along the hospital's empty, white corridors. We hear Spyros asking Marina to follow his corpse to Germany, where it will be cremated. 'When you receive my body …' continues Spyros, but Marina stops him abruptly, 'Shut up!' She suddenly stops and turns to the camera before the film cuts to a kind of reverse shot in which Marina's face is not visible. Tsangari refuses to offer a facial manifestation of emotional pain; she rather highlights it as a full-body experience, an experience that confines the body to the ground, still and blocked from movement, her head looking down, her fists clenched, an embodiment indeed of both agony and disorientation. The bodies stay silent and motionless for a bit and then the film cuts to an extreme close-up of deadpan Marina not long before she draws away from the camera and carries on pushing her father. A bit later Spyros will confess, 'I'm boycotting the twentieth century. It is overrated and I'm not sorry for leaving it. I'm an atheist old man, toxic waste of Modernism, of Late Enlightenment, and I'm handing you over to the new century without having taught you anything.' Marina does not comment on her father's lament and swan song. She just asks him what he will find where he is going. 'A giant warm pussy waiting to swallow me back', replies Spyros, only to instantly apologize for using inappropriate language.

Much like Spyros, who is oscillating between life and death, between a familiar space that is soon to be lost and the ultimate unknown space beyond the contours of life that he nonetheless sarcastically imagines as most accommodating, calling it 'a giant warm pussy', Marina experiences a similar oscillation between a home that is soon to be utterly and irreversibly lost and an unknown horizon beyond the familiar familial space that is soon to open before her as the result of the loss. Ahmed argues, as discussed above, that a loss might be experienced as a gift of an unexpected line, it might engender new directions, even ones we could not imagine or foresee. What is precisely at stake here, however? What is the meaning of Marina's loss? And what is the bodily experience of that loss?

In her final discussion with her father in the film, the two are reintroduced as if for the first time. The scene begins with a medium shot that frames Marina in the middle of a hospital corridor, her body turned away from the camera. 'Say my name', we hear her asking her father. 'Marinaki', replies Spyros who is hiding behind her. Tsangari cuts to a two-shot that shows Marina standing on the left of the frame and Spyros in the wheelchair, both facing each other. 'No nicknames', says Marina. 'Marina', says the father and Marina asks him to repeat. 'Marina.' 'Again.' 'Marina.' 'Again…' Another tedious set of repetitions continues for long enough to create once more a discomforting effect. Finally, Marina offers her hand to her father. 'Marina', she says. Spyros offers his hand back and introduces himself: 'Dad.' Marina smiles. Could that smile suggest Marina's reconciliation with her father's imminent death? Or is the whole scene nothing less than an allusion to—if not a mockery of—the orienting devices available to the body and which are eventually rendered obsolete? For one is tempted to read this tedious repetition of Marina's naming by her father as an ironic staging of the act of interpellation; namely, the act by which the subject is called into being by the signifier itself, here indeed by the very figure that has traditionally embodied the Law, that is the father.

Ahmed again explains that, in Butler's relevant formulation, becoming a subject necessarily involves an act of turning, which 'takes the form of hearing oneself as the subject of an address' (2006, p. 15). Despite admitting that this turning is not really about the physicality of the movement, she proposes that we could actually 'make this question of direction crucial to the emergence of subjectivity' by reflecting 'on the difference it makes *which way subjects turn*' (2006, p. 15). As she explains, '[d]epending on which way one turns, different worlds might even come into view. If such turns are repeated over time, then bodies acquire the very shape of such direction' (2006, p. 15). In other words, interpellation emerges as yet another orienting device that effectively produces subjectivation (indeed a turning towards a particular orientation that puts identity into effect, and in effect shapes the body towards particular directions). However, the question posed here by *Attenberg* is effectively what happens to that identity and that body when the very agent of interpellation ceases to exist? Marina demands that her father call her name again and again, looking at him directly—no turning of the body or even the head. As if she strives to prolong the effect of such an act right at the moment when she feels its expiration; as if she realizes that the death of the agent renders the act precisely ineffective, meaningless. And there is some sort of melancholic realization here; for, redemptive as it might be, there is always a sense of melancholia accompanying the loss of identity, the rupture of the subject.

On the other hand, however, what if Marina's smile and the pair's handshake at the end of the scene suggest that this loss—the loss of the father, the loss of identity itself—could, indeed, be experienced as a gift? The gift of an unexpected line? What if the death of the father could be experienced as a redemptive rupture with the 'politics of lifelines', which draw the very lines of inheritance and reproduction that haunt a body acting queerly? And, finally, what if that rupture could engender new directions for that body, ones that allow deviation from the aforementioned lines and eventually a reorientation?

Arguably, after the death of her father Marina experiences what Ahmed calls 'a migrant orientation': namely, 'the disorientation of the sense of home, as the "out of place" or "out of line" effect of unsettling arrivals [...] the lived experience of facing at least two directions: toward a home, that has been lost, and to a place that is not yet home' (2006, p. 10). Migration, Ahmed argues, 'helps us to explore how bodies arrive and how they get directed in this way or that way as a condition of arrival' (2006, p. 10). In other words, migration illuminates the ways bodies have of settling, how they effectively come to inhabit spaces that, in the first instance, are unfamiliar, how we come to achieve that 'feeling at home'. Nevertheless, *Attenberg*'s denouement is anything but a manifestation of a successful reorientation. Up to the last moment, Marina seems rather condemned to a state of perennially unsettling arrivals, in effect a perennial migrant feeling.

After Spyros's death, the film follows Marina's procedures to pay off the hospital, send her father's corpse abroad in order to be cremated and then scatter his ashes in the sea. Except for the first scene, in which Marina negotiates the hospital bill, all these scenes are marked by Marina's silence, thus highlighting the inadequacy of language to articulate the experience of loss, foregrounding it, indeed, as a matter of embodiment rather than discourse. Within these scenes Tsangari also interjects a final meeting with the engineer, shown in the same wide shot in the engineer's hotel room. The engineer is lying in bed, his naked body covered with the white sheets. He is staring at Marina, speechless, as she is getting dressed. At some point Marina turns to the side of the bed and literally lets her body drop as if dead onto the mattress. The engineer turns his head and looks at the fallen body beside him. The film then cuts to the airport cargo, where Marina watches silently her father's coffin being taken to an airplane. The next scene shows Marina staring at the black urn that carries her father's ashes, while in the film's final sequence we are at last taken to the seaside. Marina and Bella are shown driving a speedboat. They reach a certain point in the sea and stop the boat. Tsangari frames Marina in a medium shot that reveals her emotional distress as she tries unsuccessfully to open the urn. She gives it to Bella, who manages to open it. Marina takes the opened urn but hesitates a bit. Tsangari cuts to a long shot. Bella encourages Marina to scatter the ashes into the sea. As Marina pays her final debt to her late father the shot becomes more unsteady. The ashes are blown away and exceed the reaches of the frame. Tsangari cuts back to Marina's medium shot and lingers on that for a while. Marina is framed in profile; she is silent, her eyes fixed on the sea, but her body moves up and down and embarrasses the camera, which struggles to 'properly' frame it. The girls return to the coast. The film's final shot is an extreme long wide shot of industrial decay featuring the enormous smokestacks of the plant as they emerge prominently among hills of sand, mud and clutter through which lorries and bulldozers pass incessantly. The two girls, barely discernible, are seen crossing the frame left to right and reaching their vehicles. Bella gets on her bike, Marina into the car and they exit the frame. The film lingers on the empty frame for a while as the sounds of 'industrial hell' give way to Françoise Hardy's 'Le temps de l'amour'. But the song gradually fades out and the 'industrial hell' takes over the soundtrack again. The closing credits begin.

As these scenes reveal, the film's final act is, arguably, nothing more than a sequence of failed encounters, tragic departures and unsettling arrivals, which more often than not evade the frame itself. The soundtrack is, in effect, dominated by the diegetic sounds of footsteps, cargo vehicles, the boat, the wind, the sea's waves, mashing up the transient with the elemental, as both bear witness to the ephemerality of the human body, the triviality of human discourse, the monumentality of nature. As bodies and objects follow clearly demarcated routes, paths and practices, these, however, never offer an opening to productive activity. The film soon returns to the meaningless movement and the relentless inertia of the ineffectual or even, of what Harbord calls, the 'unaffectual'; space is, ultimately, foregrounded as 'a landscape where energy is blocked and intimate contact an impossibility' (2007, p. 165). Marina's new 'arrival' fails once more, condemning her to a state of perennial meandering. Perhaps this is precisely what constitutes her as a queer body, as a body that persistently resists orientation, a body that instead is engaged in an ongoing process of what Ahmed frames as 'queer orientations'.

According to Ahmed, 'Queer orientations might be those that don't line up, which by seeing the world "slantwise" allow other objects to come into view'; those that do not 'overcome what is "off line"', and hence act out of line with others' (2006, p. 106). To inhabit such a 'queer slant' is to engage in an everyday negotiation 'with the perceptions of others, with the "straightening devices" and the violence that might follow when such perceptions congeal into social forms' (2006, p. 107). But it is effectively a work that engages the 'queer' body with those alternative lines of resistance and rebellion; '[w]e would not aim to overcome the disorientation of the queer moment, but instead inhabit the intensity of its moment' concludes Ahmed (2006, p. 107).

Unlike in most of the film, where Marina strives (most of the time unsuccessfully) to align herself with the lines prescribed for her by her gender and sexuality, or even by her national and familial identity (namely, the lines of inheritance, reproduction, femininity, heterosexuality, to name a few), there are some particular moments where her body emerges as perfectly synched and aligned with another body, ironically, that of her friend Bella. We could call these moments choruses or interludes in the lineage of ancient drama's *stasima*.[3] In these interludes, Tsangari's camera captures some extraordinarily choreographed yet extraordinarily meaningless corporeal movements executed by Bella and Marina in an open space among buildings and houses of Aspra Spitia, which critics have compared to Monty Python's 'funny walks' (Rose, 2011). In these moments Marina and Bella emerge as both the film's protagonists and chorus, even though their comment upon the film's thematics is rather obscured and somewhat lost in a void of signification. Alternating between meaningless and frenetic corporeal extension into the open space on the one hand and perfectly synched animalistic behavior, framed within strictly demarcated routes and paths that the two actors 'must follow without detour' (to recall Ahmed's words) on the other, Marina and Bella's choral interludes ultimately result in nothing less than an unapologetic mockery, indeed a parody, of the act of alignment, of orientation itself. Their bodies are perfectly aligned with each other, yet often, indeed, move slantwise, extending into the space differently and shaping their own routes and pathways (Fig. 5.6). Tsangari admits that in *Attenberg* there was 'a desire to escape

Fig. 5.6 Inhabiting the intensity of the queer moment

from the tyranny of words and propriety' (Kauffman, 2011). Indeed, just as in the sequences with the father she encouraged her actors to let their words collapse into rhyming games and random animal sounds, in these interludes she manages to capture extraordinary instances of excessive movement. Through this excess the national space is produced as a space of excess, an unproductive and, thus, ultimately, hostile space, which condemns the bodies that resist to follow its long-established pathways and routes to a perennial meaningless meandering. However, ironically, these bodies, and with them the film in its entirety, do not seek to overcome 'the disorientation of the queer moment', but rather emerge as eager to inhabit and even enjoy 'the intensity of its moment'.

It would not be surprising at all if, after the final shot of the film, that gloomy melancholic shot of 'industrial decay', the film returned to the same tedious open space among the buildings and houses of Aspra Spitia only to have Marina and Bella perform one last 'funny walk', one last repetition of these alternative lines, these lines that mock and parody the straight lines of the social, these lines of corporeal rebellion and resistance, of, indeed, a queer orientation.

NOTES

1. Aspra Spitia, the name of the town, literally translates as 'White Houses'.
2. I use the word tragic here not so much in its contemporary meaning as that which causes or suffers a state of distress, but in its more classical sense as that which relates to ancient Greek drama, upon which the psychoanalytic discourse of the incest taboo is founded and which it also elaborates.
3. *Stasima* (singular: *stasimon*) were the brief interludes between the episodes of a tragedy (or a comedy) performed by the chorus. In these interludes, action was suspended and the chorus commented upon the unfolding events of the narrative.

BIBLIOGRAPHY

Ahmed, Sara (2006) *Queer Phenomenology: Orientations, Objects, Others* (Durham and London: Duke University Press).

Bradshaw, Peter (2011) 'Attenberg—Review', *The Guardian*, http://www.the-guardian.com/film/2011/sep/01/attenberg-film-review, date accessed 22 April 2016.

Felton, Patrick (2012) 'Home Video Hovel—Attenberg', *Battleship Pretension*, http://battleshippretension.com/?p=7529, date accessed 22 April 2016.

Harbord, Janet (2007) *Evolution of Film: Rethinking Film Studies* (Cambridge: Polity Press).

Heidegger, Martin (1973) *Being and Time*, trans. John Macquarrie and Edward Robinson (Oxford: Basil Blackwell).

Kauffman, Anthony (2011) 'Athina Rachel Tsangari Studies the Species in Attenberg', *New York Village Voice*, http://www.villagevoice.com/2011-03-23/film/athina-rachel-tsangari-studies-the-species-in-attenberg/, date accessed 22 April 2016.

Lefebvre, Henri (1991) *The Production of Space*, trans. Donald Nicholson Smith (Oxford: Basil Blackwell)

Rose, Steve (2011) 'Attenberg, Dogtooth and the Weird Wave of Greek Cinema,' *The Guardian*, http://www.guardian.co.uk/film/2011/aug/27/attenberg-dogtooth-greece-cinema, date accessed 22 April 2016.

Savage, Robert (2012) 'DVD Review: "Attenberg"', *Cine Vue*, http://www.cine-vue.com/2012/01/dvd-review-attenberg.html, date accessed 22 April 2016.

Serres, Michel (1994) *Atlas* (Paris: Julliard).

CHAPTER 6

Alps: Of Hauntology

Yorgos Lanthimos's *Alps* (2011) opens with a long shot of a young gymnast (Arianne Labed), as she waits to rehearse a rhythmic ribbon dance in an almost empty gymnasium; Her only audience is a man, presumably her coach (Johnny Vekris), vaguely discerned on the left margin of the frame. The film lingers on this shot, as the eminently recognizable 'O Fortuna' from Carl Orff's *Carmina Burana* takes over the soundtrack. But it is not until the song enters the chorus that the girl raises her ribbon and starts dancing. The camera follows the immaculate performance with a series of deadpan handheld and fixed shots that often decenter the moving body before it finally collapses in frustration under the fierce gaze of the coach. 'Why can't I dance to something more pop?' asks the girl, only to cede in an impassive argument with her coach, framed in an unexpected two-shot that decapitates the latter (Fig. 6.1). The film only edits in the coach's face, with a shallow-focus close-up that places his head on the right side of the frame leaving the rest out of focus, as he delivers an utterly discomforting though expressionless monologue in which he threatens to break the girl's arms and legs if she ever raises her voice to him again (something which never happened in the first place). The girl grovels and apologizes in a corresponding decentering shallow-focus close-up, which evokes both a spatial and affective isolation as she unconditionally submits to the demands of her vicious paternalistic mentor.

Winner of Best Screenplay (Golden Osella) at the Venice Film Festival (2011), *Alps* is the third feature film by Yorgos Lanthimos, and was released two years after his breakthrough film, the Oscar-nominated

© The Author(s) 2016
M. Psaras, *The Queer Greek Weird Wave*,
DOI 10.1007/978-3-319-40310-6_6

Fig. 6.1   Coercion and submission

Dogtooth. While *Dogtooth*'s success did not enable Lanthimos to access a high budget for the production of *Alps*, it nevertheless secured the new film's access to some of the most renowned film festivals around the world (Venice, Toronto, London the BFI [British Film Institute]), as well as distribution in major Western metropoles, including London, Paris and New York. Critics welcomed *Alps* with mixed reviews, either disdaining the film for its close formal and thematic resemblances to its predecessor (Watson, 2013; Rich, 2012) or lauding once more Lanthimos's distinctive visual and narrative style and appearing eager to explore the film's distinct qualities.

Indeed, the most interesting reviews were produced by those critics who were willing to trace what is distinct in *Alps* and how the film's rhetoric, while revolving around the same themes as *Dogtooth*, operates in radically different ways. Christopher McQuain notes that: '*Alps* takes the hermetic lid off the strikingly claustrophobic POV of *Dogtooth* to let it mingle, frighteningly if not corrosively, out in a much broader swathe of the world, which turns out to have its own inescapable feel of invisible but potent circumscription no matter where you go' (2012). Poly Lykourgou, on the other hand, suggests that *Alps* moves in the opposite direction from *Dogtooth*, as here 'humans try to return to their familiar shape—long for the family/relationship they lost, suffer away from it …' (2011). As she explains, whereas in *Dogtooth* 'the heroes live hypnotized in a virtual reality, which is imposed by others and thus they should escape from', 'here, the human being chooses to be deceived, voluntarily reconstructs reality […] does not escape, but on the contrary, runs in vain and with sorrow back to the past, the home, the womb' (2011). She also observes that with this film Lanthimos 'turns the camera to the actors' in an effort to investigate their own back-story as well as what makes them want to assume lives that are not their own. In her own words, 'the group members act explicitly as actors, wear costumes, stand center-stage in the life of the client, utter speech performatively, clearly and artificially. Everything is after all artificial and nobody tries to hide it' (2011). Taking its cue from McQuain and Lykourgou's reviews of *Alps*, this chapter argues that Lanthimos's film is not so much about loss and suffering as it is about the existential search for identity and belonging, about the way this search is entangled with the familiar yet always performative spaces of the family and the nation, and also about the violent regimes of oppression, coercion and submission that these spaces engender, and which the performing body can rarely escape.

In effect, the opening scene, described above, establishes some of the film's pivotal thematic and formal axes. Much like in *Dogtooth*, here too we realize early on that we are confronted with an unconventional exploration of power relations and hierarchical systems that strive to fix and regulate the human body, while at the same time an interrogation of the medium itself, its conventional representational strategies and its unapologetic collusion in the discourses of the above hierarchies is also taking place. Lanthimos's idiosyncratic framing of the human body, which assertively and systematically leaves the characters' heads off-screen, once more takes over the cinematic screen with all its confident deadpan compositions, which this time gloriously include yet another discomforting and disorienting device, the widescreen and unashamedly excessive shallow-focus cinematography. However, unlike the visible lines that sharply distinguish the human body that is in the foreground from the rest of the frame that is insistently held out of focus, 'the line separating reality and performance seems to dissipate with each passing second', as Keith Uhlich (2012) astutely points out. Indeed, as I suggest below, *Alps* obscures this line if not rendering it always already obsolete in its unearthing of performativity as a necessary condition for human relationality; a condition through which identity is (re)produced as a materialized ideal that acquires historical efficacy, thus concealing its only and true nature, which is none other than that of fiction.

It is in this sense that *Alps* fascinatingly foregrounds film's (as opposed to verbal language's) singular privilege as able to register the performing body precisely as such, prior to the formation of subjectivity, delinked from the 'I' of the performer. For in Lanthimos's third feature the space *in* the film and the space *of* the film resonate sublimely in the way they accommodate/foreground the actor as always an actor and never a subject. Hence, ultimately, *Alps* is less about the art of acting or actors themselves as particular forms of life, as particular subjectivities, as some critics have suggested, and more about the ever performing body, its meanderings through the vicissitudes of identity and the violent ways in which it is rendered precarious and disposable as an effect of its failure or refusal to perform according to norms and normalizing ideals. The film's very first scene underscores precisely this existential condition of corporeal precariousness, mirrored in the warning against the gymnast's possible defiance of her abusive paternalistic coach, a defiance which could instantly subject her to violence and suffering.

After the opening scene, Lanthimos takes a few minutes to introduce us to the other two main protagonists of the film, a nurse (Aggeliki Papoulia) and a paramedic (Aris Servetalis). A series of brief sequences shows them at work, handling the case of a young tennis player, victim of a car accident, who has just been admitted to the hospital, but also slyly eliciting information about the player's tastes, interests and habits. We are soon taken back to the gymnasium where the four main characters meet. A series of medium shots and close-ups frames the four as they discuss their group's name. The paramedic, who, as we soon realize, has assumed the role of the group's calm yet authoritative leader, announces the group's name: 'Alps'. He offers two reasons for his choice: the first is that it does not reveal in any way what they do and the second, more symbolic one, pertains to the enviable distinctiveness and irreplaceability of the famous peaks of the vast European mountain range, which 'though they cannot be replaced by other mountains can, nevertheless, stand in for any mountain' without any objection, as he argues. 'Officially I will take the name of the highest mountain, that is Mont Blanc', he continues. 'What about us?' asks the coach. 'You can choose among the names of the other mountains', Mont Blanc replies and provides each with a handout that contains a list of all the names of the Alpine mountains to choose from.

Though the purpose and function of the group still remains a mystery to the audience, this scene is important in that it effectively establishes the affective and political economy which frames this small yet rigidly structured microcosm. Much like *Dogtooth*'s idiosyncratic kinship model, this one is also underscored as a highly authoritarian (arguably quasi-familial) patriarchal construct with strictly delineated gender roles (indeed, the gender imbalance has already been established in the opening scene) and a dominant male leader, who ironically sports a large moustache, visually alluding to the mustachioed patriarchs of the classical Greek cinema of the 1950s and 1960s. In addition, though not exiled outside the contours of the broader social space—on the contrary, this time Lanthimos relocates filmic action back to Athens and has his characters live and operate within the social—the secrecy that must underlie the workings of the clan demarcates again a kind of self-inflicted seclusion, which is, however, equally impregnated with contingency and permeability, as will be revealed later. Last but not least, the visual isolation of the characters, highlighted by the conspicuous use of shallow-focus cinematography in almost every shot of the scene, suggests an equivalent affective landscape within which their relationships occur; namely, a hostile and isolating space, consistent with the highly oppressive and regulatory regime that generates it. In this way, the first scenes of the film, though barely delineating the film's narrative intentions, ingeniously introduce the audience to an ethically ambivalent narrative space, which, on the one hand dramatizes the patriarchal deployment of sex and violence (be it gendered, sexualized, emotional, physical or other) as constitutive mechanisms for the relational subject, while on the other foregrounding the subject's own collusion in the discourses that generate the structures that both constitute and oppress it.

Nevertheless, if *Alps'* rhetoric is primarily ethical, this is not merely invested in the interrogation of the problematic 'ethics' of patriarchy, but crucially in the creation of an utterly intriguing aesthetic space, which conjures up the deconstructive ethics of Derrida's 'hauntology'. As Colin Davis elucidates Derrida's highly influential project:

> Hauntology supplants its near-homonym ontology, replacing the priority of being and presence with the figure of the ghost as that which is neither present nor absent, neither dead nor alive. Attending to the ghost is an ethical injunction insofar as it occupies the place of the Levinasian Other: a wholly irrecuperable intrusion in our world, which is not comprehensible within our available intellectual frameworks, but whose otherness we are responsible for preserving. (2007, p. 9)

Lanthimos's film both invokes and renegotiates the elusive figure of the Derridean specter, questioning established frameworks of intelligibility, pushing the boundaries of language and thought and, ultimately, calling on us to take responsibility for the preservation of the Other's irreducible alterity. However, this should not imply a generic categorization of *Alps* as a ghost story, for this would make a reductive reading of the film as a whole. *Alps* rather resonates with Derrida's hauntological project in the way that the ambivalent space in which the film's narrative confines the four protagonists, and particularly the one called Monte Rosa, reverberates with what Žižek describes as 'the domain between two deaths' (1995, p. 21). According to Žižek, this space pertains to the domain between an actual death and a symbolic one, the latter realized through the prescribed obsequies that assure the burial, commemoration and mourning of the dead, their inscription 'in the text of symbolic tradition' (1995, pp. 21–23). In popular culture this domain is canonically occupied by ghosts and ghost-like creatures (vampires, apparitions, etc.), whose appearance, Davis observes, 'is the sign of a disturbance in the symbolic, moral or epistemological order' (2007, p. 2). As he explains, 'recent stories of the supernatural reproduce quite faithfully the "unfinished business" model of the commerce between the living and the dead', which might involve improper funeral rites, hidden secrets that must be revealed, 'a wrong to be righted, an injustice to be made public or a wrongdoer to be apprehended' (2007, p. 3).

In Lanthimos's idiosyncratic rendition of the popular ghost story subgenre, however, such a space is not produced by the supernatural processes of resurrection or zombification but by the protagonists' simple, yet definitely unusual trade: they are hired by people who have lost one or more loved ones to substitute for the deceased for a few hours a week to help the bereaved overcome their loss. Lanthimos does not, of course, hide his intention to clearly demarcate this space as symbolic—not necessarily in psychoanalytic but at least in representational terms—through the film's unapologetic formal and thematic defiance of verisimilitude and realism. The critics, indeed, underscore *Alps*' construction of such a 'surreal' narrative space; Boyd van Hoeij wonders, 'there is not one scene in which a mourner scoffs at the idea of someone replacing a loved one', while BFI London Film Festival 2011 critic John Bleasdale points out:

> There are some very obvious holes in the concept (no one seems to have heard of the Himalayas) but Lanthimos' *Alps*—like *Dogtooth*—is a similarly surreal, black-as-lung-cancer comedy. [...] In *Alps*, that external reality seems to have been infected by the madness. Despite the ragtag amateurish nature of this group of misfits, there are few if any voices of dissent, and their services seem to be in great demand. No one phones the police. (2011)

Clearly, much as happens in *Dogtooth*, *Alps'* spatiotemporal organization demands from the audience that they renegotiate their expectations of conventional cinematic illusionism achieved through verisimilitude and characterization. The traditional cinematic contract is rather brought to the fore and exposed precisely as such. In this way, in the film's magnificent amalgamation of content and form both the filmic and the broader social spaces are revealed as equally contractual.

Indeed, Alps' first deal is evocatively framed by Lanthimos in a way that highlights the conspiratorial workings of the contract that effectively establishes the realm of the social. Not long after Mont Blanc announces the group's name, he invites a client, a middle-aged man, into an office in the gymnasium. At the beginning of this scene, Lanthimos suggestively places the camera outside the office, thus offering only a limited view of the room. The shot is nothing short of a split-frame: in the left half, tightly and doubly framed by the office's door, the two men discuss the details of the 'contract'; in the right half, the yellow wall that separates the office from the rest of the gymnasium catachrestically occupies most of the frame, leaving only a narrow view of the gymnasium's arena on the right, through which we can discern the gymnast and the coach as they carry on with their training session (Fig. 6.2). In the following shots, namely two medium shots of Mont Blanc and the client respectively, the focus is directed to the elusive exchange of information about the appearance, habits and interests of a former captain of the Greek National Navy, who recently died of heart failure and who, as we are informed, has been a close friend of the client for over twenty years.

Fig. 6.2   In the margin, yet still within the contours of the social

Lanthimos then cuts to a wide shot of the office that places the client in the right corner of the frame as he sits alone in the room in anticipation; a view of the gymnast playing with her clubs in the background, offered through the office's interior windows, is the only evidence of movement in this unbearable interval of stillness and anticipation that echoes the audience's affective response to Lanthimos's painstaking and piecemeal unfolding of the film's central concept (which is yet to be revealed). Mont Blanc returns to the office with Mattenhof (the nickname that the coach has chosen). The client takes the captain's hat from his bag and places it on Mattenhof's head only to discover that it does not fit. Mont Blanc reassures the client that he does not have to worry, as they will make the necessary alterations so that the hat fits and also asks him to try and find his deceased friend's glasses so that Mattenhof's appearance looks as 'truthful' as possible. The client then goes and puts his arm around Mattenhof as if they were going to pose for a photograph. The scene underscores the essentially consensual and effectively contractual nature of Alps' operation, while also introducing it as the effect of a meticulous, strictly structured, well-planned and highly stylized labor. Alps are shown operating within a space which, though visibly pushed to the margins and/or in the shadow of the public sphere, is yet intrinsically demarcated by the very contours of the social, seriously affecting if not ultimately constituting it.

In effect, if *Attenberg* stages the human body's failure or resistance to delimit itself within the strict and asphyxiating contours of the social space or, as framed in phenomenological terms in the previous chapter, its failure or resistance to 'follow the lines' drawn by the 'skin of the social', *Alps* stages the body's passionate attachments to the skin of the social, its journey across the discursive landscape of its intentional or unintentional meanderings as it assumes or discards roles and identities, as it is eventually consumed and discarded by that very space it longs to inhabit. Lanthimos tells Simon Abrams with regard to his film, 'In our everyday lives, we inhabit different parts, depending on who we are and where we are and who we're speaking to and what we want to achieve' (Abrams, 2012). As the story develops the audience come to realize that the focus of the film is, indeed, not the bereaved people, their experiences of loss and the act of mourning, but the Alps themselves, the actors and the act of substituting, of performing different roles and identities, as well as how one manages these identities, or rather how one is eventually subsumed and dissolved within them.

Lanthimos's camera gradually focuses particularly on one of the Alps actors, that is the nurse, arguably the most eccentric and essentially defiant. Suggestively dubbed Monte Rosa, that is the second highest mountain of the Alps, the nurse's habitual crossings of the thin line between 'reality' and performance eventually unearth something extraordinary. As critic Landon Palmer puts it: 'In the end, *Alps* is not the ensemble piece it seems to be at first, but a portrait of a woman who lives entirely without identity' (2012); indeed, a ghost. Obliterating any sense of an identity of her own, Monte Rosa offers her body as a receptacle for various spectral subjects to inhabit both in her private and professional life, thus ironically bringing to the surface the body's own ghostly desire to surrender to the deceptive lures of identity.

Early in the film, a tracking shot follows Monte Rosa, as she walks towards a rather grubby beach, wearing a swimsuit and holding a beach towel. The scenery that opens around her retains nothing of the canonical representations of exotic and idyllic sunny and sandy Greek beaches, familiar to a foreign audience from mainstream cinema, adverts and postcards. On the contrary, an unflattering image of the Greek seaside is augmented here by the film's palette of bleak and cold colors and paired with an annoying soundtrack that foregrounds the loud noise made by the strong wind and the furious waves. Monte Rosa approaches a man sitting on a bench on the beach, gives him her keys and towel and rushes to the sea. The film cuts to a long shot of her trying to balance her body against the violent sea waves, while another cut takes us above the man's shoulder as he is watching her. Monte Rosa turns around and to the audience's surprise the two start speaking in English despite their really thick and clearly recognizable Greek accents. 'It's wonderful!' says Monte Rosa and the man asks her, 'Is it cold?' 'No, not at all!' she replies despite her visible shivering. He then asks her to come out but she begs him to let her stay a little bit longer. The film then cuts to another over-the-shoulder shot from behind the man as he watches Monte Rosa coming out of the sea; the excessive use of shallow-focus lensing once more dominates the visuals as Lanthimos does not hesitate to push the man's body to the left edge leaving the larger rest of the frame out of focus (Fig. 6.3). The film lingers on this shot long enough to irritate our vision and blur our sense of reality as Monte Rosa's body emerges slowly from the sea as if it were an apparition: not another Aphrodite, however, but more of a dark ghost approaching menacingly.

Fig. 6.3   Emerging from the sea like a ghost approaching menacingly

A few minutes later in the film, Monte Rosa accompanies her father to a ball. The scene begins with a wide shot of the dance floor, where mostly elderly couples engage in passionate salsa dancing with elaborate turns and spins before a rather indifferent stationary camera. The salsa tune is followed by a slow dance song and only then does Monte Rosa's father take the hand of an old lady and accompany her to the dance floor. The elderly couple are visibly non-matching; the lady is much taller and bigger than the nurse's father, while their moves lack any sense of passion or elegance. A cut to a medium two-shot of the dancing couple only testifies to the performative character of dance as a socially invested corporeal act, for the couple's mechanical dance moves are matched with an equally mechanical exchange of smiles. The film then cuts to a zoom shot of Monte Rosa's face as she watches her father dancing. But the camera's zooming in fails to live up to the conventional function of this long-favored cinematic technique as a psychographic penetration into the character's deeper thoughts and emotions, for it is contained by an unequivocally deadpan face.

In the next scene Monte Rosa and her father sit in her car and discuss the ball. Monte Rosa compliments her father and his partner on their dancing skills and the father expresses his sympathy for the old lady. In the last shot of the scene, the camera is placed outside the car window, framing the old man in the foreground in sharp focus while leaving Monte Rosa in the background and out of focus; the effect created by this composition is captivating as the reflection from the lights outside on the car windows in combination with the shallow depth of field visually transform Monte Rosa into a form of specter (Fig. 6.4).

Fig. 6.4   Ghost among ghosts

Ironically, her father's final words in the scene reveal, indeed, a familial space constantly haunted by ghosts: 'We used to dance with your mother a lot, too. However, not Latin; she hated Latin.' Nick Pinkerton observes:

> She plays substitute both privately and professionally, for Mont Rouge returns from work to care—like a doting wife—for her elderly widower father (Stavros Psyllakis), whose sole social outlet is trips to a senior-populated dance hall where, it's evident in one glance, ageing singles come to grab hold of a living body, so they can dance with ghosts. (2012)

Ghost among ghosts Monte Rosa emerges as yet another of the 'living dead', aligning herself with a 'path travelled by "Western civilization" in its settlement of the symbolic debt' (Žižek, 1995, p. 27), but, nevertheless, seeking to divert this path. Žižek argues, 'from Antigone's sublime features [...] through the hesitation and obsessive doubt of Hamlet [...] to the "trouble with Harry" [from Hitchcock's eponymous film]' (1995, p. 27), such a settlement is pertinent to the return of the dead as 'a sign of a disturbance in the symbolic rite, in the process of symbolization; the dead return as collectors of some unpaid symbolic debt' (1995, p. 23). The symbolic significance of the funeral rite is highlighted by Žižek in the fact that it implies 'a certain reconciliation, an acceptance of loss' (1995, p. 23). As he explains:

> symbolization as such equates to symbolic murder: when we speak about a thing, we suspend, place in parentheses, its reality. It is precisely for this reason that the funeral rite exemplifies symbolization at its purest: through

it, the dead are inscribed in the text of symbolic tradition, they are assured that, in spite of their death, they will 'continue to live' in the memory of the community. (1995, p. 23)

When something goes wrong with their obsequies they will return to settle their pending symbolic accounts; 'the return of the dead signifies that they cannot find their proper place in the text of tradition' (1995, p. 23). Of course, as noted above, in Lanthimos's 'weird' rendition of this 'fundamental fantasy of contemporary mass culture', that is the 'fantasy of the return of the living dead' (1995, p. 23), the return of the dead people occurs not quite in spectral form but via substitute bodies; ironically, it is the living that long to revive the dead through an unapologetically bizarre 'imitation of life'. Hired by the bereaved under contractual terms, these substitute bodies subject themselves to a largely makeshift, almost parodic stylization (attempted through costume, gestural and linguistic appropriations) that offers them as rather failed avatars of the deceased loved ones. In this way, in *Alps* the 'return of the dead' not only reverses the canonical fantasy, but—precisely with such a replacement of the dead body with a substitute one, which is stylized accordingly and almost ritualistically—it also renders the chasm between the actual and the symbolic death permanently insurmountable, with significant ramifications at the level of the symbolic. For if the dead body is so easily replaced by a substitute one that has the unequivocal authority to suspend life at the symbolic level (indeed, Alps' operation is never questioned or even scorned), then such a symbolic revitalization effectuates both corporeal disposability and a fetishization of the process of symbolization itself. *Alps'* unapologetic showcasing of the (dead) body's replaceability and, by extension, disposability on the one hand, and the (substitute) body's incessant succession of resubjectivations on the other, ultimately add up to an assertive disenfranchisement of the signifier from the signified (namely, the body from its identity/ies). In this sense, and with the camera fixating on the substitute body and the way—time and again—it traverses the injurious and violent pathways of resubjectivation, Lanthimos's film ultimately becomes an incisive aesthetic study of the way bodies become dispossessed in order to be finally constituted as subjects.

My use of the concept of 'dispossession' here reverberates with Judith Butler and Athena Athanasiou's contextualization of the term in *Dispossession: The Performative in the Political* (2013). At the beginning of the book, Athanasiou explicates the double sense of the term. On the one hand, Athanasiou argues, dispossession 'signifies an inaugural submission of the subject-to-be to norms of intelligibility', thus resonating with 'the psychic foreclosures that determine which "passionate attachments" are possible and plausible for "one" to become a subject' (2013, p. 1). 'In this sense,' she continues:

> dispossession encompasses the constituted, preemptive losses that condition one's being dispossessed (or letting oneself become dispossessed) by another [...]. The subject comes to 'exist' by installing within itself lost objects along with the social norms that regulate the subject's disposition to the address of the other. (2013, p. 1)

On the other hand, dispossession also involves processes and ideologies in whose name 'persons are disowned and abjected by normative and normalizing powers that define cultural intelligibility and that regulate the distribution of vulnerability' (2013, p. 2). Such processes pertain to histories of enslavement, poverty, and subjection to violence, or more recently to the operations of neoliberal governmentality and precaritization. Athanasiou observes that in both senses dispossession 'involves the subject's relation to norms, its mode of becoming by means of assuming and resignifying injurious interpellations and impossible passions' (2013, p. 2). However, whereas in the first sense dispossession appears as necessary for the social survival of the subject precisely 'as "a heteronomic condition for autonomy" through the injurious yet enabling fundamental dependency and relationality', in the second sense, it is clearly a condition 'painfully imposed by the normative and normalizing violence that determines the terms of subjectivity, survival, and livability' (2013, p. 2).

Butler builds on Athanasiou's argument by suggesting that dispossession is what effectively 'establishes the self as social' and argues that 'we can only be dispossessed because we are already dispossessed' (2013, pp. 4–5). As she explains, much of Greek tragedy relied precisely on interrogating the notion of the bounded and deliberate individual, one who is 'self-propelling and self-driven', and exposing how humans are moved by various forces (or passions) 'that precede and exceed our deliberate and bounded selfhood' (2013, p. 4). Hence, dispossession reveals the self as interdependent, 'driven by passions it cannot fully consciously ground or know' and 'dependent on environments and others who sustain and even motivate the life of the self itself' (2013, p. 4).

Although Butler points out that it is this interdependency that 'establishes our vulnerability to social forms of deprivation', Athanasiou warns that a conflation of '"being dispossessed" (as a primordial disposition to relationality [...])' and '"becoming dispossessed" (as an ensuing, derivative condition of enforced deprivation [...])' might risk a legitimization of 'an abdication of political responsibility for social forms of deprivation and dispossession' (2013, p. 5). What she suggests we should rather ask is how those foreclosures that structure our 'passionate attachments', such as the violent foreclosures of gender and sexuality, relate to various 'modalities of exposure to violence and recourse to rights' (2013, p. 6). For dispossession, Athanasiou argues, is a ceaseless procedure, mapped onto particular bodies-in-place, 'through normative matrices but also through situated practices of raciality, gender, sexuality, intimacy, able-bodiedness, economy, and citizenship', through which a variety of dispossessed subjectivities are produced and rendered either 'subhuman, or all-too-human' (2013, p. 18). Those subjectivities, she explains, are then bound 'within calculable self-same identities' and put 'in their proper place', which more often than not, and precisely owing to the violence that is inherent in their 'improper, expropriated and dispossessed' status, is one of 'perennial occupation as non-being and non-having' (2013, p. 19). The lives of these people and groups of people whose 'proper place is non-being' are described by precarity, that is, the condition in which they become 'differentially exposed to injury, violence, poverty, indebtedness, and death' (2013, p. 19). Precarity, Athanasiou explains, 'is indeed related to socially assigned disposability [...] as well as to various modalities of valuelessness' (such as racism, fascism, homophobia, abandonment, impoverishment, etc.) (2013, p. 19). Interestingly, Athanasiou invokes here Achille Mbembe's association between sovereignty and exposure to death under the term 'necropolitics', which pertains to 'a global modality of power that subjects populations to conditions that ascribe them the status of living dead' (2013, p. 20). As such, necropolitics ultimately determines whose lives matter and should be protected, and who can be disposed of, wasted—in other words, who can be deprived of the conditions for life and the 'human' itself (2013, p. 20).

For the 'place' of the 'human' is always already reserved for a fantasmatic 'self-contained, proper(tied), liberal subject', which is ironically formed and maintained on the condition of a set of dispossessions that simultaneously produce the abject and the disavowed. And here precisely lies the question of recognition. Athanasiou defines recognition as 'an apparatus that discursively produces subjects as human (or inhuman, subhuman, less than human) by normative and disciplinary terms such as those of gender, sexuality, race, and class' (2013, p. 90). Butler points out that these 'established norms of recognition bear material consequences as much for those who are intensely interpellated as for those who are partially interpellated or not interpellated at all', for 'the differential distribution of norms of recognition directly implies the differential allocation of precarity' (2013, p. 89). In other words, for those who count as human or as subjects of rights under the hegemonic norms 'precarity can be minimized through inclusion within a scheme of recognition' that automatically renders their lives as valuable and, thus, grievable (2013, p. 89). On the other hand, however, those norms simultaneously produce criminalizing and pathologizing regimes; schemes which, based on legal violence, reserve the right to kill or to let die. This happens when, as Butler astutely puts it, 'norms of recognition imperil the living, inducing precarity as an effect' (2013, p. 89). Yet even more frightening is the fact that, as Athanasiou poignantly adds, '[w]hen a life that does not figure as normatively human is violated, this violation remains unrecognized, misrecognized, or recognized in an injurious way, through terms that enable derealizing violence' (2013, p. 90).

Fascinatingly, Butler and Athanasiou's queer formulation of dispossession as the fundamental process through which the subject is formed and the self established as social reverberates with the extraordinary yet disconcerting narrative trajectory of Monte Rosa as she appropriates different roles and identities in both her private and professional life, as she strives to belong, to matter, to signify. In addition, as I argue below, the juxtaposition between the gymnast's submissive conduct and Monte Rosa's ultimately defiant conduct opens up a space to reflect on what Butler and Athanasiou frame, after Levinas, as our existential vulnerability to injury and loss and the way this vulnerability can be exploited by hegemonic schemes and norms of recognition to render the lives and bodies that do not conform precarious and even valueless—Alps itself emerging as such an authoritarian space.

First, the film underscores interdependency as an intrinsic quality of the social space by staging the way the primary form of dispossession reveals the self as dependent on 'environments and others who sustain and even motivate the life of the self itself', as Butler argues. This is most clearly achieved with one of the film's major plotlines, namely the case of the substitution of the tennis player. Early on in the film we see Monte Rosa investing in the possibility of taking up the dying girl's place, while the gymnast's interest in this particular case is also highlighted. However, Monte Rosa's position as a nurse at the hospital where the girl is admitted secures privileged access for her to both the girl and her parents. At first, we witness Monte Rosa's efforts to elicit information about the tennis player's interests and habits by spending time with her in her hospital room. At the same time, we see her attempting to build a close relationship with the girl's parents by offering them solace or hope. When the girl eventually dies Monte Rosa conceals this information from Mont Blanc and puts her plan into effect. She undertakes the gruesome task of informing the parents about their daughter's death before she, however, rushes to grasp the opportunity to offer her odd services to them. The scene in question begins with a long shot that shows the two parents sitting in the hospital's waiting area with their heads bowed, while Monte Rosa sits next to them and looks out of the window. The film cuts to a shot that frames Monte Rosa in the middle and in focus, while leaving the bereaved decapitated and out of focus on the left half of the frame. Monte Rosa's almost parodic mood swings suggestively expose the performative nature of every social interaction. At the beginning of the scene, she seems devastated and her consoling words are often interrupted by bursts of tears or silence. After a while, and as a true professional, she stands up and announces her offer to them with a deadpan face and a steady, assertive voice:

MONTE ROSA   And now I have something very pleasant to tell you. I can replace her if you want me to. Your sorrow will be mitigated and, after a short while, will completely vanish. Two or three two-hour visits a week are enough.... The end could signal a new, better beginning.... It's up to you.... You won't be charged for the first four visits.

Clearly, loss and grief are not the matter at issue here; the faces of the bereaved are conspicuously excluded from view, their anguish has no place in Lanthimos's twisted universe. What is rather highlighted is Monte Rosa's agonized efforts to claim the girl's place and gain access to a familial space, which she has herself presumably been deprived of. The schematic staging of the familiar familial positioning in contractual terms exposes the inessential and contingent character of kinship relations, while, at the same time, and significantly through Monte Rosa's persistent and assertive actions, highlighting the familial space as an indispensable environment, arguably one of the fundamental schemes of intelligibility that the (familial) self necessitates so that its life can, indeed, be 'sustained and motivated' (Butler and Athanasiou, 2013, p. 4).

As the narrative unfolds, the film goes on to stage dispossession as precisely the process which fixes and stylizes the body through a series of foreclosures that occur in the form of performative acts, which in turn effect subjectivation, indeed, the subject's entrance into established regimes of recognition. Dispossession as such a process is arguably most evidently dramatized in Monte Rosa's first visit to the tennis player's parents' house. The scene begins with an extreme close-up of Monte Rosa eating yogurt. We hear the mother saying off-screen, 'Your hair should always be tied up.... And these are not tennis shoes.' The film cuts to a shallow-focus two-shot that frames Monte Rosa in the foreground and the father out of focus in the background, both sitting in the living room. The mother is still off-screen but her voice continues to dominate the filmic space: 'What shoe size are you?' '38–39. It depends', replies Monte Rosa. A moment of awkward silence follows as Monte Rosa and the father wait for the mother to bring the deceased's shoes. The shoes arrive and Monte Rosa gladly tries them on and proudly announces: 'Unbelievable! They fit perfectly! Unbelievable!' The mother also brings the dead girl's perfume; Lanthimos once more exercises his flair for black humor, as it is none other than Calvin Klein's 'Eternity'. 'Her boyfriend bought it for her. You should meet him at some point', the mother says. The film cuts to a wide shot, which shows the provisional familial set-up re-entering the living room. Monte Rosa is now shown dressed head to toe in sportswear, her hair tied up and holding a tennis racket, while the mother is carrying a jar of water, which she puts on the coffee table in front of Monte Rosa. The film cuts to a close-up of the latter as she begins her performance: 'I was sure I would crush her. Her backhand was terrible and I knew from the start that she had no hope.' She then looks at the couple waiting for their response. 'Would you like some water?' asks the father. 'No dad, thank you', she replies. 'Usually, after a match you drink loads of water.' 'Ok, thank you.' The mother then gives her a glass of water, which she hastily chugs down; the tennis player's wristband (which was conspicuously showcased at the beginning of the film, lying on the bedside table next to the injured young girl at the hospital) is now foregrounded on Monte Rosa's hand. The film cuts to yet another shallow-focus wide shot, which keeps Monte Rosa in focus on the left margin of the frame while the shadows of her new 'parents' are in the blurred background, which covers more than two-thirds of the screen. The father orders, 'Bite your fingernails a bit.' Monte Rosa obeys. 'Enough', he then says and there follows another moment of awkward silence, as the film cuts to a three-shot that depicts the parents staring at their makeshift offspring.

Clearly, *Alps* verges on the bizarre and the surreal in its effort to unearth performativity as inherent within the trivial and the quotidian. The film, arguably, abuses the established schemes of cinematic intelligibility—namely, verisimilitude and realism, in particular—in order to expose how we are always already dispossessed by our body's compulsory stylization through particular gestures and costume. For such a process will secure a place for our body within recognizable schemes of intelligibility (a 'proper' gender, a 'proper' familial positioning and so on) and, hence, ultimately elevate us into the status of a 'self', one whose life matters and is valuable and grievable. The film arguably stages the various foreclosures that our body undergoes on its way towards subjectivation through the incessant re-stylization (or resubjectivation) of Monte Rosa's body. For much as she is made to bite her fingernails in order to be recognized as a daughter, she is equally forced to dive into cold waves and, suggestively, speak a language that is not her native one, in order to claim a place as a wife.

Indeed, much as Monte Rosa rehearses the linguistic and corporeal lines prescribed by her various 'roles', the film rehearses its relentless appetite to expose the social space, be it familial, spousal, etc., as an arena within which a set of normative, disciplinary and, often contradictory terms strive to bind the ever performing body within the fictional yet formative contours of identity. Sex emerges as a quintessential such term. In Monte Rosa's next appointment with the English-speaking man we are invited to his lighting store, where the two seem to rehearse a fight in a wide shot that frames them centrally facing each other and looking rather bored. When the rehearsal ends the man goes and locks the door of the store. Lanthimos cuts to another shallow-focus wide shot that foregrounds Monte Rosa, while pushing the bereaved to the frame's margins. The two perform the fight as prescribed—Monte Rosa even breaks a table lamp at the end of the fight, which the man has deliberately placed on the counter next to her for that purpose. Performativity is underlined in red ink. The staged fight resolves into an embrace. The camera then follows the pair as they descend the stairs to the store's basement. The man gets undressed. Monte Rosa for a moment hesitates and says in Greek: 'If Mont Blanc finds out we will have a problem. It could mean the end of our collaboration.' 'He won't find out. At least not from me', replies the man also in Greek and continues by giving her instructions on how to act during their sexual intercourse. He finally asks her to keep mostly silent and only at some point say in English 'Please, please don't stop! It feels like heaven!' Monte Rosa then lies on the sofa and the man starts performing cunnilingus on her. After a while Monte Rosa says, 'Please, please don't you stop! It feels like paradise!' The man stops and corrects her, 'Heaven.' Monte Rosa cannot help laughing, but makes an effort to concentrate and deliver the line properly. 'Please, don't you stop, it feels like heaven', she says in one breath and bursts into laughter. The film then cuts to a wide-angle shot that shows the couple on the sofa. Monte Rosa looks more relaxed in this shot and repeats the line without laughing this time. Indeed, she sounds as if she really means it.

Simulating body movements, vocal sounds and verbal indications that are typically associated with sexual pleasure is not something new, of course, in the history of cinema. Time and again, comedies, dramas and even thrillers feature female characters, in particular, who, voluntarily or not, perform such simulations in order to please their sexual partner or as part of a broader scheme of deceit. What happens in *Alps*, however, is a rather twisted version of the typical 'orgasm faking', which, much as in *Dogtooth* and *Attenberg*, not only results in a parody of mainstream cinematic representations of sex, but, most importantly, exposes the discursive nature of sex and offers it as yet another mechanism for the production of the (feminine, heterosexual, spousal) self. However, the final shot of the scene signals a turning point in the film, which resonates powerfully with the operations of identity formation. Indeed, as this shot reveals, the more Monte Rosa indulges in this morbid role-playing the more she eventually plunges into the fiction of identity, ultimately blurring the boundaries between impersonation and identification, between performance and performativity; for, as Butler taught us in *Gender Trouble*, performativity is nothing else than the repetition of acts 'that congeal over time to produce the appearance of substance, of a natural sort of being' (2010 [1990], p. 30).

However, two decades later Butler will elucidate that, although fiction, identity is not an illusion. In her own words, identity 'is meant to suggest a certain form of idealization that is historically effective. It is not precisely a "lie" or an "illusion"; it is a materialized form of an ideal that acquires historical efficacy' (2013, pp. 97–98). And precisely as a materialized form, identity is catachrestically deployed by normative and normalizing structures to produce criminalizing and pathologizing regimes that regulate the distribution of precarity. Ironically, the more Monte Rosa immerses herself in the dead personas she is expected to perform, the closer she gets to her own social death, and, ultimately, to becoming a precarious and disposable body. For, as Žižek would argue, she no longer acts as a symbolic agent, indeed an agent of the process of symbolization, which would retain the memory of the deceased at a symbolic level. She rather exhibits a forceful will to conceal the fictitious nature of this symbolization, stripping herself of an identity of her own and ultimately condemning herself to a perennial meandering 'between two deaths' as yet another Antigone. Žižek contends with regard to Antigone:

> the apparitions that emerge in the domain 'between two deaths' address to us some unconditional demand, and it is for this reason that they incarnate pure drive without desire. Let us begin with Antigone who, according to Lacan, irradiates a sublime beauty from the very moment she enters the domain between two deaths, between her symbolic and actual death. What characterizes her inmost posture is precisely her insistence on a certain unconditional demand on which she is not prepared to give way: a proper burial for her brother. (1995, pp. 21–22)

Clearly, Monte Rosa's demand is not a proper burial for the deceased (which might have happened anyway, but is not a concern of the film) but, on the contrary, a perpetual deferral of their symbolic death through the permanent substitution of their bodies with her own. Lanthimos gradually foregrounds Monte Rosa's actions as exactly the effect of such an unconditional demand, as she increasingly violates the contractual terms of her status as a symbolic agent. Indeed, we have already witnessed her consenting to have sex with the lighting retailer, despite explicitly acknowledging that this exceeds her agreed duties. In a later sequence we see her in the tennis player's bedroom, spending time with the latter's boyfriend under the unrelenting gaze of the parents, but then taking the boy to her own home and having sex with him.

Nevertheless, much as Antigone's unconditional demand renders her a member of the 'living dead', for her violation of Creon's law sentences her to expulsion outside the domain of the human, indeed to become a precarious subject, subjected to (legal) violence, Monte Rosa's violation of her position as an agent of the Symbolic, similarly renders her as disposable, sentenced to valuelessness, precarity and, hence, subjected to violence and exclusion. On her next visit to the tennis player's house the gymnast opens the door to her, dressed as the deceased girl. 'Who is it my love?' we hear the mother asking. 'A classmate', replies the gymnast and turning to Monte Rosa she recites what sounds like a rehearsed line, 'Unfortunately, I can't join you for a walk because I have to study and then attend a very important tennis tournament. See you tomorrow at school.' The next scene takes us to the gymnasium where Monte Rosa is sitting waiting for Mont Blanc. Mont Blanc comes in and stands before her holding one of the gymnast's clubs. After a calm yet utterly mordant monologue, which only exacerbates the uncomfortable atmosphere of the confrontation between the defiant employee and the authoritative employer, Mont Blanc raises the club and hits Monte Rosa hard, knocking her to the floor. Monte Rosa turns to the camera revealing her bleeding head, while on the soundtrack Mont Blanc's imposing voice announces her expulsion from the Alps.

From then on, Monte Rosa emerges as, indeed, 'an incarnation of pure drive', to use Žižek's words, as Lanthimos's camera follows her desperate efforts to pursue her unconditional demand to take up the place of the deceased tennis player as well as that of her own mother, violating the 'sanctity' of the familial space in both literal and symbolic terms. After taking care of her wound at the hospital we see her at home preparing a drink for her father. As she hands him over the glass she asks him, 'Who was mum's favorite actor?'—a typical question that the Alps used to ask about the deceased loved ones. Her subversive—if not perverse—intentions are by now clear. 'Robert Redford', says the father. She then continues, 'Mine too.... Favorite singer?', not long before she starts caressing her father's legs, slowly reaching out to his penis. The old man instantly slaps her on the face. The film cuts to a tracking shot, which follows her to the dance hall, where she finds her 'competitor', namely her father's dancing partner, dancing with another man. She pushes the man away and starts dancing insanely with the woman, finally throwing her to the floor.

The film then cuts to a low-key shallow-focus shot from behind Monte Rosa, which, reminiscent of horror films, metamorphoses her into a ghost, indeed, a member of the living dead returning to collect 'some kind of symbolic debt'; ironically, her own symbolic death. The camera follows her as she goes to the tennis player's house and rings the doorbell. Nobody answers the door, but Monte Rosa, fixated on her demand and determined to penetrate the quintessential familial space, namely the home, goes to the back of the house, breaks the large glass door with a garden chair and enters through the jagged hole. The house's alarm starts ringing frantically but Monte Rosa looks disturbingly unruffled.

Instead she walks steadily to the dead girl's bedroom, takes her shoes off and lies on the bed. She suddenly opens the bedside table's drawer, finds 'Eternity', sprays some of the perfume on her neck and then gets under the sheets. The alarm is switched off. The father enters the bedroom, pulls her out of the bed and drags her up the stairs and to the house's exit, as she manically recites the scripted lines of her macabre role all the while. As a pure incarnation of the drive, she seems relentless in pursuing her unconditional demand and quickly runs back to the broken glass door, only to be confronted by closing electric shutters. Lanthimos's medium shot frames her, face to face with the shutters, as she insists despite being visibly exhausted and puffing: 'Dad, dad can you open please? I was very good today. I won 4-2.' In the last shot of Monte Rosa's final and most tragic scene, which is also the film's penultimate scene, Lanthimos places the camera at a distance from her. Aurally dominated by an embarrassing mixture of silence, the ambient wind and Monte Rosa's gasps, this long shot augments the feeling of abandonment, exclusion and valuelessness, and haunts the viewer even after the end of the film (Fig. 6.5). Clearly, Monte Rosa violates the contractual terms of her symbolic position as well as of her quintessential structural kin position, as the last scene with her father reveals, thus exposing herself to criminalizing and pathologizing regimes—Alps itself essentially representing one of them—that violently exclude her from the schemes of recognition that would minimize precarity and secure a life for her, valuable and grievable. As another Antigone, stripped of any sense of identity, excluded from the realm of the social and

Fig. 6.5 Stripped off any sense of identity, excluded from the realm of the social

the familial, rendered valueless and disposable, Monte Rosa is perennially condemned to inhabit the threshold between life and death, a space of visible invisibility, of a haunting spectrality.

With that of Monte Rosa, the film juxtaposes the case of the gymnast, whose own trajectory, although mostly pushed to the margins of the frame or into the blurred background—with the notable exception of the prologue and epilogue of the film—emerges as significant precisely because it follows the exact opposite direction from Monte Rosa's. Arguably, the gymnast represents a completely different way in which the individual is forced into identity through performativity; one that seems to accept the provisional terms of its positioning as a recognizable subject, yet ultimately colludes in the discourses that bring into effect the normative and normalizing relational apparatuses. Throughout the film, the gymnast is witnessed either practicing her highly disciplined rhythmic gymnastics, being punished for failing to perform her various roles as prescribed, or even engaging in acts of self-inflicted violence. The contrast between the two women is highlighted in the scene where Monte Rosa goes to the gymnasium to falsely inform Mont Blanc about the tennis player's supposed recovery. At the beginning of the scene, the camera follows Monte Rosa as she enters the gymnasium and crosses the main hall. In the background of the frame of this shot the gymnast is suggestively featured hanging from the ceiling upside down and reciting the same lines over and over again. Monte Rosa finds Mont Blanc sitting next to Mattenhof—both assiduously observing the gymnast's punishment—and announces the 'bad news' to them. Despite expressing discontent with the young girl's recovery, Mont Blanc never takes his eyes off the gymnast, ordering her to keep repeating her lines. He then gives Monte Rosa and Mattenhof their pay cheques but keeps the gymnast's envelope for himself, telling her in his usual calm yet stiff tone: 'You won't get paid this month. I'll keep the money. Keep repeating. And clearer!' Monte Rosa asks what happened and Mattenhof explains that she has failed to perform as prescribed for the second time. Indeed, about 10 minutes earlier in the film, we witnessed the gymnast crying in the locker rooms, confessing to Mattenhof that she has failed to perform her lines correctly in her role as the granddaughter of an old man. The camera lingers on the gymnast's face in close-up as she looks nervously at Mattenhof, begging him to hide the incident from Mont Blanc as this might cost her the tennis player position. She even takes her t-shirt off and starts performing elaborate gymnastic postures half-naked while hailing her coach in a nonetheless mechanical deadpan manner: 'You are the king of coaches! You are the best ... (cough) ... You are the best coach in the world!' Interestingly, the film refrains from including Mattenhof in any of the scene's frames. Instead, we only hear him at the end of the scene admitting to the desperate gymnast: 'I'm sorry. I have to tell him!'

Although no physical violence is directly inflicted upon the gymnast by any of the members of the makeshift power system of Alps in any of the scenes mentioned above, her paradigm, however, highlights in the most vivid colors how control is always already a corporeal issue. The scenes portray in the most vigorous manner the highly authoritarian and violently oppressive nature of Alps as a hierarchical system that relies heavily on a patriarchal delineation of power relations, calling particular attention to the way the body is meticulously regulated, fixed, observed, punished, or to put it simply, controlled by such systems. This regimentation of the body through normative and normalizing apparatuses is, after all, the theme that underlies the film's proliferation of striking images of corporeal discipline and prescribed, regulated human movement, showcased in the scenes where the gymnast is training or where the elderly perform their uniform dancing moves. What is, nonetheless, also made poignant by these images is the fact that such corporeal regimentation is ultimately a necessary condition for the self's social survival.

In addition, it is remarkable how all these scenes that depict processes or instances of corporeal regimentation allude, especially formally, to the practice of surveillance, as indispensable for the production and perpetuation of normalizing regimes. Filmed in long wide-angle shots and consistently possessed by a visible or invisible gaze (the gaze of Monte Rosa at the dancing old people, but most poignantly the gazes of Mattenhof and Mont Blanc at the gymnast), these scenes evoke the panoptical, disciplinary mechanism of observation. One might recall here Foucault's prominent invocation of the Panopticon in his book *Discipline and Punish* (1991), whose efficiency, he claims, is maximized by way of individualizing the subjects under control and placing them in a state of constant visibility. Indeed, in *Alps*, surveillance, particularly as it is practiced at the expense of the female members of the group, emerges as a policing and punitive mechanism that, clearly, constitutes them as subjects who must be kept under control and in a state of constant visibility. The most forceful portrayal of this practice is offered in the scene where Monte Rosa is surveilled and followed by Mont Blanc, after he becomes suspicious of her unusual behavior. Strongly reminiscent of film-noir aesthetics (low-key lighting, shots through the car's rear-view mirror that foreground the observer's gaze, fragmented views of the car being followed through the moving windshield wipers), the scene shows Mont Blanc following the defiant member of Alps to the tennis player's house only to discover her duplicitous covert operation. The outcome of Mont Blanc's patrol, namely Monte Rosa's physical punishment and expulsion from the group, certainly attests to surveillance's punitive nature.

Nevertheless, Foucault also warns:

> He who is subjected to a field of visibility, and who knows it, assumes responsibility for the constraints of power; he makes them play spontaneously upon himself; he inscribes in himself the power relation in which he simultaneously plays both roles; he becomes the principle of his own subjection. (1991, pp. 202–203)

In effect, unlike the resistant and, eventually, subversive conduct of Monte Rosa, the gymnast seems to voluntarily inscribe in herself the particular power relations, becoming, indeed, 'the principle of her own subjection'. Her failed attempt to use the mechanism of seduction (yet another long-established cinematic narrative motif which is unapologetically twisted and parodied in Lanthimos's universe) as a means to distract Mattenhof from his duties as an agent of the system's rigidly disciplinary mechanisms, only verifies her function in the film as an instance of the individual's own collusion in the discourses that underpin the mechanisms that both constitute it as a subject and oppress it.

Hence, at the end of the film, the gymnast manages to achieve the status of what Butler frames as an 'intensely interpellated' subject, for Mont Blanc acknowledges her obedient behavior and efforts and rewards her generously. As we have seen above, it is eventually the gymnast who replaces Monte Rosa in the position of the tennis player while, at the very end of the film, she is even allowed to dance to pop, thus fulfilling the aspiration she expressed at the beginning. Interestingly, the film's final sequence belongs to the gymnast. Dressed in a lavish fuchsia leotard and sporting glossy make-up and a neat hairdo, the girl prances from one foot to another, twirling and tossing her ribbon with joy and grace high in the air to the sounds of Gershon Kingsley's classic electropop song 'Popcorn'. At the end of her number she enthusiastically hugs her coach telling him 'You are the best coach in the world!' And the film comes full circle with a beautiful close-up of the gymnast as she smiles replete with happiness.

Arguably, the tension between the two characters, namely, Monte Rosa and the gymnast, mirrors the 'tension between an avowed excess and a disavowed loss (the mark of melancholy)', which, as Butler suggests, is inextricably linked to the process of recognition (2013, p. 34). Athanasiou explains that if 'disavowed loss' refers to what gets abjected or foreclosed from the human, that which gets placed outside the boundary of the human, 'avowed excess' involves 'forms of life that are conferred recognition as human according to the established norms of recognizability, on the condition of and at the cost of conforming to these norms' (2013, p. 36). In *Alps*, Monte Rosa would clearly represent the former case, whereas the gymnast, of course, would represent the latter. Nevertheless, Athanasiou continues, even when those latter forms of life are ultimately recognized as human, this occurs by way of 'exclusionary inclusion', thus constituting them as 'superfluous', only 'slyly and conditionally interpellated in the all-too-intelligible categories of the normative human', and never referring to 'a fixed, ontological distinction' (2013, p. 36).

Indeed, the gymnast's position is safe insofar as she satisfies the conditions of her recognition as a subject of rights, a subject to be valued and protected. However, she can never vanquish the provisional and contingent character of her status; precarity can only be minimized, but never eliminated Butler reminds us, who, influenced by Levinas, understands precarity as an existential category, 'a vulnerability to injury and loss [that] can never be reversed' (2013, p. 20). A scene halfway through the film vividly resonates with Butler's words. We are once more taken to the gymnasium where the gymnast and the coach discuss the latter's latest replacement role as the late husband of a beautiful blind woman. At some point Mattenhof confesses: 'Sometimes she asks me to kiss her and I do it.' Then after a moment of brief silence he turns to the gymnast: 'What if you were blind. You wouldn't be able to do rhythmic gymnastics.' The girl gets visibly agitated. The film then cuts to a long shot of her as she strives to perform a ribbon dance blindfolded, yet to no avail. She tosses the ribbon high in the air, but fails to catch it back and then gets down to her knees looking for it in frustration (Fig. 6.6). From the staging of her precarious existence to the realization of precarity as a lived experience it will, however, take only ten minutes of cinematic time. Indeed, a bit later in the film Monte Rosa enters the gymnasium to find the gymnast again hanging from the ceiling, this time, however, as a result of a suicide attempt. Monte Rosa barely manages to save the girl only to hear from her that she attempted suicide because her coach had declared that she would

Fig. 6.6 Our irreversible vulnerability to injury and loss

never dance to pop. Clearly, realizing her perennially provisional status as a subject of rights, one that is apparently only partially interpellated within the established schemes of recognition, the gymnast comes across a fundamental existential impasse, which results in her self-sentencing to death. Even though she is eventually rescued and even allowed to dance to pop at the end of the film (ironically, in both cases after the intervention of Monte Rosa), one can never obliterate the unbearable awareness of what Butler frames as our irreversible 'vulnerability to loss and injury' that is insistently foregrounded in the above sequences, as in the rest of the film, installing the question of the ethical in the film's rhetoric. In effect, perhaps this awareness of vulnerability as precisely an existential condition is what constitutes the film's final shot as ironic, and, ultimately, just as tragic as Monte Rosa's last shot. For the gymnast's radiant smile that leads to the film's titles will never be able to compensate for all the violence and the injuries (both physical and psychological) that have been or in the future may still be ('legally') inflicted on both of the two women.

Nevertheless, unlike in *Dogtooth*, there might be scope for hope in *Alps*, at least to the extent that the film attests to Athanasiou's remark that, 'what gets produced outside the boundary of the human can "exceed" its boundaries and so maintain or trouble those boundaries from the outside' (2013, p. 36). As Athanasiou explains, this might result in a decentering of the dialectics of recognition insofar as this is predicated upon the operation of the 'norms that produce an "I" and an "other" in a relation of reflective and projective co-constitution' (2013, p. 64). For 'even though they might be occasionally "recognized" or "tolerated" by formal liberal reason', those 'who remain abjected by hegemonic racial, gender, and sexual norms' could engage in acts of self-recognition and self-determination that might put at risk the established apparatus of recognition (2013, p. 64.). Butler, however, warns that even in this case of such 'exceptional self-poietics', as Athanasiou names it, which aim at destabilizing the regulatory ideals that govern intelligibility, one should not forget that the point is 'not to institute new forms of intelligibility that become the basis of self-recognition,' nor 'to celebrate unintelligibility as its own goal' (2013, p. 68). For despite the fact that recognition designates our fundamental dependence upon terms that we never chose in order to emerge as intelligible beings, this does not mean that we do not need recognition. That would, indeed, risk enlisting ourselves in an impossible mission 'of self-making or self-poiesis that involves risking intelligibility, posing a problem of cultural translation and living in a critical relation to the norms of the intelligible' (2013, p. 67). And it is an impossible mission because, as Butler points out, 'we do not make ourselves as "heroic individuals" but only as social creatures' (2013, p. 67).

Athanasiou, of course, already acknowledges that, when she previously posits that the question of self-identity 'carries the genealogical burden of a metaphysics of presence' (2013, p. 17). Taking her cue from Derrida's hauntological project, Athanasiou explains that the only way to be present to one another is by 'being dispossessed by the other's presence and by our own presence to the other' for 'being present to one another takes place at the limits of one's own self-sufficiency and self-knowability, in the wake of the endless finitude of the human' (2013, p. 17). This can only happen through taking over or even giving away 'the norms through which we are established as selves and others' (2013, pp. 17–18). Hence, presence is 'haunted by its spectral absences', where 'the specter would refer [...] to the insistent and insinuating anti-ontological remains, foreclosed and yet surviving, from the normative demarcation of the self-present human' (2013, p. 16). However, it is important to highlight here that Derridean hauntology does not conjure away corporeality. In Derrida's own words, 'For there is no ghost, there is never any becoming specter of the spirit without at least the appearance of flesh, in a space of invisible visibility like the disappearing of an apparition. For the ghost, there must be a return to the body, but to a body that is more abstract than ever' (1994, p. 126). Echoing Derrida, Athanasiou contends, 'In my understanding, the specter involves a return to some sort of bodily presence, be it displaced, dismembered, enclosed, or foreclosed' (2013, p. 17).

This chapter has suggested that Lanthimos's film spectacularly projects this kind of Derridean spectral return to 'some sort of bodily presence' both through its 'weird' narrative and through its idiosyncratic form. The film constitutes an outrageous repository of shallow-focus wide shots that self-consciously sever the field of cinematic visibility (and intelligibility), insistently keeping Monte Rosa's silhouette out of focus, transforming it into a breathing shadow, an abstract body, indeed a ghost. At the level of the narrative, through her passionate attachments to impossible ideal others, her indeed impossible identifications with spectral others, Monte Rosa experiences a series of failed resubjectivations which, rather than re-enacting the terms of melancholic subjectivity, constitute her, instead, as a melancholic specter. In this way, as no longer a subject of desire but more of an embodiment of the drive, as Žižek would put it, she insistently and unapologetically violates the terms of the social contract (which takes various forms here: the symbolic contract of her structural kin position, the gendered economy of Alps' patriarchal hierarchy, the political economy of her performative placements as a substitute body) that would allow her recognition as an intelligible and viable subject. Davis emphasizes the special attention that Derrida pays to the death drives in his reading of Freud precisely 'because they elude any attempt to pin them down, circulating silently and imperceptibly yet disrupting the secure self-presence of subjects, concepts, theories and institutions' (2007, p. 16). As such an incarnation of the drive, Monte Rosa unconditionally demands to remain in the domain of the ambivalent, the uncanny, the spectral, emerging, indeed, as a collector of some unpaid debt, which, rather than symbolic is, ultimately, ethical. For, permanently dispossessed from the domain of the human and rather confined within the liminal space 'between two deaths', Monte Rosa ultimately emerges as precisely this condition of the spectral absences. She poses as this elusive spectral return that haunts subjectivity, that haunts, indeed, the living, reminding us of our always already dispossessed existence and demanding that we always aim at problematizing the boundaries that frame the intelligible, the recognizable, the human, preserving rather the possibility of an openness of meaning to the infinite and the irresolute.

BIBLIOGRAPHY

Abrams, Simon (2012) 'Yorgos Lanthimos on Alps, Greece, and the Travails of the Individual', *New York Village Voice*, http://www.villagevoice.com/2012-07-11/film/yorgos-lanthimos-on-alps-greece/, date accessed 22 April 2016.

Bleasdale, John (2011) 'Alps (Alpeis)', *Cine-Vue: BFI London Film Festival*, http://www.cine-vue.com/2011/10/bfi-london-film-festival-2011-alps.html, date accessed 22 April 2016.

Butler, Judith (2010 [1990]) *Gender Trouble: Feminism and the Subversion of Identity* (New York and London: Routledge Classics).

Butler, Judith and Athena Athanasiou (2013) *Dispossession: The Performative in the Political* (Cambridge: Polity Press).

Davis, Colin (2007) *Haunted Subjects: Deconstruction, Psychoanalysis and the Return of the Dead* (Hampshire: Palgrave Macmillan).

Derrida, Jacques (1994) *Specters of Marx: The State of the Debt, the Work of Mourning and the New International*, trans. Peggy Kamuf (London: Routledge).

Foucault, Michel (1991) *Discipline and Punish: The Birth of the Prison*, trans. Alan Sheridan (London: Penguin).

Lykourgou, Poly (2011) 'Alpeis', *flix*, http://flix.gr/cinema/alpeis.html, date accessed 22 April 2016.

McQuain, Christopher (2012) 'Alps', *dvdtalk.com*, http://www.dvdtalk.com/reviews/59113/alps/, date accessed 22 April 2016.

Palmer, Landon (2012) 'Review: "Alps" Is Exactly the Follow-Up You'd Expect From the Director of "Dogtooth"', *Film School Rejects*, http://filmschoolrejects.com/reviews/review-alps-yorgos-lanthimos-lpalm.php, date accessed 22 April 2016.

Pinkerton, Nick (2012) 'Alps: The Full Range', *New York Village Voice*, http://www.villagevoice.com/2012-07-11/film/alps-the-full-range/, accessed 22 April 2016.

Rich, Jamie S. (2012) 'Alps', *dvdtalk.com*, http://www.dvdtalk.com/reviews/58714/alps/, date accessed 22 April 2016.

Uhlich, Keith (2012) 'Alps', *Time Out New York*, http://www.timeout.com/us/film/alps, date accessed 22 April 2016.

van Hoeij, Boyd (2011) 'Review: "Alps"', *Variety*, http://variety.com/2011/film/reviews/alps-1117945956/, date accessed 22 April 2016.

Watson, Tom (2013) 'DVD Review: "Alps"', *cinevue.com*, http://www.cine-vue.com/2013/03/dvd-review-alps.html, date accessed 22 April 2016.

Žižek, Slavoj (1995 [1991]) *Looking Awry: An Introduction to Jacques Lacan through Popular Culture* (London: The MIT Press).

CHAPTER 7

Boy Eating the Bird's Food: Of Response-ability

Boy Eating the Bird's Food (Ektoras Lygizos, 2012) begins with a long tracking shot which abruptly and assertively impresses upon the viewer that there is nothing allegorical in the film's title. The tight shot foregrounds a young man's hands as they uncover a birdcage and remove the water dispenser. The camera slowly tilts up, reaching the back of the boy's head as he cleans and refills the dispenser, and then back down to his hands; his left hand is shown gently rubbing his stomach while the right removes the seed dispenser, bringing it close to his mouth. He licks one of his fingers and without hesitation takes a mouthful of the bird's food (Fig. 7.1). Yorgos Krassakopoulos of flix.gr laments, 'bearing an admittedly strange title, you'd be excused for thinking that *Boy Eating the Bird's Food* is symbolic, like the film itself. Yet there's nothing non-literal about it, just like there's nothing poetic about what's happening in Athens right now' (2012). Indeed, one could argue that unlike the stylized allegorism that infuses the films of Yorgos Lanthimos, theatre director Ektoras Lygizos's cinematic debut presents its cartography of contemporary Greece's state of material degradation and ideological disillusionment in a straightforward 'ultra-intimate cinéma-vérité style' (Dalton, 2012). Nevertheless, the film does not dispense with the medium's unequivocal representational and affective power to frame the human body in ways that often exceed the self-evident image. This chapter argues that *Boy* offers the suffering body of the young man who, admittedly, literally eats bird's food, not only as a synchronic symptom of the current economic-political moment in the director's home country, but also as a diachronic site for 'resistance',

© The Author(s) 2016
M. Psaras, *The Queer Greek Weird Wave*,
DOI 10.1007/978-3-319-40310-6_7

Fig. 7.1   Boy eating the bird's food

pertinent 'to the ordinary and extraordinary forces of endurance and survival, emerging from, and potentially dissolving, the political condition of
enforced precarious living' (Butler and Athanasiou, 2013, p. 181). At the
same time, Lygizos's distinctive style problematizes the medium's canonical means of representation by exposing the ethical implications of both
cinematic representation and spectatorship, and thus opening up a space
to attack not only the normative discourses of victimization but also their
representational means.

Loosely based on Norwegian author Knut Hamsun's classic novel
Hunger (1890), whose starving protagonist's adventures are transposed
into the present crisis-stricken Greek capital, *Boy* registers the adversities
of life in contemporary Athens through quasi-voyeuristic camerawork that
at times embarrasses the viewer with its unconstrained intimacy towards
the young protagonist. Consisting mostly of long tracking shots such as
the opening one described above, Lygizos's film follows closely—with
the camera seemingly perching on the protagonist's shoulder—an unemployed young counter-tenor's desperate foraging for food for him and his
pet canary. Despite his mesmerizing singing voice, the twenty-something-
year-old man fails to find a job that would allow him to make use of his
talent and gradually falls into a downward spiral that sentences him to
homelessness and starvation. His social and economic destitution brings

about a visible physical and emotional vulnerability but not his demise, as up to the last moment he shows an unequivocal will to resist the constant deterioration of his living conditions, determined to secure food and shelter not only for him but also for his little canary.

Premiered at the 2012 Karlovy Vary Film Festival, *Boy* followed the successful trajectory of other contemporary independent Greek films across the international film festival circuit, sweeping up a series of awards, including the Karlovy Vary Special Mention for its Lead Actor (Yannis Papadopoulos), the Quebec Critics' Award at the Montreal Film Festival, the Bronze Award for Best Film and the Best Actor at the Seville Film Festival, the Best Actor and the International Critics' Award (Fipresci) at the Thessaloniki Film Festival, as well as a nomination for the Discovery Award at the Toronto Film Festival. Impressing—and also at times disturbing—with its straightforward, tender and, at the same time, aggressive treatment of its sensitive thematics, *Boy* was critically received as a contemporary instance of 'grim' or 'Bressonian-like' 'social realism' (Dalton, 2012; Fainaru, 2012).

However, according to Martin Kudláč, the film's 'perennial pursuing of the protagonist in his martyr-like fate', 'constant scrutiny' of this single character, use of 'lyrical aesthetics' and naturalism strongly recall the work of the Dardenne brothers, whose 'poetical realism', he suggests, constitutes 'the perfect denomination' for *Boy* (2013). Indeed, the bold similarities in form and content between *Boy* and the Belgian filmmakers' films, especially *Rosetta* (1999) and *Lorna's Silence* (2008), rather place *Boy* in the context of other recent filmmaking that renegotiates and reworks the realist tradition, its claims and mechanisms, and, most importantly, its ethics. Sarah Cooper notices that the Dardennes' films not only provide a fertile ground for 'productive encounters' between ethics and cinema but are essentially inspired by and interspersed with explicit references to ethical philosophy, particularly, though not exclusively, the ethical underpinnings of Emmanuel Levinas's thought (2007). Lygizos's film, though refraining from explicit references to ethical thinking, with its daring formal experimentations and thematic provocations similarly invites ethical reflection on the screened problem and its visual representations, which heavily resonate—though again not exclusively—with Levinasian ethics.

The film combines magnificently what could be described as minimalist or austere editing on the one hand and excessive or even catachrestic camerawork on the other, which, together with its ascetic characterization and narrative structure, suggest that, as van Hoeij puts it, 'Lygizos is more

interested in observation than explanation' (2012). Through such 'observational' cinematic devices, allied with though distinct from Tsangari's
in *Attenberg*, Lygizos offers a phenomenological—rather than psychological—study of the corporeal and affective repercussions of the process,
which, as discussed in the previous chapter, Butler and Athanasiou define
as 'dispossession'. However, as suggested above, the underlying rhetoric
of such a phenomenological enquiry is, ultimately, ethical. For, by unapologetically defying realism's defining strategies and rather showcasing self-
reflexivity as its quintessential mode of address, the film emerges as both
a corrosive critique of dominant discourses of victimization, problematizing and queering them, as well as an interrogation of the medium's own
collusion in their reproduction and dissemination. In this way, Lygizos's
project arguably reverberates with Butler and Athanasiou's critique of the
machinations of contemporary neoliberal humanitarian governmentality,
which rest precisely on totalizing discourses of victimhood that erase the
victims and conceal injustices, but also with contemporary theoretical preoccupations with ethical issues implicit in visual representation and spectatorship; particularly issues that pose questions of directorial as well as
spectatorial responsibility with regard to the production and, respectively,
consumption of images of suffering.

As Athanasiou argues, 'contemporary contexts of intertwined violence,
vulnerability, affliction, states of emergency, victimhood, reparation,
benevolence, and empathic sublime […] have given rise to new complex
and contradictory forms of humanitarian government', in which 'discourses of victimization and charity are favored over discourses of political
claims and confrontations' (2013, p. 113). These forms of humanitarian government seek to objectify the victims and categorize them under
certain labels (i.e. immigrants, refugees, victims of trafficking) in order to
be eligible for state or NGO (non-governmental organization) assistance.
In this way, they ultimately generate a 'moral economy of obligatory vulnerability and compassion […] as a regulatory norm of paternalistic and
sentimental liberal humanism' that nonetheless obscures the political conditions under which these processes of victimization occur, forestalls the
assumption of relevant responsibility and even precludes the possibility of
organization and resistance (2013, p. 114).

At the same time, discourses against 'victimization' also proliferate,
particularly as a result of a neoconservative attack against the welfare
state, 'wherein the "victim" is an icon of pitiful public pathology, cultural
defectiveness, or individual failure' (2013, p. 114). In these 'anti-victim'

discourses the dire economic conditions of poor people are often attributed to their 'deficient or inept personalities', their 'failed "family structures" or "lack of strong paternal authority"', thus ultimately degrading
and delegitimizing 'individual and collective claims of harm and demands
for compensation and accountability' (2013, pp. 114–115). This is why, as
Butler argues, although 'sometimes the language of victimization strength-
ens the rationale of a paternalistic form of power (understood as providing
"protection")', we cannot completely discard it as 'at other times, it can
lead to practices of organized resistance', as in the case of the feminist protests against 'blaming the rape victim' in the 1970s (2013, p. 115). What
we should rather be alert to, are the synoptic totalities of 'otherness' and
the moral consolidations of injury produced by hegemonic technologies
of representation, as well as the collateral regimes of ineffability that seek
to obliterate the vices of oppression and dispossession. The former pertain
to discourses of over-representation such as those mentioned above; discourses of relationality, injurability, witnessing and justice, which objectify
and turn the other into an essentialist totality, too intelligible and recognizable, and thus ever only conditionally eligible to be valued and taken
care of. The latter refer to the other end of the spectrum, that is, to representational modes of unnameability, which differentially conceal injustices
and violences, engendering a 'normative reduction of the erased other to
the silenced status of abjection and victimhood' (2013, p. 132).

The challenge then is how to critically 'address the violence of rendering a person unspeakable without reinstalling a normative regime of
speakability in the form of mere naming, bureaucratic taxonomy, or formal recognition', especially when we know that 'language always fails us'
(2013, p. 133). In the face of 'proliferating forms of injurability', the task
of naming these occasions and, particularly, of 'captur[ing] the singularity
of those politically reduced to insignificant human matter, or human waste'
becomes crucial both politically and intellectually, as Athanasiou contends
(2013, p. 133). This is especially so when this singularity is 'intentionally
erased—reduced to unilaterally exposed and interchangeably anonymous
human matter'; for 'the erasure of singularity, or de-personalization, is a
crucial aspect of biopolitics' (2013, p. 133). At the same time we should
be alert 'to the normative preconditions for achieving grievability' (2013,
p. 134); namely, we should be alert to the challenge of 'how to lay claim
to a livable life without taking the embodied subject for granted as a starting point for politics', without resorting to the slippery path of an identity
politics, forged around injury (2013, p. 135). Athanasiou rejects such an

identity politics for two reasons. First, identity, as she points out, is always already intertwined with injury 'in the sense of production of embodied subjects inside the normalizing and traumatizing constraints of discourse and power', those culturally particular forces of identification and subjectivation, which, as we have seen in the previous chapter, 'imagine and recognize a viable life and a mournable death in accordance with given prerequisites of intelligibility' (2013, p. 135). Second, and perhaps most importantly, an identity politics that relies on claims of woundedness ultimately runs the risk of 'reaffirming the structures of domination that have caused the injury' (2013, p. 135).

Instead, Athanasiou and Butler propose a community centered on 'considering the vulnerability of others and recuperating collective responsibility for the lives of one another' (2013, p. 132). As Athanasiou frames this aspiration:

> Perhaps, what is at stake here is [...] an ethics and politics of post-identity subjectivities, which are consigned and exposed to the exposure, abandonment, precarity, and vulnerability of others [...] modes of response and solidarity that do not reify 'the dispossessed' and thus do not repeat the erasing of the singularity [...] but rather allow for a separateness that works as an invitation to a (political) community. (2013, p. 136)

Indeed, such a politics of social transformation is only made possible through responsive disposition, a Levinas-inspired ethical model, which enacts the assumption of responsibility for one's own position in the world and relationality to others. The source of our responsiveness and responsibility to others is precisely the condition of dispossession, examined in the previous chapter, as 'exposure and disposition to others, experience of loss and grief, or susceptibility to norms and violences that remain indifferent to us' (2013, p. 104). As Athanasiou explains:

> In a world of differentially shared sociality, if we are already 'outside ourselves,' beyond ourselves, given over, bound to others, and bound by claims that emerge from the outside or from deep inside ourselves, our very notion of responsibility requires this sense of dispossession as disposition, exposure, and self-othering. (2013, p. 106)

To care for the other, or fight against inequality is not a matter of personal morality. As Butler reminds us, 'it is precisely because I am from the start implicated in the lives of the other that the "I" is already social, and must begin its reflection and action from the presumption of a constitutive sociality' (2013, p. 107). Negotiating the antagonisms and the incommensurabilities in the social sphere is, indeed, the substance of the ethical and this idea of the interdependency of lives that are mutually implicated in one another is what eventually establishes a principle of equality and connectedness. Hence, responsibility emerges as the counter-example to moral narcissism; for when acting responsibly 'I do not augment myself with my virtuousness' but I rather 'give myself over to the broader sociality that I am' (2013, p. 108).

Moreover, 'response-ability toward human vulnerability and precarity' should be distinguished from 'the widening of the established ontological prefiguration of the human (according to the tradition of twentieth-century liberalism and pluralist modes of multiculturalism)' (2013, p. 119). It is better conceived of as an 'insurrection at the level of ontology', namely, 'the constant questioning of conditions in which the human is determined by normative and normalizing regimes of intelligibility in terms of gender, sexuality, race, nationality, class' (2013, p. 119). Indeed, to challenge the onto-epistemological foundations of the category of the 'human', is not only to undermine but crucially to dismantle the violent processes of the 'differential allocation of humanness', that is, 'the perpetually shifting and variably positioned boundary between those who are rendered properly human and those who are not, those who are entitled to a long life and those relegated to slow death' (2013, pp. 31–32). Such an enterprise, of course, assumes the category of the 'human' as always already within 'social situatedness and allocation', that is, the human as 'always the event of its multiple exposures—both within its relatedness to others and within its exposure to the normative forces that arrange the social, political, and cultural matrices of humanness' (2013, p. 32). But it is precisely through such reconfigurations that the 'human condition' is, ultimately, exposed as the 'default mechanism for upholding the intersecting matrices of colonial expansion, phallocentrism, heteronormativity, and possessive individualism' (2013, p. 32).

Accordingly, the 'barbarian, the monster and the animal', as well as the 'stranger, the sans papiers, the unemployed, the queer', generally those forms of life, historically excluded from the realm of the normative human, emerge as radicalized forces of resistance which aim at exposing or challenging the regulative fictions that produce them as unintelligible. As Athanasiou explains, 'as we struggle today, jointly and partially, in present circumstances when matters of survival are at stake, queerness, anti-racism, anti-precarity, and companion-species solidarity really matter as enactments of struggles and transformative modes of survival' (2013, p. 37). Indeed, to radically reframe the fantasy of the self-sufficient human is to think through 'amalgamation and reassemblages of the animate and the inanimate, human and non-human, animal and human animal, life and death', as well as to form 'communities with other forms of life, in social realms of co-implicated and differently embodied bodies' as Athanasiou contends (2013, p. 37). Such 'being-in-common, beyond communitarianism and anthropomorphism' can, ultimately, constitute the condition for a new politics: one that 'involves engaging with the biopolitical condition while also revisiting the humanist premises of the (bio)political' (2013, p. 37).

The question of interdependency and ethical responsibility is, arguably, already embedded in Lygizos's film's title: for the hunger-stricken boy does not merely eat bird-food but effectively *the* bird's food. And much as this is established in the film's opening shot, what is also established is the fact that *Boy*, far from attesting to melodramatic, hagiographical accounts of victimhood—typical of the genre of realism—rather prefers to undermine these canonical narratives, scrutinizing their discursive production as well as their representational rhetoric, and exposing their ethical implications by means of a largely self-reflexive point of view. The boy is not framed as a martyr who appeals momentarily to our moral narcissism, but as much a victim as a perpetrator, arguably, a symptom of a broader crisis that is material as well as ethical and representational. In this way, *Boy* draws attention to the social and affective repercussions of the Greek crisis by displacing sentimentality and rather inviting more reflective responses that call for the assumption of responsibility in relation to the production and dissemination of such devaluing narratives of suffering, but, most importantly, in relation to the perpetuation of the screened problem itself. For *Boy*'s narrative does not merely follow the story of a boy who is gradually deprived of the means for survival, but essentially the trajectory of a young man's gradual dispossession of the terms that would allocate him as intelligible and recognizable human matter, valuable and grievable, and his ultimate rendering as human waste, as a result of his voluntary rupture with 'the normative forces that arrange the social, political and cultural matrices of humanness'; namely, the family, the Church and the nation.

Arguably, what one notices from the very beginning of the film is that the central narrative theme of dispossession is crucially visually underscored by an extraordinary foreclosure of space; indeed, a formal gesture that clearly exposes the problems at the heart of representation, its ethics and limitations. Just after the introductory comment on the non-metaphorical meaning of the film's title, Lygizos abruptly and without much exposition throws us into the 'cyclone' of the protagonist's descending trajectory. A handheld medium shot shows the boy in his bedroom putting on a white shirt. A cut brings Lygizos's camera closer to the boy; sitting on a chair, the young man pours some water into his hands to rub over his stomach. With his hand forcefully pressing his upset empty stomach the boy bends his torso down to his knees before lying down on the bed next to the chair. The camera strives to follow the boy's abrupt movements and, at the same time, focus on the expressions of suffering drawn on his angelic face, but the task feels futile; the ever-elusive corporeality often embarrasses the camera, which emerges as unable to mediate the infinite and unpredictable spectrum of the body's meanderings. Then follows an over-the-shoulder tracking shot of the boy as he carelessly crosses a motorway and, after that, a soft-focus medium shot of him—indeed, a beautiful moving portrait of the handsome fair-haired, blue-eyed young man—listening to piano playing off-screen but hesitating to sing. 'Are you nervous?' asks the musician, off-screen, who accompanies him on the piano. The film cuts to a shot of the pianist's broken leg. The camera slowly tilts up, framing the pianist's efforts to stand up and walk towards the boy with the assistance of crutches. When he reaches him, the pianist extends his hand and touches the boy's chest, then demonstrates some diaphragmatic breathing exercises for the boy to copy so that he can relax; throughout the camera frames tightly the moving body parts, capturing the slightest details of their movements from an almost asphyxiating proximity. 'Do you speak German?' asks the pianist. 'No', replies the boy. 'Don't you know what the lyrics mean?' 'No.' The pianist then starts translating Bach's famous aria from the *St Matthew Passion* oratorio, '*Erbarme dich, mein Gott*'. The aria's suggestive lyrics translate as: 'Have mercy, Lord, for the sake of my tears!' The pianist explains, 'In other words, don't you see me crying?' As we hear the sound of a stomach growling, the camera tilts down focusing on the boy's empty stomach; the boy presses harder and harder on his stomach as if seeking to prevent it betraying his vulnerable state. A jump cut to an extreme close-up foregrounds the boy singing the famous aria. The camera gently moves around the boy's face as if caressing it, focusing consecutively on his eyes, mouth and ears, before it finally tilts down to the floor in search of the boy's body which has unexpectedly collapsed right at the moment he was singing the high-pitched '*Erbarme*' (mercy).

Next, the boy is framed in medium shot in the bathroom, his hair and face dripping with water. 'So I'm not right for the job', he tells the pianist. 'I'm looking for someone more experienced', replies the pianist off-screen. The boy shakes his head, his eyes fixed on the pianist, his face unreadable. 'Did I upset you?' asks the pianist. 'Not at all', replies the boy in the same inexpressive manner and stands up to leave. The pianist asks him whether he would like to eat some souvlaki. The boy politely refuses and the pianist then asks him to throw the leftovers of his meal in the bin downstairs. The camera follows the boy down the street in a long tight tracking shot, which, at first, shows him putting the plastic bag with the food next to the bin, but seconds later, after making sure that the pianist is not watching over from his balcony, quickly picking it up to take it home.

'Obsessively shadowing the main character while negating any view of the surrounding world, the director's camera performs a psychosomatic inspection of the young futureless man', Celluloid Liberation Front's blogger notices (2012). Clearly, *Boy*'s spatiotemporal construction, despite— or precisely owing to—the 'obsessive shadowing' of the lead character's movement in space by the camera, departs from the classical narrative cinema's paradigm, where, as Deleuze has argued in his discussion of the 'movement-image', a valorization of the protagonist's agency predominates in relation to the production of filmic spatiotemporality.[1] More of an unproductive expenditure of cinematic spatiotemporality, often refusing causality and disappointing the viewers' expectations, Lygizos's film is more interested in foreclosure rather than disclosure; an uninhibited, yet futile navigation through an increasingly shrinking space.

This brings to mind again Janet Harbord's conceptualization of the 'space-time' image, examined in Chapter 5, in which cinematic space, much as time in Deleuzian thought, becomes indeed, the 'product of movement, rather than a frame within which action takes place' (2007, p. 164). As Harbord usefully points out, cinematic movement is to be crucially relieved of its historical theoretical link to concerns with productivity, understood instead in the form of mobile relations between things that, ultimately, expose it as more of 'an emotional state' (2007, p. 164). For, to articulate movement as a spatial category of relational energies is to shift attention away from action towards affect, it is to open 'analysis on to an affectual understanding of filmic space', one which considers cinematic space as a 'landscape produced through the relational contracts of things', rather than a mere 'container for action', 'a static backdrop to events' (2007, p. 164). Arguably, the primary relational contract in *Boy* is none other than that of the camera itself in relation to the body of the protagonist. The camera constantly haunts the body of the boy, following him literally everywhere: in bed, in the bathroom, in the metro, in the streets. By having an ever-moving camera fixating on an ever-moving body, while marginalizing—if not thoroughly obliterating—the broader space (both the physical and the social) within which action takes place, *Boy* constructs a claustrophobic space *for* and *through* its main character, in which movement is rendered unproductive, if not catachrestic, and more often than not merely reduced to a compulsive drive to satisfy elemental biological needs; the only teleology that, arguably, underpins the boy's (as well as *Boy*'s) temporality.

In effect, as the camera confronts the hunger-stricken body of the boy, increasingly foregrounding it acting and reacting in unpredictable if not convulsive ways, the audience comes across an astonishing foreclosure of space. After picking up the leftovers of the musician's food from the recycling bin the boy returns home. Lygizos's by now familiar handheld tracking shots follow the boy walking up the stairs and, suddenly, with an unexpected twist of the body, jumping over the railing. On entering the flat he hastily rips open the plastic bag and gobbles down the souvlaki. In the shots that follow, the boy's diminishing means of survival are highlighted, as he boils the milk to check if it has gone bad, as he unscrews the light bulb from the kitchen ceiling to use it in the bathroom, as he pays a visit to his elderly neighbor only to steal from his sugar jar. And then the film returns again to the boy's morning routine, showing him filling up the water and seed dispensers of the birdcage and taking it to the balcony for some fresh air. The camera never stops capturing from extreme proximity the boy's excessive motion in the constricted space of his flat, as he stretches and leans against the railings, as he extends his arms to reach the seed dispenser above his head, as he drops a sock from the balcony as an excuse to pinch a couple of figs from the neighbor's back yard. The encaged bird soon becomes a metaphor, a mirror of the boy's own state of entrapment within the gradually condensing physical and social contours of his urban surroundings, a mirror of both the boy's as well as our own entrapment within the constantly diminishing contours of the cinematic frame, as the camera menacingly stalks his ever-moving body. And the convulsiveness of his body might precisely be an indication of his (and our) wish to escape the frame of the camera, to escape the limited and limiting contours of the representable, the intelligible, the knowable; it might precisely point towards a world that will never be our own but one that will always haunt our sense of the self and the other.

These limitations of film representation and spectatorship and, most significantly, the ethical implications that arise from them, are addressed by Libby Saxton, who, drawing on the ethical philosophy of Emmanuel Levinas, argues against the manipulation and exploitation of the other's image and suffering by mainstream film and the dominant visual culture, in a way that, in effect, elucidates Butler and Athanasiou's equivalent warnings about 'the synoptic totalities of "otherness" and the moral consolidations of injury produced by hegemonic technologies of representation' mentioned above. As Saxton writes, Levinas's philosophy 'manifests an abiding suspicion of the aesthetic and the visual, which he associates with forms of domination and violence' (2010b, p. 95). As she explains, even though the French philosopher describes ethics as an 'optics', he separates the ethical relation from the field of the visible, owing to the 'propensity of images to blind and deafen us to the Other' (2010b, p. 97). In Levinas's own words: '[ethics] is a "vision" without image, bereft of the synoptic and totalizing objectifying virtues of vision, a relation or intentionality of a wholly different type' (1994, p. 23). Taking his cue from the biblical Second Commandment, which prescribes the proscription of images, Levinas invites us to reflect upon this proscription away from its religious connotations and rather within an ethical enquiry of our relation and responsibility to the other. For the prohibition against representation acknowledges the transcendence that characterizes our relation to the Other, something which is unattainable through perception:

> This transcendence is alive in the relation to the other man, i.e. in the proximity of one's fellow man, whose *uniqueness* and consequently whose irreducible *alterity* would be—still or already—unrecognized in the perception that stares at [*dé-visage*] the other. (Levinas, 1999, p. 75)

Saxton draws attention to the equivocal meaning of the French verb *dé-visage* that Levinas uses in the above sentence, which can be translated as either 'stares' or 'defaces'; in the latter case, the verb denotes a central concept in Levinas's thought, that is the face (*visage*) of the Other, whose uniqueness evades/resists representation. It is important to clarify, however, that the Levinasian 'visage' does not necessarily or exclusively pertain to the human face; it rather refers to 'the way in which the Other presents himself, exceeding *the idea of the Other in me*' (Levinas, 1994, p. 50), it is 'what cannot become a content, which your thought would embrace; it is uncontainable, it leads you beyond'

(Levinas, 1985, p. 87). The face reveals itself 'without the intermediary of any image', as Levinas insists (1994, p. 200) and Saxton elucidates, it rather '*expresses, signifies* and *speaks*, addressing and commanding me from a position beyond the perceptual field' (2010b, p. 99). Hence, insofar as representation reduces the face 'to immobility, re-appropriate[s] its alterity and silence[s] its address' (2010b, p. 99), the prohibition against representation emerges as the ground of ethical relations, calling the subject to a responsibility for the other. Reflecting upon filmic representation and spectatorship through Levinas's ethical philosophy becomes then a challenging task, particularly when acknowledging that the subject–object relation that has been traditionally ascribed to film spectatorship by psychoanalytic theory is inherently a form of what the philosopher names 'altericide', or 'the Other's reduction to an object of my perception' (2010b, p. 92). Saxton wonders:

> How could a visual medium reveal alterity or call us to responsibility in the manner described by Levinas? Is it possible to conceive of ways in which cinema might expose us to this face without 'defacing' or 'effacing' it—without reducing it to an object of perception? Is the prohibition against representation signified by the face not always already violated as images of the other are captured on celluloid or translated into digital data? (2010b, p. 100)

Indeed, so long as the viewer is placed in a dominant position over the object viewed, so long as the camera effectuates a mediation of otherness and a manipulation of our look, then the ethical encounter as envisioned by Levinas, immediate and spontaneous, but also asymmetrical (with the Other calling the self into question rather than the other way round) is rendered impossible through film, Saxton argues (2010b, p. 100). Nevertheless, Levinas's misgivings about representation might be challenged by alternative filmic practices and strategies that reframe the canonical psychoanalytic paradigm of spectatorship, which was after all founded on mainstream narrative cinema, opening up the possibility for establishing viewing relations that 'preserve the proximity and separation proper to what Levinas calls "a relation irreducible to the subject–object relation: the *revelation* of the other"' (2010b, p. 100).

In her reading of Claude Lanzmann's *Shoah* (1985), Saxton identifies such 'revelatory' filmic strategies not so much in what the film depicts as in the film's omissions and refusals. For Saxton, Lanzmann's documentary about the Holocaust is both 'a visual critique of the visual' as well as a paradigm of the way film 'might expose us to alterity without domesticating or simply effacing it' (2010b, pp. 103–104). As she explains, the film communicates its 'mistrust of images of atrocity' through its refusal to offer direct images of the past or images of the dead. In its fixation on the deadpan faces of the witnesses, which resist any definitive reading, as well as in the juxtaposition of their oral testimonies with 'the empty, derelict and deceptively tranquil murder sites to which they return in the present' the film 'directs attention beyond itself towards an otherness which cannot be recuperated in images', thus emulating the Levinasian ethical encounter in yet unpredictable ways (2010b, p. 103). For, despite the practical limitations of cinema, which obstruct the recreation of the 'unpredictable, unmediated, unique and daunting confrontation with the Other from which Levinasian ethics derives', Lanzmann's film still rehearses 'a relation irreducible to the subject–object relation' (2010b, p. 105). By 'impeding our vision and frustrating our desire to see', *Shoah* disturbs 'the illusory positions of sovereignty and transcendence afforded to viewers' in psychoanalytic accounts and instead implicates our gaze, charging it with responsibility (2010b, p. 105).

Consisting of tracking shots that, despite following closely the protagonist's foraging for food, effectively efface his surroundings, *Boy Eating the Bird's Food*, much like *Shoah*, disturbs the subject–object relation of viewing, posing questions and problematizing the task at issue, namely, the representation of extreme suffering (in our case the experience of hunger), as well as the use of the camera to construct intimacy with its subjects. As the scenes analyzed above reveal, Lygizos's film is rather one of unexplained drama, overshadowing the protagonist with an ever-shaky camera, penetrating the smallest details of his material, corporeal and affective experience of the crisis, but, at the same time, refusing the audience much exposition in terms of narrative space and time. On the contrary, *Boy* ceaselessly forces the ever-moving body of the protagonist, and at times his impassive face, to the foreground as a partition that impedes our vision of the broader collapsing cityscape, indeed 'frustrating our desire to see', to know, to make sense. Lygizos's claustrophobic framing emerges, thus, as an essentially ethical act, which disturbs the viewers' 'illusory positions of sovereignty and transcendence', pointing towards an alterity that is beyond our reach, 'an otherness which cannot be recuperated in images', to use Saxton's words.

This is further emphasized by the film's refusal to turn the boy's character into an object of psychological study. For, much as we are made complicit in this bizarre stalking of the boy's quotidian meanderings, bearing witness to the slightest details of the deteriorating material conditions of his life, so we are denied any access to his emotional vicissitudes, confronted either with a deadpan face that resists interpretation or with his back insistently and suggestively turned to the camera as a deliberate act of ef-face-ment. In a subsequent scene, Lygizos's tracking shots follow the young boy to a telephone company, where he tries his luck at the company's call center. The handheld camera frames him tightly from behind, while he makes phone calls to prospective customers. After a few failed attempts to hook new customers he picks up the phone again but this time pauses for a second, turns around to check if anybody is watching him and quickly dials a number. The camera remains fixed behind his shoulder revealing little, if any, of his facial expressions. Filled with the call center's unedited noise, the soundtrack denies any audio access to the call. Seconds after he dials the number the boy closes his eyes tightly, listening but not talking (Fig. 7.2). But, this facial gesture is barely discernible, as the camera refrains from taking advantage of the privileges afforded by what has long been one of the cinema's favorite devices, that is the facial close-up, rather preferring to remain by his side. The tight framing of the character thus offers no access to his personal drama; and the boy rushes to hang up the phone, take his bag and vanish through the building's corridors, before we grasp what the scene is about.

Fig. 7.2   The camera and the boy's physical proximity, yet emotional distance

Lygizos's treatment of the close-up is, indeed, quite poignant throughout the film and, certainly, in line with the film's overall ethical engagement. The director's framing choices break with the cinematic tradition
of deploying the close-up as revelatory of a hidden interiority;[2] *Boy* refuses
to transform the face into 'a spectacle, an incarnation of unspoken or
unspeakable truths', to foreground it as 'the locus of a privileged relationship to the real', as Saxton comments in relation to *Shoah* (2010b, p. 102).
Our encounter with the boy's face is instead either foreclosed by the camera's insistence on framing his body from behind, even or especially at
moments of emotional tension, as is evident in the scene described above,
or, in the rare cases that we are afforded the luxury of closeness to his face,
contained by a frustrating confrontation with indecipherable expressions,
as in the scene with the pianist. Following Saxton's reading of the use
of the close-up in *Shoah*, I would like to similarly suggest that, through
its idiosyncratic relation to the camera, the visible face in *Boy* becomes a
reminder of the way the Levinasian 'visage' always 'eludes our vision and
escapes our grasp'; through its resistance to being reduced into '[a] source
of knowledge or [an] object of aesthetic contemplation' it unearths the
possibility of 'an opening onto alterity' (2010b, p. 102).

In these ways, Lygizos's film emerges as a 'weird' cartography of the
Greek crisis; an ethically laden formal attack against the vices of over-
representation that characterize the normative discourses of victimization
proliferated by dominant media, which, as Butler and Athanasiou warn,
turn the victims into essentialist totalities. Through its unconventional
visuals, the film creates the perfect formal platform to accommodate a narrative of suffering that departs from the moralistic rhetoric of mainstream
discourse, which, imbued with the narcissistic sentiments of paternalism
and compassion, may obliterate political claims and confrontations. As
Saxton again notes, recent debates on visual narratives of suffering draw
attention exactly to the propensity of such images to 'abstract or sani-
tize their subject-matter or turn it into an object of voyeuristic fascination', thus simultaneously posing questions about the ethical implication
of those for whom these images are produced and distributed through
the various visual media, namely the viewers (2010a, p. 65). Saxton references Susan Sontag and Lilie Chouliaraki, who both object to sentimental
responses to images of suffering and advocate instead critical reflection
on both the imaged violence as well as on the images themselves. In
Chouliaraki's thinking, the 'regimes of pity' produced by the news narratives of television 'construe suffering as an aesthetic spectacle', which

rather than inducing action and the assumption of responsibility 'pro-duces narcissistic emotions about the suffering "other" that cannot move the spectator beyond the reflex of caring only for those like "us"' (2006, p. 13). In this way, these discourses ultimately reflect and consolidate the asymmetry of power between those who watch and those who suffer, thus reinforcing contemporary economic and political divisions (2006, p. 4). In a similar vein, Sontag warns against the 'imaginary proximity to the suffering inflicted on others' offered by televisual images, which suggests a link between the viewer and the faraway sufferer 'that is simply untrue, that is yet one more mystification of our real relations to power' (2004, p. 91). For, this paradoxical 'tele-intimacy' obstructs critical response and rather engenders dispositions of sympathy that 'proclaim our innocence as well as our impotence' (2004, p. 91). Instead, such images should be regarded as 'an invitation to pay attention, to reflect, to learn, to examine the rationalizations for mass suffering offered by established powers', to 'stand back' and, indeed, consider how we ourselves are implicated in the screened suffering (2004, pp. 104–105).

Clearly, these discussions are preoccupied with the ethical implication of viewers of 'real' images of violence diffused by mass media, and primarily by television. However, as Michele Aaron argues, the issue of ethical response and responsibility is also pertinent to film spectatorship, since this is 'inherently contractual and hooked on the "real" or imagined suffering of others' (2007, p. 112). Aaron draws on the classic psychoanalytic paradigm in her explication of the contractual nature of spectatorship: underwriting mainstream 'film's management of perverse desire (its socio-moral scale) and illusion (its fiction-status)', psychoanalytic theory has unearthed the disavowing strategies of mainstream cinema, which sought to maintain the 'safe distance between the spectator and the dangers suggested by and within the cinematic spectacle, be they emotional or psychological (or even ethical)', while simultaneously allowing him/her to indulge in (ostensibly 'authentic') fantasy (2007, p. 92). However, as she points out, certain filmic practices, found for example in films such as those of the Dogme 95 movement, deliberately break the contract, by 'aggravating the act of "artful forgetting"' and/or pushing the limits of the representable (2007, p. 112). Devices such as self-reflexivity, for example, expose 'the mythic processes at the heart of classical cinema: the safe distances that characterize (fetishistic) spectatorship' (2007, p. 97). As she explains, self-reflexivity 'performs that radical Brechtian practice of distanciation, drawing attention to the myth of separation, of dissociation, and the necessary fiction of self-coherence' (2007, p. 98). By questioning our 'mythic distance and safety, the irresponsibility or neutrality of looking on', self-reflexivity can expose film spectatorship as 'intimately connected to the issue of responsibility', as it is nothing less than 'a negotiation of personal pleasures and others' interests', indeed, 'a marker of socio-political responsibility' (2007, p. 88).

Aaron's invocation of the responsibility that is immanent in film spectatorship is also invested in Levinasian ethics, and particularly in the philosopher's notion of intersubjectivity. As she explains Levinas's thought, our face-to-face encounter with the other is what crucially engenders our sense of self: 'our subjectivity is constituted through our response to somebody's difference from us. This response becomes respons-ibility, both as a kind of subjectivity-in-action (a reflexive state of self-constitution) and as our obligation to the other' (2007, p. 111). This obligation arises from our implication in the other's potential death insofar as 'my existence necessarily compromises someone else's' (2007, p. 111). In Levinas's own words, '[m]y being-in-the-world or my "place in the sun", my being at home, have these not also been the usurpation of spaces belonging to the other man whom I have already oppressed or starved [...]?' (1989, p. 82). Applying this line of thought to film spectatorship Aaron contends that, so long as film viewers are implicated, not only as consumers but also 'as consensual parties in the generation of characters' suffering for our entertainment', spectatorship emerges as 'intrinsically ethical', as it 'depends upon our intersubjective alignment with the prospective suffering of others' (2007, p. 112).

In this sense, film spectatorship is not entirely distinct from any other form of consumption of images of violence, be they staged or unstaged, 'real' or fabricated. After all, as Saxton illuminates drawing on Sontag, the boundaries between entertainment and information, between reportage and spectacle, in contemporary modes of image-production diffused via televisual or other mass media are increasingly obscured (2010a, p. 68). Nevertheless, in contrast with mainstream media's inexorable proliferation of images of violence and suffering as spectacle for mass consumption, cinema can constitute a site of resistance to their 'altericidal practices' and numbing 'unreality-effect', to the 'ghosting of reality' that is effected by the 'hyperarousal' caused by violence in films and on the news, as Saxton proposes following Geoffrey Hartman (2010a, p. 69). Practices and strategies, such as self-reflexivity, intertextuality, stylistic excess, interpretational vacuity, 'minimal visuality'[3] and 'counter-shots'[4] are only some examples of the ways cinema, and visual media generally, can call into question our relationship to the production and distribution of images of violence and suffering, interrogate, indeed, our own collusion as viewers in the exploitation and sensationalization of the suffering of the other.

In effect, *Boy* is replete with such *non-altericidal* practices. The 'interpretational vacuity' registered on the deadpan face of the boy, as well as the 'minimal visuality' that is achieved through the restriction of the visual field by the body of the boy which operates as a partition between our vision and his broader physical and social surroundings, constitute, as already suggested, instances of resistance to the totalizing perspectives of mainstream (over-)representation, while also alluding to the fact that other forms of suffering and vulnerability are under-represented or even left unmarked. At the same time, combining the above unconventional visual experimentations with an absence of melodramatic soundtrack, Brechtian acting style and a profoundly anti-heroic trajectory for its protagonist, *Boy* emerges as an exemplary progeny of the European art-house tradition of self-reflexive cinema. For, echoing the paradigms of Dogme 95 and the Dardennes, Lygizos's film self-consciously breaks the contract, both 'aggravating the act of "artful forgetting"' and pushing the limits of the representable. Through such defiant form and spatiotemporal construction, the film arguably achieves a break with the moral economy of mainstream narratives of suffering, sketching rather an elliptical, yet controversial portrait of its protagonist, which refuses to attest to normative discourses of victimization.

Just after the scene at the call center, we witness the boy stalking a girl, who works at a hotel. The scene follows the boy's obsessive, yet discreet attempts to keep the girl's body in sight as she moves about the hotel lounge, appearing and disappearing behind counters and glass partitions (Fig. 7.3). The camera's quasi-improvisational movement, as it strives to track the boy's erratic movement and also register his voyeuristic maneuvers through a playful change of focus, mirrors our own attempts to get a clear glimpse of the world around the boy; attempts which are often frustrated by the omnipresence of the boy's body in the frame as a permanent obstruction to our vision, as well as a constant reminder of a world beyond our reach. The girl exits the hotel and the boy follows her down the street as she walks towards another building. Entering the building, she stops momentarily at the concierge's door. The camera, insistently hovering behind the boy's shoulder, reveals only partially his point of view, as the girl turns unexpectedly towards him and acknowl-

Fig. 7.3   A nod to our perennial spectatorial position as 'Peeping Toms'

edges his presence with a smile. Lygizos offers no reaction shot here: the camera rather seems to have been taken by surprise, stumbling over the boy's footsteps as he rushes away. Suddenly, the scene looks familiar; as the boy looks through the glass doors of the hotel, gluing his gaze to the girl's movement in space while keeping his own body hidden and at a safe distance, he, arguably, emerges as yet another onscreen surrogate for us in the act of looking, reminding us of our perennial spectatorial position as 'Peeping Toms'. The scene, indeed, becomes nothing short of a self-reflexive gesture: a staging of our own act of looking on through the cinematic keyhole, augmented here by the camera's intimate relationship to the boy's body. And the girl's corresponding act of looking back, which arrests the boy's gaze as much as our own, arguably does nothing but expose the always already voyeuristic nature of cinematic spectatorship. In this way, the scene's staging of the act of voyeurism ultimately emerges as an incisive interrogation of our own relentless appetite as consumers of a visual culture that irrepressibly bombards us with images that objectify the Other, while its emphasis on the boy's shadowy status as a voyeur alludes to the disavowing strategies of this culture that have ensured its perpetuation by preserving the illusion of the safe and irresponsible position of its consumers, namely the spectators.

Another scene that powerfully breaks the contract, exposing the ethical implications of film representation and spectatorship, and thus challenging the mainstream narratives of suffering is, arguably, the explicit scene of the boy's masturbation, which constitutes Lygizos's most daring attempt to complicate our viewing position and contain any probable sentimental responses. The scene begins with the camera placed outside the bathroom, shooting through the half-open door, and thus offering only a restricted view of the masturbating boy, whose body is pushed to the right margin of the frame. The voyeuristic nature of our viewing position is not only evoked here by the shot's composition, which features a double-frame effect, created by the door on the right hand side and the wall/partition on the right, but also by the decentering of the boy's body, which ironically showcases it as the object of our voyeuristic desire by precisely concealing it. However, a cut (the only one in the scene) gives way to the film's most controversial shot; a graphic shot that unapologetically verges on the terrain of pornography, stretching the limits of the representable at the same time as it poignantly comments upon the spectatorial voracity for corporeal and sexual exposure. The shot at issue is nothing less than another tight tracking shot, which here roams over the boy's naked body vacillating between his sweaty face and his right hand, which is foregrounded stroking his fully erect penis. Astonishingly, the single shot of the fully exposed real act of masturbation lasts for more than a whole minute, including the climactic ejaculation and the boy's unexpected gesture of eating his own semen, narratively compelled by his severe state of hunger.

'A bold move, to say the least, by both the actor and the filmmaker', as *Indiewire* blogger Carlos Aguilar observes (2013), the explicit scene of the boy's masturbation provides Lygizos with yet another opportunity to unravel the illusions offered by the comforts of mainstream cinema, attacking, thus, the disavowal at the heart of film spectatorship. This might be better understood in light of Žižek's hypothesis in relation to the unnamed prohibition of explicit depictions of sex in the lovemaking scenes of mainstream cinema, which is, ironically, tested here in the most unpredictable, yet palpable manner. As Žižek suggests, the interjection of explicit sexual content in such scenes 'would derail us, for the rest of the movie we would be unable to regain our balance and follow the narration with the usual disavowed belief in the diegetic reality. The sexual act would function as an intrusion of the real undermining the consistency of this diegetic reality' (1995, p. 111). Accordingly, the inclusion in

Boy's narrative of a shot more than a minute long of an explicit sexual act emerges as yet another self-reflexive strategy which disturbs the canonical contractual disavowed belief in the film's diegetic reality by functioning precisely as a derailment from it. This gesture assists the film in suspending identification and, generally, an empathic viewing of the boy's drama, as is canonically the case with visual narratives of suffering that are invested in realism. Obstructing, thus, such 'dispositions of sympathy', as Sontag calls them (2004, p. 91), *Boy* unmasks the spectatorial complicity in the traditional cinematic illusion and encourages critical reflection on both the medium's and the spectators' agency and responsibility with regard to such superficial, and by implication delusive, narratives.

In effect, the recurring narrative device of the girl, who reappears a few times in the film as the boy's object of desire, in conjunction with the explicit scene of the boy's masturbation—and its highly self-reflexive undertones—amplify the film's refusal to surrender to a conventional hagiographical representation of victimhood, rather emphasizing the fact that the boy is as much a sexual being as he is a hungry one. By offering such a complex portrayal of the victimized protagonist, the film thus refrains from facilitating sentimental responses to what might otherwise have masqueraded as a moralized, abstract or sanitized subject-matter, namely, the state/process of the boy's material and social deprivation, hence appealing for more complicated and critical responses to the problem itself; responses that challenge the dominant discourses of victimization, questioning their ethics and politics.

The protagonist's de-sanctified portrayal is further augmented by another recurring narrative device, that of the frail old neighbor, through which *Boy* achieves an extraordinary defiance of monolithic representations of the crisis, showcasing instead its protagonist oscillating between victimhood and perpetration in his effort to satisfy his biological needs. This characterological volte-face is already evident in the very first scene in which the old man appears. After receiving a call, the boy goes downstairs, opens the door of his neighbor's flat with his own copy of the key and goes to the living room where he finds the old man on the floor. Lygizos's long tracking shots follow the boy closely as he helps the old man get back on his feet and put on his slippers, before he goes to the kitchen to bring him some water. Taking great care not to make a noise, the boy suddenly starts looking around the kitchen cupboards and the fridge for food, but he cannot find anything more than a half empty sugar jar, from which he helps himself. The scene definitely suggests a close relationship between the boy and the old man that is clearly characterized by mutual respect. However, the question that hovers over the scene is to what extent does the boy's act of compassion for his disadvantaged fellow man, as well as his own destitute state, justify the act of theft that is graphically foregrounded by Lygizos's camera. In the subsequent scenes that feature the boy's ethically problematic relationship with his old neighbor the questions proliferate and become, indeed, importunate. Unable to pay the utility bills, the boy finds the water supply cut off. Desperate and puzzled, he takes a plastic tub and goes downstairs to his neighbor's flat. Again taking great care to avoid making noise he walks towards the kitchen and fills the tub with water, while also snatching some biscuits from the cupboard. Walking down the corridor to the flat's exit the boy fails to keep quiet and the old man, who is sitting in his bedroom reading, notices him. Holding the tub with the stolen water, the boy looks at the old man and apologizes. Gazing with the boy once more via Lygizos's signature over-the-shoulder tight shot, the audience catches a vague glimpse of the neighbor's response, as he subtly smiles at the boy, takes off his glasses and closes his eyes in silence (Fig. 7.4). The camera slowly pans to the boy's face, but once again fails to mediate his embarrassed state of mind; we can actually only presume it by the way he keeps his gaze fixed in the old man's direction.

Fig. 7.4   Between victimhood and perpetration

The last, and perhaps most ethically intriguing encounter between the boy and the old man, occurs halfway through the film, when the boy, after having been evicted from his own flat, decides to reside in his neighbor's. After opening the door, he walks towards the old man's bedroom—Lygizos's camera steadily following him from behind. Suddenly, the boy stops at the door and looks down off-screen. The film, however, refrains from disclosing what the boy sees with an eye-line match. It rather cuts to the kitchen where the boy tries to ease his prolonged state of hunger and then to the bathroom where he takes a shower. Desperate as he may be, the boy does not neglect to also offer water and food to his canary. Seconds later and as the camera follows his movement around the old man's flat, we suddenly witness him walking over his neighbor's body, which lies on the bedroom floor, presumably dead. Astonishingly indifferent to this presence the boy switches off the lights and lies down on the sofa. However, unable to sleep he soon gets up again, searches for the phone and dials a number. 'Mum … did I wake you up?' we hear him asking. Once again, Lygizos avoids offering any visual or audio access to the boy's interlocutor. We hear the boy uttering intermittent words but no actual conversation is mediated to the audience. The boy rushes to hang up after some prolonged moments of silence and abruptly starts slapping his face. The camera draws slightly back and then slowly follows the boy's footsteps as he walks back to the sofa. The phone starts ringing but the boy firmly shuts his ears and eyes. Lygizos then cuts to the next morning, showing the boy opening the window to allow in some fresh air, picking a few of his belongings, including the birdcage, and exiting the old man's flat once and for all, leaving behind him the corpse on the floor.

Arguably, the narrative device of the frail old neighbor, which culminates in the boy's shockingly unresponsive behavior to the old man's death, offers Lygizos the opportunity to utterly de-sanctify his protagonist and complicate his position as an ethical agent. With such a controversial representation of victimhood, the film thus resists attesting to the moral economy of piety and charity that underlies dominant discourses of victimization, which, by appealing to a narcissistic, self-affirming sentiment, forestall the political debate. On the contrary, it exhibits a meticulous perseverance in reinstalling the question of interdependency and responsibility as quintessential for an ethical reframing of these discourses. Without obliterating the complexities, antagonisms and incommensurabilities inherent in the sphere of the social, but rather foregrounding them through the occasional reversal of the protagonist's profile from a victim to a perpetrator, *Boy* insists on responsibility as the ethical precondition for the renegotiation of the terms that govern our always already precarious existence and the discourses that reproduce those terms. And responsibility is showcased—both at the level of visual representation as well as at the level of the narrative—as an unconditional opening to alterity, one which is arguably realized via a post-humanist conceptualization of interdependency.

After refusing to pawn his laptop for a ridiculous price, the boy pays a last visit to what looks like his familial archive, saved on the computer's hard disk. As the film's frame merges with the laptop screen, photographs of elderly people—presumably of his mother and father—as well as of a dog appear on the screen looking directly at the camera, arresting our gaze, which is left once more wondering, paralyzed before the sparse slices of a past familial time that will never be recovered. For, apart from his highlighted classical music background, the snippets of further back-story information scattered sporadically in the narrative allow only for some partial speculations that are, nonetheless, never verified. Clicking from one picture to another, the boy finally stops before the image of an old lady; following his lead the camera lingers on that frame for a while. But it is not long before the boy finally clicks back to the desktop moving this particular folder to the recycle bin, deleting, indeed, the last reminders—if not remainders—of his private familial history. The boy then puts the laptop in a bag, which he carefully places on the doorstep of an apartment. He rings the bell but quickly rushes down the stairs to hide himself. He pauses for a moment behind the staircase to listen to the door opening. Fixed on the boy's face the camera denies any view of the action upstairs. We only hear the door opening and, subsequently, a man's voice shouting 'Yorgo!' twice. But our gaze is permanently directed at the boy, who is now seen running down the street and, suddenly, falling over the pavement and injuring his leg.

Astonishingly, this is the only time in the film that we hear the boy's name—if Yorgos is, indeed, his name. Arguably, the overt 'unnameability' of *Boy*'s protagonist, its distinctive elliptical rhetoric in both formal and narrative terms, emerges as an ethical act against the vices of naming, against de-facing the other's alterity, against erasing singularity and reducing the project to (injured) identity politics. Instead, the film's elliptical tone 'opens ways for thinking the materiality and affectivity of embodied agency without restoring the body as a hypostatized foundation of identitarian action and agency', to use Athanasiou's words (2013,

p. 178). For, insofar as the film's self-reflexive mode of address defies realism, claiming rather the terrain of a critical—or, better put, ethical—allegory, it thus captures singularity beyond identity, beyond references to a particular embodied subjectivity. *Boy*, indeed, rather offers the body of the boy as a receptacle for all those singularities reduced to 'insignificant human matter', thus paving the way for rethinking the medium as a unique means to surpass the limitations of language and imagine, indeed, 'modes of response and solidarity that do not reify "the dispossessed"', 'an ethics and politics of post-identity subjectivities, which are consigned and exposed to the exposure, abandonment, precarity, and vulnerability of others' (2013, p. 136).

Re-enacting the Levinasian ethical imperative, the film deploys what we could name as '*non-altericidal*' formal and narrative strategies; strategies which invite us to reimagine the world as, indeed, one of 'differentially shared sociality', taking responsibility for the others' suffering and for their care without striving to fix them under intelligible categories that will constitute them as eligible to be taken care of. In addition, the film foregrounds the possibility of reinventing the humanist premises of the biopolitical through breaking with the social norms and discourses that regulate the production of humanness as well as through enacting ethical communities with differently embodied bodies, indeed, other life-forms. Much as the boy deletes the familial faces from the memory of his computer, and, arguably from his own memory, so he effaces himself from the social and familial field of visibility. Indeed, the delivery of the laptop to the unseen man foregrounds instead the boy's own effacement from the social scene, an injurious rupture with the space that has traditionally been regarded as most accommodating and protective, namely the family.

His leg bleeding, the boy hobbles to a pet shop to buy some birdseed for his canary, and then heads to the deserted building where he has hidden his pet, after his eviction from his flat. But to his surprise, the building's entrance is firmly sealed with a metal door and he cannot reach his feathered friend, despite his agonized efforts to break in. Exhausted and distressed he makes his way to a nearby church. Inside the church, the camera registers the movement of the boy's gaze as he watches an old woman—who resembles his mother—lighting a candle and then kissing the icons. A cut back to the boy shows him also lighting a candle and then taking a seat behind the woman. After a moment of silence, the boy starts singing Bach's hymn, which accompanied our introduction to him at the beginning of the film. With the camera fixed behind his shoulder, we see

Fig. 7.5 'What a beautiful voice.... You made me cry'

the old lady turning round and glancing at him visibly touched, before she turns back again to wipe her tears with a tissue (Fig. 7.5). 'What a beautiful voice.... You made me cry', we hear a voice whispering. The film cuts to a close-up of the boy only for the audience to realize that it is his own voice whispering, making up a fictitious dialogue, in which the woman supposedly offers him some beef with rice, which he refuses because he is fasting. 'Why are you fasting?' 'Because ... I want to confess', he finally mumbles. Much as the film forecloses the familial space, rendering it as inept in responding to the boy's drama by underscoring the paradox of its ubiquitous absence, it equally foregrounds the Church as inadequate to provide refuge—both material as well as spiritual/ideological—for the crisis-stricken body. Juxtaposing central concepts from the ecclesiastical lexicon, from the canonical Greek Orthodox rituals of candle-lighting, icon kissing, fasting and confessing to the universal axiom of compassion through the boy's grotesque dialogue/monologue, the scene emerges as nothing less than a caustic parody, a tragic cry against an excessively ritualistic, pseudo-spiritual institution that does nothing but reproduce the discourses by which individuals are de-instituted and reduced to human waste. The scene attains particular resonance in the light of contemporary manifestations of the Greek Orthodox Church's highly intolerant agenda; particularly the repetitive homophobic public statements made by high-ranking clergy, as well as the revelations about political and economic support of a part of the ministry to far-right, neo-Nazi political groups and their extremely dangerous racist and homophobic discourse and acts.

In the film's final scene, a long shot from above—a shot very rarely used in the film—shows the boy using a ladder to access the basement of the deserted building where he had hidden his canary after their eviction. Walking among a clutter of rubble, old furniture and broken statues of heroic figures from the nation's past glorious history the boy reaches the birdcage, which is suggestively covered with the Greek national flag (Fig. 7.6). Ironically, the quintessential symbol of a nation that has failed to assume responsibility for its dying children's lives is reduced here to a mere coversheet, devoid of respect, stripped off its glorified status. The boy uncovers the cage and lovingly follows his own caring ritual of providing his little friend with food and water, in a scene that recalls the film's opening shot. But this time the camera holds back. The shot is still shaky but not tight anymore, as if it does not want to intervene, to invade the private moment between the boy and the bird. The bird starts chirping as if to thank its human friend for taking care of it. Among the rubble and the ruins of national disillusionment another form of interdependency emerges, another form of collectivity not marked by identity or similitude; indeed, a post-humanist enactment of response-ability, which considers

Fig. 7.6   Among the rubble, yet still surviving, still struggling

the other's vulnerability beyond identitarian claims or other 'normative forces that arrange the social, political and cultural matrices of humanness' (Butler and Athanasiou, 2013, p. 32).

As the camera lingers unsteadily on this shot, foregrounding a crumbling national space reduced to a clutter of meaningless narratives, the bird's song—much like the film in its entirety—emerges as a '*cri de coeur*' against the very terms that differentially render diverse forms of life as precarious, disposable, un-grievable. Contesting the oppressive regimes that govern the discursive matrices of memorability and recognition, particularly family, religion and the nation, the film reinstalls the relational condition by foregrounding 'forms of interdependency, persistence, resistance, and equality that […] create a counter-socius in the midst of hierarchical and regulatory power regimes' (2013, p. 175). The final shot, with the boy and the bird still surviving, still struggling, still singing, in spite of being wholly dispossessed and disposed, indeed discarded, among the rubble of the nation, ultimately emerges as an imaging and imagining of such forms of collective resistance; or, to use Butler's eloquent phrasing, 'a defense of our collective precarity and persistence in the making of equality and the many-voiced and unvoiced ways of refusing to become disposable' (2013, p. 197).

NOTES

1. According to Deleuze, people have mistakenly regarded the classical cinematographic image as necessarily being in the present. Indeed, narrative time might seem consistent with the time of the story; however, the viewer can recognize that time appears in a condensed form, represented through a character's movement in space. This, for Deleuze, constitutes the movement-image, which is fundamentally linked to an indirect representation of time, time in its empirical form. This is achieved by the sensory-motor schema, which governs the movement-image, both spatializing time and rendering it linear according to the needs of causality and narrative coherence. The sensory-motor schema takes the form of action-image, which 'comprises received movement (perception, situation), imprint (affection, the interval), and executed movement (action properly speaking and reaction)' (2009, p. 260). Through the physical actions of the protagonist, which provide the logical link between spatially and temporally disjointed images—even if these are moments of flashbacks,

dreams and/or fantasies—the viewer never experiences time passing in and for itself, but always in a singular, linear and literally edited version.

2. The revelatory qualities of the cinematic facial close-up were noted in classical film theory, with Béla Balázs famously describing the device as 'film's true terrain': 'In close-ups every wrinkle becomes a crucial element of character and every twitch of a muscle testifies to a pathos that signals great inner events. The close-up of a face is frequently used as the climax of an important scene; it must be the lyrical essence of the entire drama' (2007, pp. 102–103).

3. 'Minimal visuality' pertains to visual practices, such as those found in the videography of Holocaust survivor's testimonies, where, as Saxton explains Hartman's contention, 'the restriction of the visual field to an individual embodied voice maximises the "mental space" opened up by the image and creates a new "affective community"' (Saxton, 2010a, p. 69).

4. 'Counter-shots' refer to the heterogeneous perspectives that, according to Serge Daney, can be registered in cinema and 'bear witness to a certain *alterity*', as opposed to the uniform perspective, that is '*the point of view of power* of "le visuel"', namely the televisual electronic spectacles (Daney, cited in Saxton, 2010a, p. 69).

BIBLIOGRAPHY

Aaron, Michele (2007) *The Power of Looking On* (London: Wallflower).

Aguilar, Carlos (2013) 'Foreign Oscar Entry Review: Boy Eating the Bird's Food', *Indiewire*, http://blogs.indiewire.com/sydneylevine/foreign-oscar-entry-review-boy-eating-the-birds-food-greece-ektoras-lygizos-foreign-language-oscar-submissions-academy-awards-2014-international-film-business, date accessed 22 April 2016.

Balázs, Béla (2007) 'Visible Man', in Erica Carter (ed.) and Rodney Livingstone (trans.), 'Béla Balázs, *Visible Man, or the Culture of Film* (1924)', Screen, 48/1, 91–108.

Butler, Judith and Athena Athanasiou (2013) *Dispossession: The Performative in the Political* (Cambridge: Polity Press).

Celluloid Liberation Front (2012) 'A Behavioural Report on the Greek Crisis', *Film International*, http://filmint.nu/?p=5142, date accessed 22 April 2016.

Chouliaraki, Lilie (2006) *The Spectatorship of Suffering* (London: Sage Publications).

Cooper, Sarah (2007) 'Mortal Ethics: Reading Levinas with the Dardenne Brothers', *Film-Philosophy*, 11/2, 66–87.

Dalton, Steven (2012) '*Boy Eating the Bird's Food*: Karlovy Vary Film Review', *The Hollywood Reporter*, http://www.hollywoodreporter.com/review/boy-eating-birds-food-karlovy-festival-346508, date accessed 22 April 2016.

Deleuze, Gilles (2009 [1985]) *Cinema 2: The Time-Image*, trans. Hugh Tomlinson and Robert Caleta (London: Continuum).

Fainaru, Dan (2012) '*Boy Eating the Bird's Food*', *ScreenDaily*, http://www.screendaily.com/reviews/the-latest/boy-eating-the-birds-food/5044107.article?blocktitle=Latest-Reviews&contentID=1479, date accessed 22 April 2016.

Harbord, Janet (2007) *Evolution of Film: Rethinking Film Studies* (Cambridge: Polity Press).

Krassakopoulos, Yorgos (2012) 'KVIFF 2012 Review: "Boy Eating the Bird's Food" by Ektoras Lygizos', *flix*, http://flix.gr/en/kviff-2012-review-boys-eating-the-birds-food-by-ek.html, date accessed 22 April 2016.

Kudláč, Martin (2013) 'IFFR 2013: The Passion of the Everyman in Boy Eating the Bird's Food (2012)', *Film International*, http://filmint.nu/?p=7427, date accessed 22 April 2016.

Levinas, Emmanuel (1985) *Ethics and Infinity. Conversations with Philippe Nemo*, trans. Richard A. Cohen (Pittsburgh: Duquesne University Press).

Levinas, Emmanuel (1989) 'Ethics as First Philosophy', in Seán Hand (ed.) *The Levinas Reader* (Oxford: Basil Blackwell), pp. 75–87.

Levinas, Emmanuel (1994 [1969]) *Totality and Infinity: An Essay on Exteriority*, trans. Alphonso Lingis (Pittsburgh: Duquesne University Press).

Levinas, Emmanuel (1999) 'The Prohibition Against Representation and the "Rights of Man"', in *Alterity and Transcendence*, trans. Michael B. Smith (London: The Athlone Press), pp. 121–130.

Saxton, Libby (2010a) 'Ethics, Spectatorship and the Spectacle of Suffering', in Lisa Downing and Libby Saxton (eds.) *Film and Ethics: Foreclosed Encounters* (Oxon: Routledge), pp. 62–75.

Saxton, Libby (2010b) 'Blinding Visions: Levinas, Ethics, Faciality', in Lisa Downing and Libby Saxton (eds.) *Film and Ethics: Foreclosed Encounters* (Oxon: Routledge), pp. 95–106.

Sontag, Susan (2004 [2003]) *Regarding the Pain of Others* (London: Penguin).

van Hoeij, Boyd (2012) 'Review: *Boy Eating the Bird's Food*', *Variety*, http://variety.com/2012/film/reviews/boy-eating-the-bird-s-food-1117947921/, date accessed 22 April 2016.

Žižek, Slavoj (1995 [1991]) *Looking Awry: An Introduction to Jacques Lacan through Popular Culture* (London: The MIT Press).

CHAPTER 8

Epilogue

In *Dogtooth*'s final scene the father drives his car to work as usual. The old Mercedes crosses Lanthimos's extreme long shot left to right and stops in the middle of the frame and in front of the big factory. The father gets out of the car and enters the building. The film then cuts to a closer shot of the Mercedes's boot and lingers on that frame for about half a minute. A disconcerting quietness pervades the film's final shot. It is a moment of suspension, of suspense, the agonizing silence of anticipation, during which the viewer's desire to see the boot opened grows. For *Dogtooth*'s final shot is haunted by the preceding sequence, in which the audience have witnessed the older daughter breaking her dogtooth with one of her brother's dumbbells and then hiding herself in the car-boot in an attempt to escape the oppressive contours of her totalitarian familial space. However, Lanthimos once more disappoints our expectations. The film cuts to black before the end credits appear. The film's denouement acquires a resonance that is both tragic and enigmatic. For, rather than offering a meaningful closure, Lanthimos's film dissolves in yet another meaningless foreclosure; indeed, in the foreclosure of meaning. As the Mercedes's boot remains firmly closed denying any access to the older daughter's fate, the film itself opens a gap, a void in the realm of meaning. One might wonder what this gesture is all about. I would call it an ethical one.

As Gilles Deleuze demonstrates in *Cinema 2: The Time-Image*, traditional 'narration always refers to a *system of judgment*' (2009, p. 133). As he explains, classical narrative cinema insists on an 'organic' narration, which claims to be true by preserving 'the legal connections in space and the chronological relations in time' (2009, p. 133), thus offering an indirect representation of time, as a consequence of action, dependent on movement and inferred from space (2009, p. 128). Through this structure, with what Harbord calls 'the revelatory acts of narrative, bent on exposing error and reasserting a moral order', normative cinema 'implicitly stages a higher moral authority, a transcendental legislation' (2007, pp. 157–158). However, this 'notion of a greater or absolute truth' is collapsed in post-war cinema and cinema cultures of the margins, which privilege repetition or the accumulation of acts with 'no "greater" meaning', without performing 'a revelation or exposure of "truth" that suggests an appeal to justice' (2007, p. 158).

Taking Deleuze's and Harbord's above considerations of the ethical implications of cinematic spatiotemporality a step further, Galt (2013) makes the case for a queer 'default cinema', whose construction of time and space, as discussed in the Introduction, defies meaning altogether, thus manifesting a radical queer response to contemporary histories of economic crisis. Despite the contextual differences, the Greek films examined in this book display thick connections with the strand of global art cinema that Galt dubs 'default', not least in the way they respond to the ongoing moment of the Greek crisis precisely by exhibiting what Edelman calls a radical 'refusal of meaning' (2004, p. 120). This is the point where, as I have proposed, the 'weird' intersects with the 'queer', arguing that the current cinematic trend's radical rhetoric can be articulated as an 'essentially' queer ethical response to the alarming moment of the crisis and the concomitant crisis of meaning it has engendered.

Indeed, the Greek films discussed in this book offer neither a reestablishment of moral order nor a definite resolution, their denouements rather encompassing a relentless negation of meaningful closure and, at the same time, an ethically laden opening of meaning to the indefinite and the irreducible. In *Dogtooth*, Lanthimos refuses to open the carboot; in *Hardcore* Martha escapes from the city to an obscure destination before the uncanny image of the child in the photograph comes to life; in *Attenberg* Marina gets in the car, having scattered her father's ashes in the sea, and simply drives out of the frame; in *Alps* the gymnast dances to pop music, but the smile on her face is haunted by the image of Monte Rosa before the closing shutters of her imaginary family home; in *Boy* the young man reunites with his pet canary, but this reunion is devastatingly compromised by his tragic state of extreme destitution; even in *Strella* the images of the otherwise joyous New Year's party are undermined by the vagueness that underlies the affective (and erotic) structure of the relationships between the members of the newly reassembled queer family. The films unapologetically refuse a definite closure; they refuse indeed to signify. And this refusal to signify, this ambivalence and indeterminacy that imbues not only their endings but their entire construction of time and space, ultimately construes a cinematic spatiotemporality which this book, following Galt, understands as queer.

Through a queer defiance of narrativity and identity, undermining the referentiality of language and images, and exposing the futility as well as the oppressiveness underlying the discourses that seek to infuse time and space with meaning, these films materialize the 'queer refusal to signify' (Galt, 2013, p. 62), articulate precisely the moment of negation without recourse to futurity, opting to remain vision-less, indeed meaningless. For, even in the case of *Strella*, which Chap. 4 reads as an instance of what Muñoz calls the 'aesthetic queer utopias', the film's utopian sensibility, as I have argued, relies more on a negation of the present, on a polemic reframing of existing totalitarian discourses and structures, rather than the projection of alternative queer worlds. The films, indeed, do not strive to 'overcome the disorientation of the queer moment but rather inhabit the intensity of its moment' (Ahmed, 2006, p. 107).

However, to inhabit the intensity of the queer moment is to attend to its critical, oppositional and resistant aspects. The intense queer moments created as a result of the films' vision-less, meaningless, indeed 'weird' form and narratives, are heavily laden with an all-encompassing trenchant critique, both deconstructive and repudiating, of a particular set of meanings. For, to recall Edelman's words once more, 'The narrative that raises meaninglessness as a possibility [...] necessarily bestows a particular meaning on such meaninglessness itself' (2004, p. 120). The films demonstrate a relentless vehemence in deconstructing and reframing the nation's favorite narratives as these have been enmeshed with capitalism, channeled through the nation's quintessential ideal and structural core, namely the 'sacred' Greek patriarchal family, and reproduced and disseminated by a series of state-supported and supporting discourses (the educational system, the Orthodox Church, the mass media), including, of course, the cinematic medium itself. By unapologetically attacking those narratives, as well as the discourses and technologies that have diachronically produced and reproduced them, these films align themselves with a long tradition of subversive Greek cinema, which, as outlined in the Introduction, has consistently advanced its oppositional aesthetics against the nation's official historicity, imagery and imaginary. At the same time, however, as has become evident, the films discussed in this book clearly also depart from that tradition for, faithful to the queer moment of negation, they refrain from proposing an alternative vision, opting to attend to the intensity of the moment, registering cinematically, indeed, the 'crisis of meaning'.

In effect, the films' sustained negation of the intertwined meanings of capitalism, (Greek) nationalism and patriarchy, is simultaneously an invitation for a radical opening of meaning, a radical openness to difference as a register for the unthought, the irreducible and the indefinite. This bold move is achieved through the affective surplus produced as a result of the films' subversive aesthetics and defiant construction of cinematic space and time. As images, spaces and bodies appear and withdraw without temporal coherence or narrative significance, the cinematic gaze, often disembodied and fragmentary, is impregnated with ambivalence and indeterminacy rather than a reflection of subjective meaning and experience. Whether decentered or center-staged, the characters are often denied agency, as their actions are rendered excessive, unjustified and unresolved, while the deadpan acting style refuses access to the experience of time and space as meaningful and productive. Instead, wasteful time, what Harbord describes as 'inertia', is foregrounded, not necessarily because the films are devoid of action, but, because action is deliberately separated from productivity, rendered excessive. In this respect, the films reverberate with contemporary theorizations of queer time as unproductive and queerness itself as 'wasted time, wasted lives, wasted productivity' (Schoonover, 2012, p. 73).

Time, indeed, emerges as a key issue at stake in these films. Through their defiant representation of national and familial time, as well as their unconventional construction of cinematic time, the films attest to no simple conceptions of temporality. At a superficial level, time, of course, appears as linear and chronological, but it is also effectively repetitive, comprising an alternation between dissociated fragments of quotidian time, characterized by boredom and unproductive expenditure, disjointed moments of fantasy or performative intervals, and acts of temporal rupture, marked by violence, incest, death, dispossession; all accumulating without 'greater' meaning. Futurity is contested and, ultimately, negated. For, on the one hand, such spatiotemporality results in what Harbord understands as a 'fetishization of action, a repetitious re-enactment of the quotidian' (2007, p. 156), which, nonetheless, acquires particular resonance insofar as it unearths performativity as precisely constitutive of identity, space, and time. On the other hand, the repetition of the seemingly trivial and insignificant is constantly undermined and haunted by the possibility of rupture. This fascinating conflation of the temporal conditions of repetition and contingency ultimately exposes performativity's structural reliance on the absence of essence, its dependence on the emptiness of the Signifier, and meaning itself as a matter of contingency, an act of imagination, subjected to a ceaseless reframing, a perennial deferral of closure(s). Harbord concludes, 'as the causal chain of narrative events disappears in modern cinema, a gap opens, a void appears in the midst of the thinkable. Here cinema portends to the unthought, or brings us to an encounter with the limits of the thinkable' (2007, p. 162).

In this sense, the films' defiant queer sensibility engenders profound paradigms of non-representational logic, which not only defy the canonical disavowing contract of cinematic illusionism but, crucially, emphasize the limitations of representation, the perils of narrativity, the contingency of meaning. The films, thus, attack the medium itself, critiquing its collusion in the reproduction and dissemination of the nation's totalitarian oppressive discourses, but, most importantly, gesture towards the unthought and the uncanny that always eludes our sense of the self and the other. But meaning, as we have seen, is attacked and problematized not only at the level of form but also through the films' idiosyncratic thematization of language and *logos* as the singular privilege of the humans. In *Hardcore*, the pragmatic construal of language is questioned, as Martha's voice-overs often obscure rather than illuminate the events of the narrative, displacing meaning in an uncanny domain that oscillates between fantasy, desire, nostalgia and the drive. In *Strella*, Greek grammar is reframed and reimagined, as the gender agreement between determiners, pronouns, nouns and adjectives collapses and the morphemes that define gender become 'floating signifiers' subjected to queer creativity. In *Dogtooth*, semantics is extensively and excessively defied and manipulated by an unapologetic reconfiguration of signifiers and signifieds in the service of the oppressive patriarchal regime. In *Attenberg*, the communicative value of language is defeated as the film performs a catachrestic use of dialogue, where words lose their semantic gravity and gain value only for their sonic qualities, or dissolve into raw sounds and mimicking of animal voices and bodily gestures. In *Alps*, language is exposed as a primary mechanism for the performative construction of identity, as dialogues are rehearsed and replayed and eventually congeal into illusions of meaning. Finally, in *Boy*, language collapses altogether as sentences remain unfinished, questions unanswered, monologues masquerade as dialogues, as the gaps proliferate and ellipsis and silence eventually take over the human soundtrack.

Breaking with the canonical paradigms of both human and cinematic language, the films then resolve into a queer fascination with the body or a fascination with bodies acting queerly. The films, indeed, constitute a repository of bodies that refuse the patriarchal order as much as they resist the neoliberal structures of productivity and 'responsibilization':[1] from the inert and desexualized bodies of *Dogtooth* and *Attenberg*, through the disintegrating, convulsively acting and, eventually, castrated body of the *Boy*, to the transgressive bodies of *Hardcore*'s *sinthomosexuals* and *Strella*'s incestuous lovers, and, of course, the spectral body of Monte Rosa, which emerges as yet another embodiment of 'the remainder of the Real internal to the Symbolic' (Edelman, 2004, p. 25). Showcasing a subversive deconstruction and, simultaneously, rearticulation of the normative discourses of the body, these films are ones that ultimately point towards more ethical ways in which the medium might capture, edit, exhibit, reframe and reimagine it.

If the 2008 riots in Athens (and the many others that followed the eruption of the crisis), have been construed as manifestations of meaninglessness, if the primary affective response to the crisis has been indeed articulated as a 'crisis of meaning', the contemporary trend in Greek cinema construes and articulates this moment of meaninglessness as an eminently queer one, it bestows on this meaninglessness an essentially queer 'meaning'. However, the void of vision inherent in this meaninglessness should not be understood as an annihilation of political discourse. This void of vision does not, indeed, forestall the confrontation as precisely political; it only suspends its meaning as one of fixed and fixated identitarian claims. It is, ultimately, the vision of the void as precisely a call for a perennial deferral of a clearly demarcated vision, a call for a perennial contestation of and opposition to the reproduction of the oppressive regimes that have interchangeably regulated the allocation of rights according to their own terms of recognizability: patriarchy, heteronormativity, nationalism, capitalism, neoliberalism, neocolonialism, the Church, and so on and so forth. Indeed, the 'weird poetics' emerges as, ultimately, queer in the way it essentially constitutes a paradigm shift in how the medium can serve as an unexpected platform for putting forward both an ethics and a politics of difference.

Halfway through *Dogtooth* the family is sitting peacefully at the dinner table. All of a sudden the older daughter asks: 'Mother, what is pussy?'

Despite her visible astonishment the mother replies calmly, 'Where did you see that word?' 'On a case on top of the VCR', says the daughter. The mother then glances surreptitiously at the father and replies rather uncomfortably: 'Pussy is the big light. Example: The pussy went out and the room was plunged into darkness.' The family, then, looks up at the big light above their heads. Silence ... I wonder whether in this dialogue we could replace the word 'pussy' with 'cinema'.

NOTE

1. As Butler and Athanasiou explain, 'responsibilization' names the condition of social therapeutics put forward by neoliberal govern-mentality, which is 'premised upon a morality of self-government, possessive individualism, and entrepreneurial guilt' (2013, p. 103).

BIBLIOGRAPHY

Ahmed, Sara (2006) *Queer Phenomenology: Orientations, Objects, Others* (Durham and London: Duke University Press).
Butler, Judith and Athena Athanasiou (2013) *Dispossession: The Performative in the Political* (Cambridge: Polity Press).
Deleuze, Gilles (2009 [1985]) *Cinema 2: The Time-Image*, trans. Hugh Tomlinson and Robert Caleta (London: Continuum).
Edelman, Lee (2004) *No Future: Queer Theory and the Death Drive* (Durham and London: Duke University Press).
Galt, Rosalind (2013) 'Default Cinema: Queering Economic Crisis in Argentina and Beyond', *Screen*, 54/1, 62–81.
Harbord, Janet (2007) *Evolution of Film: Rethinking Film Studies* (Cambridge: Polity Press).
Muñoz, Jose Esteban (2009) *Cruising Utopia: The Then and There of Queer Futurity, Sexual Cultures* (New York: New York University Press).
Schoonover, Karl (2012) 'Wastrels of Time: Slower Cinema and its Labouring Subjects', *Framework*, 53/1, 65–78.

INDEX

© The Author(s) 2016
M. Psaras, *The Queer Greek Weird Wave*,
DOI 10.1007/978-3-319-40310-6

225

157, 158, 163, 165, 166, 171–4,
178, 182, 183, 185, 193, 195,
198, 200, 203–5, 208–10, 222
Bordwell, David, 25
*Boy Eating the Bird's Food/ To Agori
Troei to Fagito tou Pouliou*
(2013), 29, 185–214
Brides, The (2004), 21
Butler, Judith, 28, 80–3, 130, 131,
139, 149, 166–9, 171, 173,
179–82, 186, 188–90, 196, 200,
223n1

C
Cacoyannis, Michalis, 16, 30n4, 102,
103, 119n5
Callas, Maria, 93, 111, 113, 114
camp, 55–7, 111, 114, 115
Cannes Film Festival, 17, 30n6, 64
capitalism, 12, 27, 68, 69, 82, 84,
133, 219, 220, 222
Cassia, Paul Sant, 9, 10, 70
causality, 17, 25, 47, 133, 194, 213n1
Chalkou, Maria, 23, 27
Chouliaraki, Lilie, 200
Christmas, 53, 54, 57, 93, 96, 116,
117, 119
clientelism, 10
compulsory heterosexuality, 68
contingency, 5, 8, 71, 83, 159, 221
Cooper, Sarah, 187
crisis, 1–31, 42, 83, 95, 125, 134,
186, 192, 198, 200, 206, 211,
218, 220, 222

D
Dalianidis, Yannis, 17
Dardenne, Jean-Pierre and Luc, 31n8,
187
Davis, Colin, 159, 160, 183

de Lauretis, Teresa, 41, 70
Dean, Tim, 58
debtocracy, 42, 61n3
Deleuze, Gilles, 145, 194, 213n1, 217
democracy, 6
Derrida, Jacques, 182, 183
dictatorship, 20, 30n3, 108
disavowal, 144, 205
disposability, 166, 168
dispossession, 28, 166–9, 171,
188–90, 192, 220
distanciation, 25, 201
Dogme 95, 201, 203
Dogtooth/ Kynodontas (2009), 4, 23,
24, 28, 31n11, 63–90, 125, 128,
141, 156, 157, 160, 161, 173,
181, 217, 218, 221, 222
Downing, Lisa, 59, 60
drag, 102, 104, 111, 114, 115, 120n6
Dyer, Richard, 117

E
Edelman, Lee, 40, 41, 49, 50, 52, 58,
61n4, 89, 218, 222
Child, 50, 52, 61n4, 61n5, 218
negativity, 40, 50, 52, 58
reproductive futurism, 49–51, 58,
61n4, 61n5
sinthomosexual, 49, 50, 52, 57, 60,
61n4
Eleftheriotis, Dimitris, 22
El Greco (2007), 21
emancipation, 23, 118
ethics, 10, 13, 79, 97, 107, 115, 159,
187, 190, 193, 196, 198, 202,
206, 210, 222
Europe, 3, 19
eurozone, 3, 21
excess, 18, 24, 40, 50, 57, 59, 93,
114, 136, 153, 180, 202
Eyes Wide Shut (1999), 46